Melanie Klein and Object Relations

An International Journal Devoted to the Understanding of Object Relations

VOLUME 15, NUMBER 3, SEPTEMBER 1997

Envy
Papers in Memory of Harold N. Boris (1932-1996)

MICHAEL EIGEN	357	Boris for Me
EDWARD EMERY	361	Remembering Harold Boris
HAROLD N. BORIS	365	Envy in the Psychoanalytic Process
EDWARD EMERY	397	Mnemosyne: Death, Memory, and Mourning
RICHARD P. ALEXANDER	417	Some Notes on the Origin of Despair and its Relationship to Destructive Envy
JOSEPH H. BERKE	443	Womb Envy
RICHARD E. VILLEJO	467	Insights on Envy: A Kleinian Analysis of Shakespeare's *Othello*

Ghosts, Time, Language

JEAN-MICHEL RABATÉ	475	Beckett's Ghosts and Fluxions
BETTINA L. KNAPP	493	Beckett's *That Time*: Exile and "That Double-Headed Monster... Time"
GERALD L. BRUNS	513	Otherwise than Language
	541	*Notes on Contributors*
	543	*Instructions to Authors*

esf PUBLISHERS
BINGHAMTON & CLUJ

JOURNAL OF MELANIE KLEIN AND OBJECT RELATIONS is an international quarterly published in March, June, September and December of each year by *esf* Publishers, Binghamton, NY, USA.

THE ANNUAL SUBSCRIPTION RATE for volume 15 (four issues) is $60.00 (Canada and US) for individuals, and $100.00 (Canada and US) for institutions. All orders outside Canada and US, add $24.00 postage. Back and current issues are available at $20.00 per issue (orders outside Canada and US add $6.00 postage). *When subscribing, indicate whether you desire to start with the current issue or the current volume.* All prices quoted in US dollars. All payments should be made by check, (international) money order through a US bank, Visa and Master Card. Payments from outside the United States should be made in US funds. When ordering from Canada and paying by check, please write on your check either "Pay in US funds" or send C$84.00 (individual subscribers) or C$140.00 (institutional subscribers). Subscriptions and address changes should be sent directly to: *esf* Publishers, 1 Marine Midland Plaza, East Tower– Fourth Floor, Binghamton, NY 13901, USA.

BOOKS, PERIODICALS AND ADVERTISING INQUIRIES should be sent directly to the publisher: 1 Marine Midland Plaza, East Tower–Fourth Floor, Binghamton, NY 13901, USA. All books and materials received will be listed under BOOKS RECEIVED and ARTICLES NOTICED. All advertisement should conform to the standards of the journal and its publisher. Advertisement guidelines and rates are available upon request.

PERMISSION to reproduce any material in this journal by any means must be obtained in writing from the publisher.

REPRINTS of the articles may be requested directly from the authors.

PRODUCED BY SFRTPF, Inc., a non-profit, tax-exempt professional organization. © SFRTPF, Inc., 1997 (unless otherwise indicated).

INDEXED in *Language and Language Behavior Abstracts, Psychological Abstracts*, and *Sociological Abstracts*. For reference purposes, use the abbreviation *J. M. Klein Obj. Rel.*

Effective with Volume 14, Number 2, the journal is printed on acid-free paper. The paper used in this publication meets the minimum requirements of the American National Standards for Information Sciences—Permanence of Paper for Printed Library Materials, ANSI Z39.48-1984. ∞

ACKNOWLEDGMENTS: Several papers in this issue have been reprinted by kind permission of the following persons and publishers: Mrs. Carol Boris and J. Aronson, Inc. for "Envy in the psychoanalytic process" by Harold N. Boris, © H.N. Boris; Editions Rodopi B.V. for "Beckett's ghosts and fluxions" by Jean-Michael Rabaté, © Editions Rodopi B.V.; Pennsylvania State University Press for "Beckett's *That Time*: Exile and 'that double-headed monster... time'" by Bettina L. Knapp, © Penn State U Press; and Yale University Press for "Otherwise than language" by Gerald L. Bruns, © Yale Univ Press.

ISBN 1-883881-28-5

Manufactured in the United States of America

Harold N. Boris (1932-1996)

BORIS FOR ME

Michael Eigen

Hal Boris is one of the last of a vanishing breed. A true analyst who did not go through official analytic institute training. He became an analyst the old fashioned way by working at it, living it, tasting it with every fiber of his being. Analysis become him, lived through him, went to new places with him. The world will be poorer without him, and without the kind of quirky, goat-like development he represents.

Not everyone who has some contact with a Bettelheim or Rapaport or Erikson will make the use of it he did. Contact with such people can raise existence to new levels. But not everyone is open to uplifting, not everyone risks inspired living. Not everyone has a Daemon to follow.

Love of the work of Wilfred R. Bion brought Boris and I together. We met only once. When I was Program Chair for the National Psychological Association for Psychoanalysis. I created a series of programs on Bion and Winnicott, and invited Boris to give a talk and seminar. The first moment of meeting felt so loving and free. He seemed almost a giant puppy, arms akimbo, fluttering, face open, great white wisdom beard. Delicious.

After his evening talk, his love of wine and food seemed part of a flowing generosity. But there was precision, incisiveness. He chose the wine carefully yet sent the first bottle the waiter opened back. There was something in the taste that did not meet his expectation. It wasn't right enough. But the next bottle was acceptable, and so was the bottle after that.

The next morning was the seminar. The laser quality of his thinking became more intense, dark, ferociously sharp, delicately biting. There are movie scenes where heads are cut off before the victims realize it. His thinking could be like that—piercing illusion after illusion, heads rolling everywhere, light as air. A soul or psyche samurai. We had a blood-curdlingly, marvelously, uplifting morning. Whatever Boris did came out of genuine contact with something real, something important and valuable. Like it or not, he kept you close to something you needed to be close to. What joined us was love of psychic reality—which is what, independently, led us to Bion. Sooner or later, psyche lovers seek each other out, join hands across worlds.

I think it important to say that, at least indirectly, Boris reached out to me before I reached out to him. Some years earlier, I learned that he wanted me to discuss a paper he was giving at an American Psychological Association meeting. My father had just died and I was not into meetings, so I declined the invitation, given by an interested third party. Years later, I regretted it, and partly made up for it by providing some recognition for Boris's achievement. The point is, he knew about me before I knew about him. This is a tribute to the sensitivity of his antennae, his ability to pick up on simpatico currents, his immediate access to certain scents. Boris was deeply into Bion more than a decade before I even knew about the latter.

A terrible marvel is that Boris was ill the several years I knew him. For a long time, treatment sapped his energy. He depicted rising for a few minutes at a time, writing a little, then out again. He published three books (1993, 1994a, b) during this period. I was honored to write a Foreword to one of them (1993). All probe and open psychic realities.

They feature essays written over many years—intensely alive books. His last writings, with death near, were among the most alive of all. These essays shed skin after skin, closer and closer to the naked psyche's twists and turns. As Boris prepares to leap through death, the pace of psychic unfolding quickens.

There was an important side to Boris's work that always scared me. Not his luminous penetration of falsehoods, frightening in a good way. But his dedication to a strain of "survival of the fittest" thinking, which sticks in me like a poisoned apple. He has passages where he talks about the coupling and pairing of the best, the brightest, the most beautiful, the interplay of the ideal and everyday life, the ideal and instinctual. Should I hold out for Ms. Right or go for Ms. Right Now? (In reality, I'm beholding to Boris's holding out and capacity for selection for some good wine at dinner—and his choice of me as a kind of penpal.) Enlightening as so many of his passages are, there is a "superman" element to his Darwinian strain that makes my hair stand on end.

His descriptions (e.g., 1993, pp. 47-50) of Edelman's use of Darwinian ideas to describe cellular processes eerily parallels a disease in his future. To some extent, Boris transposed Edelman's transposition of Darwin to processes of choice and selection in psychic life. A yawning gap opens between those who make it and those who don't—those who are fit (the best) and those who are not (runts of the litter, the weaker or less endowed, who "get shunted aside by the stronger, richer, or better endowed" [1993, p. 47]). Who can deny areas of applicability of such cruel, naturalistic processes? Surely, one must look truth in the face, no matter how ugly.

Without sticking my head in the sand, I'm not ready to concede that evolution works only the Darwinian way. I'm not sure the fittest always survive or the lesser die out (are you and I the fittest?). Biblical emphasis on reversal hints that the logic of development might be a great deal more subtle. There may be more wisdom than meets the eye in the idea that the meek will inherit the earth (after the strong kill each other off). A Taoist picture of "evolution" seems a lot more hopeful (Boris tends to see hope as self-deception).

Within the world of specialists on evolution, there is turmoil concerning what evolution is, how it works. In an essay on the neuropsychology of "soul" or "spirit," Joseph (1996, pp. 268-319) sees evolution more in terms of metamorphosis than natural selection. Bion's use of the term "transformations" leaves this open. The verdict is out, but I can't help feeling Boris squeezed himself into a depiction of evolution that harmed him, too harsh to take.

Nevertheless, there emerges in Boris's work a sense of what it is like to be one of the unselected and unchosen in a world of better people, a world where envy gnaws the innards. Few things are more important than working with what makes people feel horrible about themselves. Ghastly self-feelings lime the underside of power. The gap between destructive "haves" and destructive "have-nots" taints what it feels like to be alive.

Few people have conveyed as acutely as Boris the plight of an unwanted fetus or baby self fighting to live—or die. He has located a nucleus that feels it ought not be alive, yet pushes for life. Does one have a right to be alive? Can one live—in what way, to what extent? Few have conveyed vicissitudes of self-hate as keenly. One gains from Boris ever more accurate appercep-tions of what life has to go through to live.

Boris can be dazzlingly and terrifyingly sharp yet wonderfully gentle. He does not rest on laurels of the moment before, but pushes edges of the future. He milks the surfboard of the present for dear life, rides it like a wild bronco, stays on it microseconds more than most of us. As ever, he seemed to be just picking up steam when he vanished.

Perhaps the finest tribute I can offer, is to convey what I heard in the voice of a patient of his who called me. She spoke about what a tough time she was having finding another analyst. Hal was a tough act to follow. She was thinking of consulting with me, if she visited New York. She never came. I heard something in her voice that made me quiver. Many patients and therapists develop loyalty to one another. But the loyalty of someone touched in that special way that makes all the difference in the world has an unmistakable sound.

After word of his death, I felt badly over our aborted friendship, a friendship that never quite took off. We valued each other and in another decade or so, might have grown together. An odd and beautiful thing about human being is that sometimes death brings souls closer than life. I never felt closer to Hal than now—and, I suspect, in years to come closer still. In human life, what could have been is often more important than what is. A friendship that could have been can become more powerful than one that was.

Hal, sing on. I hear your spirit ditties of no tone. They work in me. You have worked well. Your music is in the air. Now and then our songs become counterpoint. We sing together.

REFERENCES

Boris, H.N. (1993). *Passions of the Mind: Unheard Melodies, A Third Principle of Mental Functioning*. New York: New York University Press.

―― (1994a). *Envy*. Northvale, NJ: Jason Aronson.

―― (1994b). *Sleights of Mind: One and Multiples of One*. Northvale, NJ: Jason Aronson.

Joseph, R. (1996). *Neuropsychiatry, Neuropsychology, and Clinical Neuroscience*. Baltimore, MD: Williams and Wilkins.

225 Central Park West
New York NY 10024
USA

Remembering Harold Boris

Edward Emery

Harold Boris cannot be categorized. We can, however, accurately say that he was that genre of analyst we might think of as neo-Kleinian. His passion and synthetic imagination found its consumate Other in encounter with Wilfred Bion. Yet, true to the spirit of Bion, to say this of Boris is already to fit him into a slot. As one who was especially sensitive to fits (as, for example, between a nipple and a mouth), Harold Boris did not fit easily into the way the group mind divides up the conceptual universe.

Hal's was the mind of a gadfly. Peripatetic, he had a voracious appetite for questions and for taking the received view and twisting it between 30 and 350 degrees until the familiar idea took on freshness and transformed into something new and original.

Like that other gadfly Socrates, Hal was a master ironist. He loved words, their meter and rhythm, their sound and tone. He loved to move them around, create juxtapositions, let them rub against each other, pair and couple, and form through this mix a discourse that was at once poetic and lucid. As one who was suspicious of the foreclosures in which story-telling could wrap desire, he was a consumate story teller. His writing had the flavor and dance of unconscious mentations displacing and condensing toward the highest levels of abstraction, all the while anchored in the lived and the immanent of experience in order to sight enduring truths.

> Like other children, I was fascinated by the mote dance in the sunbeams and the spiral nebula in the galactic broth of the lightly pressured cornea. What butterfly net (Abercrombie and Fitch? Whorf and Sapir?) could capture these swirls without in the process of reducing them to rubble? In what way, against the background sounds of my own life and croons, growls, and struts of others, could I reach beyond the now and the then to the almost was and the yet to be? (Boris, 1994, p. vii).

I first found Hal through his paper on Bion ("Bion revisited"). Here, I thought, was a mind on fire. His was a mind that slid back and forth between what Kant called the sublime (the unfathomable) and the aesthetic (the beautiful). He later told me that of all who were to have impact on his life and development (Erikson, Rappaport, and Bettelheim—to mention but a few), Bion was decisive, in the sense of being both disorienting and expanding. It was, he said, like hitting your head against the top bunk.

I never asked Hal the obvious: who or what occupied that top bunk. He implied, however, that whatever primal scene or thick memory or dense nothing was the denizen of the overhead, it took up too much room. Hal found his way through the limit of this woody obstacle and onto his own path betwixt and between.

This achievement is, of course, never without price. Among its costs is the toss up between the dread of being chosen and so defined by the other, and the agony of not being chosen and so left without anchor, on—as we say—one's own. This tension became a persistent theme runing through all of Hal's work, from the early papers on anorexia to the later series on envy:

> So, what many of us fear most, starvation unto death, becomes the best riposte to what the anorectic fears most, enslavement by the desirability of the other; and, when projected, enslavement by the desire of the other; and when dissimulated into the food-hunger condensation, enslaved by food and the effects of food, namely weight (1994, p. 167).

And later:

> The envious die a thousand deaths; it is heartwrenching, the pain they go through, because their self-preservation inclination is such that they cannot resign themselves to the one and only death" (*ibid*, pp. 97-98).

Then, faced with the choice of being himself or the other, there is Boris on Boris:

> When, after another several phone calls, he (Bettelheim) granted me an interview. . . he had only one question for me:
> "What is your name?"
> I told him my name, and of course he asked again. I told him again, a little more loudly.
> "I am asking you: What is your name? and you do not appear to wish to answer."
> "I am answering!" I replied, stung, and repeated my name.
> "Boris is not a surname. What is your real name?"
> "Boris!" I replied in what must have been nearly a shout.
> "My name is Boris and that's the only name I have."
> I wondered briefly if there was somewhere I could get another one. But what should the new one be: "Bettelheim"? (*ibid*, p. xviii).

He was, to the end, Boris.

REFERENCES

Boris, H. (1986). Bion revisited. *Contemp. Psychoanal.*, 22(2): 159-184. [Reprinted in *Sleights of Mind*, pp. 225-252.]
—— (1993). *Envy*. Northvale, NJ: Aronson.
—— (1994). *Sleights of Mind. One and Multiples of One.* Northvale, NJ: Aronson.

15 Brewster Court
Northampton MA 01060
USA

UNDER FIVES STUDY CENTER

CHILD AND FAMILY PSYCHIATRY
UNIVERSITY OF VIRGINIA
CHARLOTTESVILLE, VIRGINIA, USA

INFANT OBSERVATION CONFERENCE

April 30 - May 2, 1998

APPLICATIONS IN
TRAINING, TREATMENT AND RESEARCH

The Tavistock model of infant observation has stirred interest in the United States. Multi-disciplinary panelists from England, Canada and the U. S. will discuss papers on the current use of this model as it influences treatment, training and research.

The conference will take place at the historic and beautiful University of Virginia, Charlottesville, Virginia, USA

Write for conference information :

Under Fives Study Center Conference
Child and Family Psychiatry
One Boar's Head Lane
Charlottesville, Virginia   22903

Tel: 804-243-6950   Fax: 804-243-6970
e-mail: heg2e@virginia.edu

ENVY IN THE PSYCHOANALYTIC PROCESS

Harold Boris

> To pay their respects to the Lord came three men. As befit his station in life, the one who was arrayed in gold was the first to present himself at the altar. "Forgive me, O Lord," he prayed. "I am nothing."
>
> The second man then stepped forth. He was arrayed in silver. "O Lord, forgive me. I am nothing," he prayed.
>
> The third man then came to the altar. He was disheveled, his robes tattered and torn. "O Lord," he prayed. "Forgive me. For I am nothing."
>
> At this, the first man nudged the second: "Look who's calling himself nothing!"

Although analysts of all persuasions attend to them intuitively, the dynamics of envy have not (until now, perhaps) been available for systematic therapeutic investigation and relief. In this paper I hope somewhat to remedy that omission. Unlike other writers, I do not regard envy as primary. I shall therefore focus on fantasies concerning selection, on hope, and on that handmaiden of hope, time.

The explicit role of envy in the therapeutic endeavor has for the most part been confined to the analysis of the negative therapeutic reaction. In his encyclopedic work, *The Fundamentals of Psychoanalytic Technique,* Etchegoyen (1991) provides a summary of these contributions beginning with Freud. In "Remembering, repeating and working through" (1914), he warned that the patient's worsening condition might be used for his own ends. In "The economic problem of masochism," Freud (1924) changed his terms somewhat; rather than the sense of guilt Freud refers to the need for punishment. In 1923, in *The Ego and the Id*, Freud links the condition to guilt generated by the superego; the patient, who ought to have the right to improve, worsens because the superego does not assign this right to him.

Abraham (1919) wrote that such patients cannot understand that the aim of the treatment is the cure of their neurosis and indicates that narcissism, competitive rivalry and envy are important impelling forces. Horney (1936) noted the paradoxical nature of the backward movement. There is a puzzling worsening of the patient when there should be progress. Horney wrote of the narcissism and sadomasochism of the patient, which distort the reactions to interpretation and make the patient a rival of the analyst. Joan Rivière (1936) proposed that, in the advent of the depressive position, the anticipation of a depressive catastrophe is particularly intense and that feelings of omnipotence figure large in the manic defenses employed to control the analyst and the analysis. She pointed out that such patients come not so much to have themselves cured as to find a cure for their damaged internal objects. Reflecting on the curious mix between entitlement and dread which I have myself emphasized, she observes a conflict between conscious egotism and unconscious altruism.

Homer tells the story of Penelope awaiting the return of her husband, the father of her son. As Queen, she is under vast pressure to consider her long overdue husband Odysseus dead, to remarry, and give order and continuity to the monarchy. Pressed, finally, to stipulate a time by when she will do this, she promises to do so when she has finished the robe, the winding sheet, she is weaving for Odysseus' sick and dying father, Laertes. It is as if in this she asks only to put a wrap on her former marriage. "So spoke she," recounts Antonious, "and our high hearts consented thereto."

But what Penelope wove in daytime, she unraveled by night.

> Such wile as hers we have never yet heard that any of the women of old did know . . . . Not one of these in the imaginations of their hearts was like unto Penelope (*The Odyssey*, pp. 18-19).

The generosity of this estimation was doubtless prompted by Antonious's effort to save face among the wooers who, for more than three years, were taken in by her. Penelope had higher hopes, almost higher even, it was to turn out, than for Odysseus. But in fact undoing what was done in order to rearrive at square one is a device probably as old as time itself.

Regarding time, Adam Phillips (1993) puts the pith of the traditional psychoanalytic view, which regards the intervals (frustration, absence) between being contentedly with the object and being with it again as at once the source and seat of mental life. One could ask the following "slightly absurd question, Is the first thought the absence of mother or the presence of time?" (p. 91) "I think where I am not, therefore I am where I do not think," writes Lacan (1977, p. 166). Indeed—but this is time in the COUPLE. I begin with time, but time in the PAIR.

Many of those who harbor doubts as to whether or not, or to what extent, they are meant to flourish, feel that it is only a matter of time before their status as one of the unselected will come into view. But that is only part of it. There is in these instances a need to be reborn or otherwise transformed consonant with one's hopes (see Bollas below). Such travelers cannot long tarry. If therapy were a place they could be out of before all was discovered or before time ran out on hope, that would be one thing. Failing that, there are not many options. They can leave (sometimes at a moment's notice). They can make it look as if they are there against their will (this is not tactically disconnected from the first). Or they can continually reset the clock to zero. (This makes schedules a favorite battleground with rules coming a close second, particularly those concerning coming late and leaving early, and rescheduling; if the therapist has a taste for skirmishes, all he needs are a few rules.) Whichever way they take, they cannot but envy the comfortably vast sense of time that psychoanalysts enjoy (as expressed, for example, in the aphorism "These things take time"). Envy's need to disestablish time and continuity is acute or acutely chronic. Through all of these, of course, runs the anguished argument—who decides?

The patient's often covert anxiety about getting well, becoming better, being different, indeed, becoming or getting anything, must occupy the center of the analysis, if there is to be one. At the core of this is the patient's use of analogues to decrease feelings of being tormented by differences he can neither use nor forget. These analogues serve (often enviously) to blur distinctions and so at once reduce desire and increase similarity. They thus serve the PAIR at the expense of the COUPLE. When distinctions are heightened, the loss of these fondly fashioned analogues represents, accordingly, not one, but two frightening events; a sense of being at one with the group is jeopardized and the now-no-longer-just-like-me portion or person becomes open to relationships featuring either xenophobic attack (stranger anxiety) or abject desire, both of which had been finessed by blurring the vast distinctions between "more than" and "different from." There then, after a long interval, lurks a renewal of the awesome otherness of the other.

How hard people who fear the pain of feeling envious work to make the analysis someone else's and not their own! When they arrive it is because they are sent. While they are here it is to assist the analyst with clear or obscure purposes of his own, for which he never seems sufficiently grateful since he is always carping about something or other. When at length it begins to dawn on very envious patients that they may just possibly be here for purposes of their own, they threaten to leave, wait to be dissuaded, and then resume their care of their needful analyst. After each interval the question seems to arise anew: if I have to want, or know I want, it won't be you I choose. Analysts who themselves need a sense of alliance are often tempted to regain one by filling out the space the patient is leaving. And indeed if one doesn't, one's own serenity and dispassion seem so enviable as to inspire havoc. Rather than succumb, the patient might rather die or starve or give himself or herself to others. Part of the difficulty is that people justly fear selection; they know that the more ardent their desire the fewer the choices. They sense, correctly, that the analyst is making selection after selection, choosing this aspect of the patient over that. What will they be like when they are over?

> P. You know, when I sleep around like this I am at risk of contracting AIDS. Yes. But not, at least, of contracting aid.
> Ψ When I was little we played tag. Being the smallest, I was often "it." And being little often I could not catch the others, so I had to stay "it" for a long time. [Silence.]
> Ψ My turn to be "it."
> P. Can you hear me?
> Ψ Only when you make yourself audible.
> P. But you could hear my question?
> Ψ I can hear you when you make yourself audible. I can "hear" you when you make yourself "heard."
> P. [Inaudible.] Did you hear that?
> Ψ I "heard" that.
> P. But did you hear it?
> Ψ Some choice!

But as in any argument, there is the equal and opposite position. The famished wish to control time propels an intent to own it. And the surest sign of owning something often seems to be that the owner can do anything he wants with what he owns. Furious at being spooked by time, the envious patient makes waste hastily. Nothing takes too long, and there would be time for everything were the therapist not so impatient. In his novel *Mr. Palomar*, Italo Calvino (1985) writes:

> "If time has to end, it can be described, instant by instant," Mr. Palomar thinks, "and each instant, when described, expands so that its end can no longer be seen." He decides that he will set himself to describing every instant of his life, and until he had described them all he will no longer think of being dead. At that moment he dies (p. 126).

Then too there is what Calvino approvingly (elsewhere—1988) quotes from Carlo Levi. Levi is speaking of Laurence Sterne's *Tristram Shandy*.

> The clock is Shandy's first symbol. Under its influence he is conceived and his misfortunes begin, which are one and the same with this emblem of time. Death is hidden in clocks, as Belli said; and the unhappi-

ness of individual life, of this fragment, of this divided, disunited thing, devoid of wholeness: death, which is time, the time of individuation, of separation, the abstract time that rolls toward its end. Tristram Shandy does not want to be born, because he does not want to die. Every means and every weapon is valid to save oneself from death and time. If a straight line is the shortest distance between two fated and inevitable points, digressions will lengthen it; and if these digressions become so complex, so tangled and tortuous, so rapid as to hide their own tracks, who knows—perhaps death may not find us, perhaps time will lose its way, and perhaps we ourselves can remain concealed in our shifting hiding places (p. 47).

Thus when envy is acute there is also a therapist who must be prepared to live with nothing being settled. Indeed, if the therapist is so unwary as to permit himself a sigh of relief now and then because things seem to be going better, he will soon enough come to feel his sigh was overheard, for it is promptly followed, as if by magic, by the recrudescence of old issues that have come unglued again. Under such circumstances, perfectly competent therapists can be forgiven if they turn from helping their patients understand the forces driving them to teaching, confrontation, even jeremiads—those sentences that begin with, "You know...."

The envious person generally tries to rid himself of his disease by inducing the illness or trauma instead in the analyst, grafting it to whatever remnants there are of the analyst's own. This is the parasitism that characterizes the patient's idea of object relations. The patient's relation in the PAIR with his introjects is the first job of the analysis; the analyst should endeavor not to expose himself for emotional discovery until well into that work. For the patient, if he cannot flourish without exposing himself to murderous retaliation from his split-off hatred, cannot thank the analyst for leading him to this.

When the patient's greed, anxiety, and envy converge on issues of ownership, for the analyst too there is a deeper question: which of the rules and structures are necessary for the work to progress, and which the hand-me-downs of tradition maintained in therapist's professional PAIR and GROUP—the latter of which I shall call the academy. In making this distinction between function and tradition, I do not mean to say that the affiliation with tradition is not important to the therapist. The therapist needs to feel a part of things, particularly when being exposed to the relentless doubts insinuated into him by the envious patient. For perhaps the greatest pain for the analyst arises out of the patient's unrelenting assertion that the analyst has bad intentions and therefore, even if he does his best, nothing he can do will be right. Often this assertion is not made verbally, but indicated in sighs and moues, small rollings of the eyes, and quick, slight movements of the shoulders. For all that the analyst may try to understand that this unrelenting attitude contains those qualities of the survivor—backbone and resolve—the fixed quality of this stubborn asseveration can get unnerving.

All the same, the lighter the analyst travels, the less there is to protect because, when excessively envious, the patient suffers from an insufficiency of unconsciousness and so needs to enlist the therapist's resistances to augment his own. The envious patient, if he is going to look into psychoanalysis at all, is not likely also to be willing to see it—or see it through. He will do what he did as a baby, he will "cut" the analyst. He is simply not going to be found wanting; every indication of want discovered will have to be the analyst's want of him. He leaves a vacuum for the analyst to fill. The analyst finds this vacancy tempting, for certainly the life he hears about and the person he encounters seem distressed indeed. He may feel further tempted by the fact that if he does not get actively to work nothing much will seem to be happening.

Impatience, boredom, irritation, desolation, doubt all help the therapist not to listen or closely attend. By inspiring these feelings in the therapist, the patient can get the therapist to join in finding little significance to what he says. Not a few patients achieve the same ends by provoking in their analysts an increasing disbelief in the analytic process. The patient will drone on or become hit or miss, and the therapy will soon begin to seem like a nothing. In short, the therapist will soon find himself with every reason to want actively to help his patient out or out. If he does not help, the therapist will begin to be afraid of becoming sick with uselessness, helplessness, rage, and guilt. By organizing their lives into a downward spiral, the patient dares the therapist to continue what seems to have become too little or too late. Every point at which the therapist moves away from the business at hand to pick up on something peripheral to it is a moment in which the therapy can be vitiated. This places the therapist in a cleft-stick. If he sets the therapy aside to see to the downward spiral of the patient's life, he shows his care and concern for the patient, but he also demonstrates a lack of respect for the therapeutic endeavor.

Not all patients have to split the therapist like this nor all analysts to feel split. But when, out of acute envy, the patient needs insofar as he can to sever the therapist from his therapeutic potency, the analyst needs to know his own needs. Does he need assent to what he says? Does he need progress —for the patient to get better or change—for the patient to be different? What does he need by way of cooperation—regularity, promptitude, talk? The prudent therapist will know his limitations and make his rules accordingly. If he asks for no more and no less than what he absolutely needs, it follows that the rules and structures he requires can be non-negotiable. If he can settle for what the black-pajamed patient can afford him, he will spare himself from dreading the next appointment or yearning for the end of this.

So envious can envy become that it has no interest even in the self, except an envious one—ever alert to snuff out or punish any indications that the self is flourishing. Since this means that the patient cannot get well without exposing himself (really, those he is identified with in the PAIR) to terrible abuse for doing so, the patient can only turn himself to an interest in the other and getting him more ill. (It is in this sense that Meltzer [1967] talks of analysis as being a salvage operation.) Such a self, gorged by the identifications that go to make up first PAIRING, then GROUPING, so seriously lacks the relations involved in COUPLING that it is almost choked.

> As I drew closer, I saw what was happening. She [a bag lady on the streets of NYC] was *imitating the passers-by*. . . . But it was not just an imitation, extraordinary as this would have been in itself. The woman not only took on, and took in, the features of countless people. She took them off. Every mirroring was also a parody. . . .
>
> This woman who, becoming everybody, lost her own self, became nobody. This woman with a thousand faces, works, personalities—how must it be for her in this whirlwind of identities? The answer came soon—and not a second too late (sic): for the build up of personas, both hers and others' was fast approaching the point of explosion. Suddenly, desperately, the old woman turned into an alleyway which led off the main street. And there, with all the appearances of a woman violently sick, she expelled, tremendously accelerated and abbreviated, all the gestures, the postures, the expressions, the demeanors, the behavioral repertoires of the past forty or fifty people she had passed (Sacks, 1985, pp. 117-118).

To ask the self to identify with the analyst in what is sometimes called the therapeutic alliance is a disservice. It means opening up the inclination to look for, mayhaps to lust for, the very differences of which COUPLING is made. And it means the terrible loss of the identifications out of which the self is constructed (often ingeniously and with concealed pride).

> Each individual is made up of what he has lived and the way he has lived it, and no one can take this away from him. Anyone who has lived in suffering is always made of that suffering; if they try to take it away from him, he is no longer himself. Therefore, Mr. Palomar prepares to become a grouchy dead man, reluctant to submit to the sentence to remain exactly as he is; but he is unwilling to give up anything of himself, even if it is a burden (Calvino, 1985, p. 125).

It follows that it helps very much if a patient's progress, or lack of it, is his own business, and not the analyst's. Therapists are not immune from envy; indeed some portion of their practice enacts and visits upon their patients an envy screened from view by their membership in the psychoanalytic group. If the analyst can stand for the therapy to belong to the patient, there is less reason for the patient to try to "get his own back." Envious patients often ask their analysts to help them cheapen and degrade speech, free association, personal encounter, and anything else that they cannot yet use with pleasure and confidence.

The initial experience of envy is naturally at its most acute when concentrated. The infant who can take his time about discovering the features of the breast is less traumatized by the envy with which it inflames him. That same sort of time taking will be required by the infant self as it comes into contact with the analytic provider. But when envy is rife, it dilates rapidly, and with only a brief amount of time to contain it, it quickly reaches explosive proportions. The infant self doesn't know what its successor selves know about time. But though successor selves come into being, the infant self survives until it feels able to mourn its own passing.

Many people are asked or allowed to discover their analysts far too soon. There may have to be a series of encounters at the beginning, though the fewer the better, having to do with rates, times, and other housekeeping matters. And there may have to be a series of encounters in which the analyst must demonstrate that he understands that the patient will expect him to have something to ask or even to say, before he can get back out of the patient's way. But these early interventions can be used to make manifest the analyst's conviction that psychoanalysis is a matter of talking of experiences in which both analyst and patient participate and has nothing whatever to do with talking *about* experiences, particularly those the analyst only hears about. This, when repeatedly demonstrated, helps the patient to recognize himself as the vital part of the enterprise, an experience essential to any analysis, but especially to one in which the patient's envy is a prominent feature. If the therapist can forget about his designs on the patient, including those he has been taught are necessary and correct, the patient has a chance of forgetting about the therapist and getting on with what he came to do. This is to create, or recapture, and then display a series of half-forgotten experiences. Later on, should he feel two heads are better than one and that there is something to be said for an-"other" perspective, he will ask the analyst for an interpretation of what he has been at such pains to display. This leaves the value of having a contribution to the matter by the therapist to the patient where, of course, it belongs if it is to be his and not the therapist's therapy.

If, by the time the patient is ready to discover him, the analyst's COUPLE-relationship (his or her libidinal transferences) and the PAIR-relationship (his or her identity and work as a member of a psychoanalytic PAIR and representative of the psychoanalytic GROUP) have been thoroughly investigated by the analyst, he may indeed have something to say. For he will by then know what he wants to say—and also, no less, why he wants to say it. That is why it helps so much when therapists can, first, wait to be asked; second, be really sure what it is that they are being asked; third, be clear about what they have to say; and then be fully informed as to why they want to say it. But in such self possession, there is little foothold for the patient, who may then accordingly raise the ante by becoming ill, getting in trouble, or wanting to leave. Analysts who until then have been studies in forbearance may come undone.

> In her sexual life with her new lover, P. is not feeling realized. There are some key elements in the original primal scene that are not finding their way into her current one. She is hesitant to complain, because she feels that others, particularly her lover and her analyst, might find her ungrateful. And she is ashamed to confess that she is secretly preoccupied by the admittedly unlikely possibility that her gentle and considerate lover might suddenly hit her or force her. But little by little she is "sneaking back" to her prerelationship masturbation fantasy, the main feature of which is that others are watching her undress, dance, or have sexual intercourse until they can stand it no longer. At this point the fantasy bifurcates. In some renditions the others are envious of her sensuality and beauty; they hope by interrupting and pressing money upon her to drag her down into being a prostitute. In other renditions, they are so beside themselves with desire that they must have her no matter the cost to them in money and humiliation.
>
> Even in the richly textured warp and woof of this material, there is no missing the bright, anguished thread of loss. Past images, past hopes are going unselected by current events. It is as if (as a dream of P.'s soon puts it) P. has become a department store where people come and pick and choose whatever they like. Her fierce, desperate wish to have a hold on them through their passions is being frustrated, and in her shame of that wish, which, after all, concerns life and death, she cannot assert her ferocity, save by sneaking back to her fantasies.
>
> As the new relationship goes from good to better, and she grows daily happier, her heart sinks. The evident contentment of her lover makes her want to wail and gnash her teeth. Death, already implied in the unmistakable passage of time away from her youthful imaginings, and expressed in the cruel fates of the fantasy, now makes its appearance garbed as AIDS and as pregnancy—each definitive, hence final, so fatal. Afraid, and furious because she is afraid, she alters the love making with her lover until it

begins to resemble a scene in a movie in which, to practice safe sex, each person crawls into a body-sized condom. Her lover, instead of becoming rapacious, begins to have occasional difficulties with his potency, something that leaves P. feeling guilty and more afraid. She becomes fearful lest her lover leave, she feels she is now living on borrowed time.

How to put an end to ending? How, instead, to force time's own pace?

P., feeling compelled to outgrow her childish ways long before she could grow out of them, has grown up fast. She has become an adept at developing a taste for things before coming to an appetite for them. A young woman in a hurry—ever impatient—it took time before she could feel convinced that where she hurried to was wherever she could take all the time in the world. Death too is something to be gotten over with as soon as possible. Perhaps after the pain of death is over one can relax and enjoy life. She has long felt that only if she were already married to him could she sit back and escape the turmoil of a first date. It is painful for P. to leave each session; on knife's edge, she has been unable to immerse herself in the time she has. It seems she comes too often for what she is able to accomplish; her analysis seems to be taking forever.

  Ψ [Suggests that deep down P. feels she should have more frequent sessions, but hates both ideas—of more frequent sessions and of thinking she should have them.]

  P. Why would I want to come more often? This is such a waste of time, as it is, that it's only because I only come as often as I do that I can put up with it!

Is this waste cause or consequence? Had she more time, wouldn't she need less? As this begins to occur to P., she begins to feel endangered.

  P. [Turns from lying prone on the couch onto her side. She sees the analytic foot.] "I am allowed to see your foot. I am not allowed to look at you, but I am allowed to see your foot." [She has earlier been talking of how she lies and steals.] "Your shoe. Do you remember how I always want to eat your shoe. I used to think about that a lot—that's how I realized it. I feel you are angry and impatient with me. You looked angry and impatient when I came in today. I thought of it as a projection. But maybe you *are* angry and impatient with me. Maybe it's you, not me. Are you? *Are* you? I buy a lot of shoes, you know." [Silence.] "I am sure it is your influence, though I can't see how."

To relate is to choose. To relate certain observations by supposing, for example, that to all actions there is an opposite and equal reaction is to rule out all the other possibilities that might previously have seemed determinate. Objects are merely objects—appendages—until they are discovered to be in a relationship, whereupon they take on significance, being at once signified and signifier. It is the discovery of their role in a relationship that excites envy— or, when envy can be borne, jealousy.

A patient sighs, says:

> I hope I do not let the whole thing go haywire again. [She means the *"hole"* thing, an interpretation Ψ has used for her, so her decision not to use the phrase is today probably a proximate source of her worry.] Today I feel it, I feel second rate and I know it is a result of my wish that K. treated me better over the weekend, that I wasn't left feeling such a slob, so defective, with this, this, and this wrong with me. And today I feel you are listening, really listening, ya know? But I know you *do* listen. But today I can say it to you, let you know I know. But I am afraid. I am afraid that this will all go physical on me—out of the realm of the emotions. Into mindland: panic attacks, nausea, fatigue. And that "the looking funny" doesn't come back. I hate that worst of anything. I cannot control it when it happens and everything looks funny. Not funny. What is the word I want? Surrealistic, out of kilter, dislocated. Everything. You have said it is my making it "everything" is to keep it from being any particular no-thing.

Meanwhile P.'s sessions seem to be going badly.

At length, P. remarks about her silliness in thinking Ψ could help with something that after all is between her and her lover. She suspects Ψ thinks she is being paranoid.

Ψ agrees, reminding her that Ψ often thinks this to be her defense against feeling frightened. Ψ adds that she sounds annoyed at being able correctly to guess what Ψ thinks.

P. I think *you* think I ought to come more often, but I can't, and I don't think you understand that I can't. [This is said bitterly, as if there has been or is an empathic failure on Ψ's part.]

Soon P. declines to speak, instead lying in each session as if in a pool of anger, waiting for things to change. In P.'s silence, Ψ hears this:

"I have given you all the information that anyone with an ounce of intelligence and sensitivity requires before doing something to h-e-l-p. Going back to free-associating, which I know is what you expect me to sooner or later do, would be going along with what you want—allowing you, once more, to have your way. In fact, you are probably only too anxious to interpret matters as they now stand, as if it were not you who were responsible but some distant figure from my past, now reincarnated in you. Well, I say 'only too anxious,' but in fact you believe that time is very much on your side. Not only do you get paid no matter what, but you can let me either sink or swim or to stew in my own juices until I come around to your way of doing things."

This fear enrages P.

"I will not allow myself to be subjected to these intimidation tactics, not again, not now at my age. You're running a con. You lulled me with your sympathetic, nonjudgmental manner, and I fell for it. I turned myself inside out for you, but each time it is the same: never satisfied. Well, forget it! I'm not going to be that kind of sucker, not now, not ever. D' you seriously expect me just to roll over and play dead?"

P. [Talking aloud to Ψ] "Do you expect me to just roll over and play dead? And—*don't turn this around!*"

As if in some anxiety lest Ψ do just that, P. now gets up from lying down and sits on the edge of the couch. She is calmer now, enough to look at Ψ. But something in Ψ's steadfast, musing gaze sends a lightening flash of pure rage through P. Words like "just sitting there" carom past.

P. I don't have to put up with this bullshit, you know! [P. gets to her feet, walks to the door grasps the knob.] "Well, have you got anything to say, because if you don't . . . ." P. turns the knob, opens the door slightly.

Ψ I do have something to say, but could you at least sit down?

[P. sits on the very edge of the chair that was the starting off place many months ago. The door from the consulting room to the waiting room is left slightly ajar. Ψ here goes on to say what, in the turmoil, Ψ can find to say.]

Such moments occur in some form sooner or later in any therapy in which the patient's (or the therapist's) envy has a preeminent role. The time we use to allow matters to evolve and recohere and the quiet we employ to listen for our dawning intuitions conveys menace. Since so much of this is supposed to go without saying—indeed, cannot quite be said—one must (the pregnancy analogy is deliberate) bear this in mind. One's own capacity to tolerate nothing quickly becomes an issue central to the analysis. If one can regard the torment of experience as a hateful fact, analysis is possible. If one succumbs to the temptation to replace the no-things with something —well, one soon is out of the analysis business and into the transfusion business. Envy in effect blocks anything and everything the other can do until the other does what the self wants, in this case, until Ψ does what P. wants. The end need not come abruptly, in a big bang, as in the illustration it appears to be doing. The stripping away of Ψ's potency can be gradual and chronic.

The precise event P. illustrates can be understood in several ways. That there are several hot potatoes being tossed back and forth, concerning which of the two must own up to unrespectable qualities or intentions, is apparent. P. wishes to disassociate herself from being the source of these and to reassign their ownership to Ψ, something, it seems, P. feels can only be done securely if and when Ψ acts consonantly with them. These involve being greedy, grasping and indifferent to time. And they involve something called "turning things around."

Ψ is reluctant to act consonantly with what P. attributes to him (or her). He "holds" them, in the sense of knowing them, but only when the door opens outward does Ψ make a grab for P. Does Ψ then do what P. fears? Does he, for example, interpret the transference?

After all, much of what P. has been experiencing can be accounted for very easily by explanations having to do with transference. The transference has rules in it to the effect that displacements can fan out or contract as to objects, can split subject and object (as in "part of me" or "part of you") and can reverse, as to subject and object, wholly or in parts. It is not so much the nouns that matter but the verbs—not *who* does what and with which and to whom, but the nature of what's *being done*. You can do it to me or I can do it to you, so long as we *do* it. The transference embodies this, primarily in the exploration and exploitation of differences: in part-object terms, mouth-breast, penis-vagina and so forth; in whole-object terms, prey-predator, younger-older, man-woman and so on. Thus we can imagine that P.'s opening statement, consisting of P. lying on the couch like an unchanged infant might lie about neglected in a puddle of urine or feces, reflects the recurrence, in present time, of a very distressing state of affairs in which P. once again is waiting for someone, in the present instance Ψ, to change her—but not, of course, in any therapeutic sense. The fact that Ψ is not doing this for P. and, to make matters worse, is relying on the potency of his skills as a therapist not to have to change the dirtied, uncomfortable, neglected P., adds insult to injury—and the sheer gall or effrontery of this posture of Ψ's stimulates P.'s envy. P. intends to denude Ψ of his (or her) therapeutic powers, of his wherewithal, because these stand between P. and getting cared for.

On the other hand, P. is trying out leaving, and Ψ plainly needs to afford her the time to do so. Though tempted, Ψ may not have to tell P. such things as that he can find another Ψ for P. or that he will save P.'s hours for a while so that they are there should P. elect to return. He may instead be able to say: "*Of course* we must put a stop to what you are finding so intolerable, even if that means an end to this session, or an end even to our work. *No one* should be asked to go through what you have been going through." P. may experience this as a Trojan horse designed to insinuate Ψ's own projections or to reposit P.'s projections into P. But what if Ψ means what he says?

The tension at this juncture cannot be overestimated. P. is at the edge of discovering that she may not in fact be able to conceive and give birth to herself—that Ψ is necessary as something more than a stage property. The current disparity is one in which Ψ is onlooker, is the infant in the primal apotheosis out of which, in P.'s as yet unreconstructed history, another infant, a little boy, was indeed born. Proud P. is going this time around to mother and father the as-yet-unformed baby of herself. *And don't turn this around!*

But it is—slowly, inexorably, as if huge plate tectonics are crushingly on the move—getting turned around.

> A patient says: "I am always on my back. I am a turtle or a beetle, on my back, soft underbelly up, being or anticipating being used, fucked, or devoured. Why can't I turn over? Why do you refuse to let me sit up?"

Manifestly, this woman's language is in the COUPLE; it seems sexual in nature, inviting associations of cannibalism, rape, premorbid autopsy. It is placed there defensively, because, as the image of beetle and turtle suggest, there is a carapace to be found. Translated into the language of PAIR and GROUP, which at the moment is latent to that of the COUPLE, the issue shows its darker side. In this language the turtle might refer to the length of life tortoises enjoy, while the beetle might suggest the prolixity of the beetle among extant creatures. Beyond that, moreover, is her vulnerability to the prying eye: that eye empty of remorse or charity, that espying eye that asks, "What are you doing here? Haven't I long since told you to be dead and gone by now? Your place is with the invisible chorus, yet whom do I see—You!"

When envy is on the boil, there are only two distillates: only two positions in the world and only one → way for objects to relate. There is "it" and only more of "it." The arrow may swing, but it is the same arrow. If the arrow is ↓ down up, its alternative is up ↑ down, if it is I am being ← fucked, it can only invert to → you.[1] It is easy to see therefore that changes in Ψ's approach to P. can all too easily be seen not as empathic accommodation, but as a capitulation. P. consciously desires such capitulation, but unconsciously capitulations degrade Ψ in P.'s connoisseur eyes and in doing so stimulate a good deal of guilt. The patient can often only escape such guilt by persuading himself that the analyst isn't worth feeling compunction about. And he will provoke the analyst until the latter conforms to the justifiable profile. But when the patient takes relief from such disparagement he loses out on whatever remaining value there is to the analyst. A victory for envy in the PAIR is a loss to the patient in the COUPLE.

Such divergences of opinion come about when Ψ misunderstands the bone of contention. P. is being stubborn because her understanding from day one (whenever day one was) was that she is meant to give over and die, as a result of which she can only want to—or want to become a changed character (cosmetic surgeons do very well out of this need). It has taken every ounce of P.'s resolve not to take these orders. That resolve, moreover, has alienated P. from herself, because in the PAIR she is not meant to resist; she is meant, rather, to carry out instructions as every good soldier must. The *resolute* quality of the nonreceptive object—the object made of stone and bone—becomes itself an object of envy, for its presumptive indifference is much coveted by the personality that feels itself at sixes and sevens due to the force of influences playing upon it. But if Ψ attempts to find relief by active efforts to engage the patient, he will be shown—though he may not notice—the patient's increasing triumph and relief that it is now the analyst! who needs and wants—the tables have been wormed; the cinder is on the other foot.

In the face of a feeling one should get on about dying, any status quo can only be attractive indeed. The analyst may feel that the analysis has locked into an impasse, but what is for the analyst an impasse is for the patient an anchorage:

"I felt so scared I couldn't move," says the woman alone in the dark.
"I couldn't breathe, I couldn't draw a breath."
"I shrank, I tried to make myself as small as I could without moving," says the man out late in the parking garage or the deer caught up in the headlights.
"I closed my eyes," says the little boy.
"I can't go on like this!" says the woman rent by the pea under the mattresses, but mutilated by the fear that she might want nonetheless to go on.
"I covered up my ears and made noise in them by clapping my hands over them," says the little girl.
"I began to hallucinate," says the trembling gent in the corner. "The voices took charge and started screaming orders."

There has to be some way of controlling the angel of death. The envy of the unselected is atavistic, perhaps because their anxieties are so close to the fundament. I have, for example, never worked with such a patient who did not have a secret and engorged fascination with ova-positing—that quick, passing fascination with insects that immobilize their victims and make them unwilling host to their eggs and larva. But neither would I have caught that line of fantasy had I not been alert. There is much shame to it, as one might expect, since shame itself, being a social anxiety, is a function of the PAIR, and ova-positing a violation of the precepts of the PAIR that we use one another as self-objects and sources for mutual identification. But ordinary reproduction is a function of the COUPLE, and, as such, not a remedy for the illicit and defiant determination to cheat death of its proscription against progeneration. The initial wish, to deposit experiences not yet processable by symbol formation, thought, and affect formation turns ugly. It *must* penetrate the barrier of the self-contained (or other-containing) object. The frustration of its efforts to penetrate in a straightforward way produces a surplus of hatred and feelings of persecution. These in turn stimulate the wish to murder the object—or, failing that, at least to *be* murdered *by* it. The discovery of murderous impulses in the object is tantamount to the discovery of life where all was deadness—stone and bone. The wish to be murdered (an apotheosis) is a variation on the wish to be created/selected.

> P. [Returning to the subject.] You tell me I should come more often. But my friends always ask me when I am going to terminate. I have to tell them you don't think I am done. My God, if I told them how many times a week I am still seeing you, they would think I was crazy—I don't mean crazy crazy, I mean crazy to let you make me keep coming like this. You know, you may be over estimating me. You may think I can go farther. But it could be that I have reached my limit. Maybe I don't have what it takes. Maybe I am just not one of those people who are cut out for deep therapy. What do you think? You never tell me what you think. People ask me, "When are you going to be through?" And I don't know what to tell them.

Though P. has not come out and said so, she is bringing public opinion to bear: "friends," "people." Size figures here: the agglutinative impulse of establishing more of the same makes many of few and more of many. The public enters as if comprised of legions. Armies. Under these circumstances it is not difficult to see why murdersome Ψ, too, might come to feel by turns murderous and its dead opposite, but in either case, ready to augment *himself* also through numbers. He will invoke his group, *his* academy. And as always the academy is ready to respond. Not only will Ψ find some analysts who, in the name, say, of Margaret Little, recommend touching, but other analysts who recommend a good old fashioned dose of reality, à la Freud's precedental work with the Wolf Man.

Eckstaedt, for example (1989), writes:

> For more than a decade, analysts in all parts of the world have noticed that some analyses are incomparably more difficult than others, if not impossible. In 1972, Limentani expressed the opinion that ego-syntonic neuroses, as he calls these disturbances, constitute an irreversible stumbling block to analysis. Khan provides a candid and vivid description of

how he spent years working in analyses where, so far as he could tell, nothing was happening or developing until he began to notice how annoyed he was with these patients and how necessary it was to counteract the situation (p. 502).[2]

Eckstaedt herself remarks that unless modified, such analyses are likely to be "as-if" analyses: "It is as if the analyst were assuming the role of a victim whose sacrifice is that of his analytic competence" (p. 503).

This is an ambiguous issue. Surely it would be a relief to P. to know something of the mysterious depths of Ψ's hatred and surely P. would like to know that she can affect Ψ. The capacity to affect the other is the great equalizer. It is often the way people know they are alive, are there. Thus it is probable that the more greatly P. feels affected and influenced by Ψ, the more she will insist on a turn about as no more than fair play. If, at such junctures as we are considering, P. obliges Ψ to alter his methods, limits, or boundaries, there will be a diminution of envy, to the point, moreover, that the so-called negative therapeutic reaction may be averted. It may be that Freud's imposition of a time limit upon the Wolf Man was less a confrontation— putting the heat on, lighting a fire under—with that man's frozen state than an unfreezing of Freud's usual determination to "stick coolly to the rules." This is what makes such doses of reality equivocal. It is true that many patients, feeling themselves to be in abject masochistic surrender to the sadistic analyst, can only feel that as they turn the tables, the analyst will then be in the same position relative to them. (And then in danger of another turning, which can only return them to being on their backs.) The introduction of what Eissler (1953) called "parameters" is, thus, an intricate undertaking.

As I noted, Dante placed the envious in the Inferno, where they milled about leadenly with their eyes sewn shut with leaden thread. One can discern in this a punishment for their greedy and covetous eye, for their looking for the worst, for the deadness of their presence in the light of good fortune, cheer, and levity. But in the more primitive taliation, they suffer for their attempts to blind others to their status as "illegal aliens," their impostorship, their counterfeiting of belongingness. They are should-not-haves masquerading as have-nots. In fact, of course they *are* have-nots; there is an irony here. The masquerade is that they are *pretending* to be have-nots when in fact that is exactly what they are. P. is bound and determined to see whether Ψ too is an impostor. If Ψ is, P. will feel rampant and deprived of an opportunity to increase his wherewithal; if Ψ isn't an impostor, although P.'s envy will increase, P. can continue to believe that something may come of the therapeutic endeavor. In fact, there is no choice: P. is bound to have a nose for how Ψ moves about in the world, for no pretense is safe unless the fooler can find someone willing to be fooled.

We left Ψ in somewhat of a quandary. P. was rather stubbornly about to decamp. Moreover, P. had made clear that anything Ψ might try to say would probably be construed by her—*and in addition her* GROUP—as actions that could only make matters worse. When thinking earlier about how this worked, we saw that P. was rather successfully compromising Ψ's therapeutic potency. There is in this a condensation of death and potency, of life and generativity. If there is to be a generative relationship, it seems that it will have to be with P. as the container. Quite apart from this rousing homosexual panics in patients who are or are feeling male, it means that female patients must *willy-nilly* conceive, gestate and bear Ψ's "offspring." This spells death to each one's wishes to achieve generational life in—or also in —the inverse manner.

Suppose, therefore, that P. wants to generate something that requires Ψ to be the container. Ψ's dominion over the analytic situation requires (or seems to) that P. kill off that generative strain in herself and instead submit to Ψ's in or outpourings. For P. who is close to feeling the need to give way to death as it is, this additional requirement is likely to feel like the last straw. P.'s doorway stand can be understood as a last ditch effort to get her point of view into Ψ's container. P. first tries to put a stop to Ψ's flow: she is, as it were, halfway out the door and then orders Ψ, "And don't turn this around!" Then P. continues her outpouring of grievances intending to project them so decisively into Ψ's container that they stay there long enough to affect Ψ's contents. People whose envy is chronic may allow Ψ to pour what Ψ will into them, but they may only have the conception and change afterwards. That is, they may leave or terminate the work, seeming to be essentially unaffected by the experience, but go on to "get well" on their own or with some other, more deserving therapist.

The provisioning function of the breast—vital in the COUPLE—has, as a counterpart, a receptive function, no less vital to the PAIR, for the reception and processing of projective identifications, particularly those having to do with the infant's dread. That such sympathetic imagination is essential for the analyst goes without saying, but that this differs from empathy and understanding is not so well known. The distinction is simple: empathy and understanding are issued and taken in relation to the patient's conscious communications and feelings. Sympathetic imagination is directed to fathoming and conceiving what the patient and analyst are unconscious of. Bion (1970) put it this way:

> To the analytic observer, the material must appear as a number of discrete particles, unrelated and incoherent. The coherence that these facts have in the patient's mind is not relevant to the analyst's problem.

His problem—I describe it in stages—is to ignore that coherence so that he is confronted by the incoherence and experiences incomprehension of what is presented to him. . . . This state must endure until a new comprehension emerges (p. 12).

The comprehension or conception here is of the unconscious, of preconceptions that are as yet unrealized. In Winnicott's (1962) description, it is a leading out from the unconscious (p. 167). An inadequate but familiar example is the slip of the tongue. A patient is telling what she knows of what she experiences, when suddenly the slip occurs:

P. When it comes to men, I am a shrinking violent. I mean. . . .

Although (because) the unconscious has got a word in edgewise, as often as not the patient wants to correct the slip and go on. Some analysts will bring the patient back to the slip and ask for associations: "Violent . . . ?" In contrast to this linear extension of consciousness, the thrust of sympathetic imagination is toward the curve of brow or shape of belly that this new addition gives to the figure in the carpet that seems to be emerging. This will include the use to which what is told is being put—how it is designed to create or modify the analytic relationship. For example, the coalescence of the two images—violet and violence—is vivid in the way that the peace posters that featured putting a daisy into the barrel of a gun were vivid. Yet in those messages the relationship was explicit: no one could doubt that the flower was meant to replace the ammunition and nullify the violence of the gun. But can the same be said of the "violent" replacement of the flower with the word violence? In the latter instance, given the divergence of the two images, P. might have been doing violence to the analyst by making it problematic as to which associational line to follow.

To happen, the patient has to gain access to the medium, and as we saw earlier, the analyst who is unable to serve as a container for the patient will either leave the patient defeated or push him toward more and more violent ways of conveying the message into the medium. The extent to which the therapist is "saturated," as Bion called it, by his own transferences or therapeutic mission is the degree to which the analyst cannot be available to who and what the patient is. The analyst is the medium in which the patient happens. It is the patient occurring within and upon him that provides him the data. It is necessary for the analyst to ignore the patient who is in his consulting room in favor of the patient who is happening at the very center of his own inner experience.

To be so ignored does not (at least not initially) ingratiate itself with any patient, and when envy is rife the conscious self that is directing the action can only persecute the borning self that is being afforded the analyst's medium. This often stimulates a double-barreled counter-attack. Material dries up—dreams, slips, and associations give way to strictly narrated material about which the patient has all the information and the analyst none (the analyst who goes for this material finds himself asking who, what, where questions in some forlorn hope of keeping up). And the patient does whatever he can to make the analyst unable to profit from his intuitions and empathy. At such times one may find one's self feeling closed off, petulant and judgmental, and much inclined to ruminate about using special measures to confront the patient even while wondering wistfully where one's capacity for imaginative identification has fled. It is possible to so hate feeling dour that one feels tempted to reassert one's receptivity to such doubting Thomases, and so to linger late over sessions, invite telephone calls, or otherwise (by "being more human") display a good spirit. These measures only confirm to the patient that the analyst's receptivity has gone and that the analytic relationship has turned into one where both can fake it.

Faking it has an awful but compelling appeal to someone when he does not want to be recognized for who and what he is because to be so could mean exposure and humiliation or arrest and execution. The patient may persuade himself (or allow himself by the manifestation of a very accepting attitude) to believe that somehow Ψ may be able to thrust his sentence aside. Because he never sees the doorways from which the analyst emerges in the daytime and returns at night, prudence dictates that P. be ever careful of what he lets Ψ know. Such analyses spend a ferocious amount of time being trials. There are explanations, testimonials, confessions, spirited defenses, counter-accusations. The trial is the more Kafkaesque in that the examining magistrate does not exactly press charges, cross examine the defendant, or in other respects give him a case to answer. In hideous fact, he acts as if there isn't even a trial. Under the circumstances, free association is a derisive notion. The patient must bring the case material in from outside. And in any event, how can one who lives or dies by the analyst's judgment of him, dare freely to associate with him?

Poor Ψ may like to think he is a good and civil man, a Stracheyean figure, mutative in his interpretations and effects. But who knows? In any case, gods are needed: without them there can be neither apology nor confession, nor least of all redemption. Once the analyst is imbued with such powers—or, worse, cultivates them, he is secretly feared and hated. (Surely these are overtones in P.'s Salomé-like images in which the judges are finally humiliated by the power of her beauty and desirability and revealed for the Circean pigs *they* are.) The therapy becomes symbiotic. In return for his therapist's good graces, the patient, now hostage, makes his ongoing explanations, his continuing obeisance. What the patient will come to establish, reestablish, remember, or invent, is a different sort of process.

In this, as Bollas (1979) says,

> The mother is less identifiable as an object than as a *process* that is identified with cumulative internal and external gratifications. [The mother is] *a transformational object...* that is experientially identified by the infant with the process of the alteration of self experience; an identification that emerges from symbiotic relating where the first object is known not by cognizing it into an object representation, but known as a recurrent experience of being—a kind of existential, as opposed to representational, knowing.... The mother is not yet identified as an object but is experienced as a process of transformation, and this feature remains in the trace of this object-seeking in adult life, where I believe the object is sought for its function as signifier of the process of transformation of being. Thus, in adult life, the quest is not to possess the object; it is sought in order to surrender to it as a process that alters the self (p. 97).

When Bion used the term, *capacity for reverie* he meant by it not merely the capacity for vicarious understanding, but the capacity of the other to contain in reverie what the infant self calls up *without necessarily discharging it into action*. This means that although, as Bion also said, "one must say what one means and mean what one says," the analyst should say what he says sparingly. The patient has to do his own transformational work if he is to establish a process capable of transforming him. The first process, after all, failed signally to transform the patient into someone worth selecting; this time, if one gives up faking it, there can be no mistakes.

P., in leaving or threatening to leave, tries to force some portion of herself into Ψ, the message now having reached the status of a massage. Let us be as clear as we can about what is at issue. At its simplest, she would wish Ψ to know how she feels, sadistically, perhaps, to go through what she goes through. I shall suppose that P. is afraid of having to die unfulfilled—that there is something either in the process or in the transference that makes P. feel that she is dying and has to do something quite drastic to have it stop. Is this dread of her personal death? Or is she in dread of having been fated to die before she can fulfill her destiny? Is the insinuation of her dread into Ψ all she wishes to achieve? Or does she wish to impregnate Ψ with something else as well?

In P.'s particular instance, we have seen the conjunction between AIDS and pregnancy. In this, something more is at stake than her personal demise. To the question of whether she may be borne as a child, there is the question of whether she may bear a child. And, if not, whether she can realize that child elsewhere. Selection in the GROUP is indifferent to the individual fate of the particular person. Selection is concerned with the successful perpetuation of the GROUP as species. When frustrated, the urge to be transformed turns from symbiosis to parasitism. The self wishes to reproduce and clone at the expense of the other—and then becomes acutely fearful of retaliation in kind. Selection by the other is bound to be regarded as pernicious—as an attempt at seduction, rape, or more mystical intercourse. Seepage, tendrils, infiltration—these are the fears associated with the parasite. They amount to the hostile take over the self wishes to set in motion against the unyielding contained object. The living-dead self wishes to invade the other and deposit both ego and reproductive capacities in it—forcing it by stealth and strength to breed offspring.

The remarkable ability of the therapist to take in and process material makes him a perfect container for such "Ova." But a difficulty arises when the therapist appears to have quite similar designs on the patient. Sooner or later the patient's material, having been processed by the therapist, is returned to the patient, where, to be elevated about it, it is designed to take root and grow. Since the patient, by virtue of his projections of intent, will inevitably suspect the therapist of harboring attempts to impregnate or gestate his ova in the patient, conscious or unconscious attempts by the therapist to effect cure or change will for a long and confounding time only confirm the patient's worst suspicion—that the very marrow of him is under attack. The envious patient wants tremendously to give birth to himself; any attempt by the therapist to imbue him with a clone or variation of the therapist's self will be staunchly resisted. But sharing is a very difficult matter.

A patient says:

> I know I am not finished yet, that there's more to do, but I can't somehow convey that. I can't say, "My analysis is very important to me. I am much more troubled than I ever let on." I just can't say something like that. And it's not so much that I am afraid someone will say, "Aren't you taking yourself too seriously?" because I don't hear it coming from them. It comes from me—"Aren't you the serious earnest one. . . ." Very mocking. [Momentary silence.] I must be going crazy, I swear I am going crazy, because just now, I mean just then, I heard this voice saying, not a voice, but you know what I mean, saying, "If you tell him about last night, I'll kill you!" Now I suppose you are going to say, "Well, what about last night?" But do me a favor—don't. I really can't tell you now, not if my life depended on it.

This patient is caught in the no-person's land between academies. One academy—speaking now of organized psychoanalysis and psychotherapy—has standards it considers secular; many observers have noted that these standards are not far removed from religious standards, values, and structures (Bion, 1966; cf. Eissler, 1965). These in turn derive from the sense of an ultimate. Given our nature as human beings, there is really no escape from a devout belief in an ultimate. As I have noted repeatedly, the ultimate is some form or fashion of an eugenic ideal, a better approximation to the divine or the natural or the philosophic ideal. Science and religion may contest the scientific method or faith, revelation or experimentation, inspiration or perspiration, as artists and engineers might dispute intuition or trial and error, fiction and fact. But none of these contest that there is something better—as in good, better, best—that makes the argument passionate and important. Even cynics and nihilists, even eclectics and other flower children have articles of faith. The academy has goods and betters in mind for itself and for its clientele. Not only do we speak of patients getting better, but we have ladders for development, others for pathology.

The envious have academies of their own, of course. These are contra-academies. They tend to emphasize either nature or nurture. The nature is genetic or biological, and that is where cure lies. The nurture is economic, ethnic, or ideological, and in changes of these is where the cure lies. It is not that these assertions are true or false, one-sided or otherwise. It is how they are used that distinguishes the scholar from the demagogue. To promote a particular point of view, one must of necessity minimize another, but there is a wide difference between minimizing and diminishing. The demagogue is a creature of arrogance in the sense Bion (1957) has used the term. That is, he would like to feel that invention serves well-being more than does discovery, and that invention is in inexorable danger from discovery by those who make discoveries. Many physicians who believe in the scientific method know that psychoanalysis is a bunch of hogwash. Envious at their certainty, I wish I knew that.

But the academy has value for the group precisely in its ability to promote assertion over proof, the more so when proof is imperceptible to others. The matter of resistance is a case in point. Resistance was first used by Freud to describe the ego's anxiety lest its reconfigurations of previous and prospective experience be undone by renewing the original experience or discovering something that would invalidate currently held experiences of experience. It was as such an intrapsychic experience concerning the return of the repressed. By various means and for various purposes, however, resistance came to mean antagonisms to the precepts of the academy. As a "No" from a patient might mark a resistance to an interpretation, so a "No [nonsense]" from other academies was taken also to mark a resistance. That there is sense to this is irrefutable. Psychoanalytic findings arise from the particular methodology of psychoanalytic investigation and those using the method first on the couch, then behind it are the only ones able to attest to the validity or usefulness of those findings. But why then should others be expected to accept its findings on the basis of a simple say-so? If this has truth to it in the struggle among the academies to survive and propagate their own, surely this will have truth in the consulting room as well.

In the consulting room, an interpretation can also be an assertion of the academy. If it is, it is a statement marked by arrogance, a political statement dressed up to look like a therapeutic one. I think Ψ might not dare to say to P., whose hand is on the doorknob, if still the inside one, "You are resisting," even though, in the corrupted meaning of the word, P. most decidedly is resisting. If Ψ did so it would be a matter of arrogance meeting arrogance, head on, and if P. were the sort of plucky person she seems to be, her hand would soon be on the knob on the other side of the door. Yet there is a paradox here too. Ex cathedra assertions by the analyst are often employed exactly because the patient habitually diminishes what the analyst says.

"So, boiled down, what you are trying to say is. . . ."

"Yeah, well, I did what you told me to and. . . ."

"Well, last time you said—I don't remember, something about, uh. . . ."

Sticking to Essentials

What is the alternative? What is it that we may usefully do? What is it that I mean by *the* therapy or *the* analysis? In its essence, the analytic process is a search for meaning—what this means and what meanings are attached to that. It is an exercise in hermeneutics. It rests on the assumption that when experience becomes intolerable and cannot be changed in the world of affairs, it is changed in the world of mind. That is, the unbearable meaning of the event is changed, and substituted for it is an alternative set of meanings or meaninglessnesses. It would be pleasant to think that the psychoanalytic process restores meaning, but it doesn't altogether; too often it must get by on supplying meanings. All the same, as the patient enters into the psychoanalytic domain, he immediately becomes meaningful, even if no one yet knows what those meanings are.

When the patient's envy is deeply rooted in feelings of being unselected as against others' ability to walk astride the earth as if they belonged there, the discovery of meaning is the fulfillment of the patient's deepest wish. In her paper on the adhesive pseudo object relationship, which deals with fantasized survival mechanisms in earliest infancy, Mitrani (1993) uses the phrase, "[He] was conceived by his mother, but not *conceived of* by her" (p. 33). With admirable concision this phrase expresses the plight of the unselected, pointing directly to the importance to being conceived of—that psychoanalytic activity, par excellence. In my view, such conceptions through the discovery of meaning need to take place in what I have called a hermeneutically sealed room. In this room there is interpretation, interpretation, and very little else. By interpretation, I join with Etchegoyen (1991) in his definition: "Interpretation . . . always indicates something that properly belongs to the patient, and of which he has no knowledge" (p. 321). The difference between interpretation, confrontation ("confrontation shows the patient two things in counterposition, with the intention of making him face a dilemma, so that he will notice the contradiction" [p. 316]), clarification ("clarification seeks to illuminate something the individual knows, but not distinctly.... I think clarification does not promote insight but only a reordering of information" [p. 321]), and information ("information refers to something the patient is ignorant of about the external world... something that does not belong to him") "is very great and will serve to define and study interpretation" (p. 321).

The preoccupation with whether he is worth keeping is not easily dispelled by the discovery of meaning; indeed it occludes it. Judgment rules the day. Hardly a fact can see life without immediately acquiring a penumbra of judgmental implications. Nothing less than survival is at stake and, for the infant self, the thrust toward survival entails alteration of the econiche. As not many pages ago we saw with P., the infant self is a mover and a shaker, whose orientation is toward changing the environment—namely Ψ. P.'s very livelihood seemed to depend on Ψ's valuation of her, something else she could not afford to leave to chance. Each time Ψ speaks, he seems to open a door, and behind each door there is, as always, the Lady or the Tiger. (With her hand on the doorknob, P. was quite literally turning the doors on Ψ.)

The hermeneutically sealed room requires that the analyst leave the academy at the door. The less he knows about good, better, and best, the better. Interventions other than interpretations are all too easily confusable with efforts to inculcate, recruit or convert, when one would want the patient's efforts in these regards to be prominent instead.[3]

Thus the analyst may find it helpful to treat those who consult him as members of some other academy come to do some basic research. Were this research to be into a matter of physics or physiology, I doubt he would offer interpretation to his newfound colleague unless and until he or she saw interpretations as being of some possible use. Indeed, he might well not take those who consult him into analysis unless or until the need for a many sessioned week employing free association emerges in a way that convinces them both it is worth the try. (The *DSM-III* and all it represents lives in a different universe. It is the expression of a particular academy, one that knows people from their worlds and bumps and not from themselves. There is a certain kind of psychotherapy that follows from that, but it has nothing to do with what I am talking of here.) It follows that the analyst would be ever ready to abandon the attempt when and if it proves sterile— or simply not worth the effort. I cannot emphasize too strongly that before analysis is undertaken, its potential usefulness as a method must be obvious to both parties and both must be prepared for the enormous work it entails.

When would interpretations come into it? When the transference prevents new and present experience from developing, which is to say while the past remains doggedly in the present and before it can be remembered and forgotten. The mandate for interpretations, has, I think, to be renewed on a daily basis. They must be offered only when wanted, and not when the analyst needs to alleviate his discomfort (see Boris, 1991).

> A patient takes a rare leave of absence from her therapy to attend a conference in her field. On her return she reports she was glad she attended because, as she hoped, the conference was of great practical value. She also reports that she has for some reason been giving a lot of thought to her mother, whom she "fired" some years ago. She begins then to speak with feeling of a precisely recollected mother, a marked contrast to what she did while her mother had been fired. But by the next session this new-won access has sealed over, and P. is beside herself with frustration and fury: "I hate the whole world and everybody in it, but most of all I hate myself'."
>
> Ψ [waits for a while to see where P. will take this, but P. has retired into a hapless mixture of "it's no use" and "I don't give a damn." Ψ draws P.'s attention back to the "everybody" in the world the patient hates, and suggests that this must surely include her. But P. merely stares disgustedly at the ceiling.]
>
> Ψ "You may have sought to make a compromise, by hating first your mother and now yourself in the hopes we might have something to work on. Could it be that you hoped to bring your feelings about me into it but to leave me out of it?"
>
> P. [is outraged by this breach of her compromise and tells Ψ how much she hates Ψ's need to bring herself into everything.] "You must think the sun rises and sets because of you! Well, there are other people just as important to me as you."
>
> Here P. goes on to speak of a male friend who was at the conference with her, ending with, "Maybe he's so sensitive because he's gay."
>
> Ψ And the mother-me is so in sensitive because we are not?

Envy is here, of course, and this patient is envious even of herself. To the self, the self is an object like any other, and is treated accordingly. One has to think in terms of subject-self and object-self and, of course, other. Either of the selves can and does form relations with the other self in dynamics that are linked to their relation with the other. The other can be internal or external to the psychological surface of the skin, which surface can coincide with the actual skin or, as in skin disorders, can be a part of the one rather than the other self. (Tustin [1981] has written on this phenomenon in relation to psychological autism.) Or the one can be above the waist, the other below. Or,

P. I think in my head that. . . .
P. I know in my mind. . . .

Of special note is that the subject-self can envy the object-self—or fear the latter's envy in respects little different from the relations between self and other. Thus, as changes begin to take place in a therapy, especially between the subject-self and the therapist, the object-self can get quite huffy:

P. I don't know whether I mean what I am telling you or not. I mean, I mean it, but when I say it a little voice in me says, "Oh, come off it you're just telling him what he wants to hear." Just now when I told you the dream, it kept saying, "Oh, aren't you something—such a sig-nif-i-cant dream. I'm impressed." You know, real snide.

I wish there was some way of telling you stuff without having to do so out loud. Couldn't you read my thoughts? It's weird I say that—about you reading my thoughts. That was my worst fear when I first came here. But now it's as if—if you could read them, and I wouldn't have to say them out loud, I could tell you anything. . . every thing. But it's like I can't stand over-hearing myself. I know it's crazy, but that's how I feel!

In the consulting room it does not matter whether we are looking into the relations of the COUPLE or of the PAIR, or into the relationship between narcissism and object love, or the death and life drives. The reader who has followed me thus far will have heard countless resonances with formulations proposed by others, for example, with Rosenfeld's dissociated duo, the omnipotent narcissistic self and the dependent infantile self, or with Fairbairn's libidinal and anti-libidinal egos, or even with Freud's superego, Bion's super-superego, Meltzer's tyrant, these on the one side, and the id, the object-loving or the sexual self on the other. I have, of course, distorted my own presentation in favor of demonstrating the particular biopsychology of selection and survival that I think opens Klein's primary envy to further analysis. In real life analysis, the COUPLE and its passions are ever at play, contributing eroticism (e.g., sadism and masochism) and longing in equal measures. It must not be forgotten that P. (as a member of the COUPLE—one might say, as a "member of the wedding") was living out in the analysis a highly excited masturbation fantasy, one which was not finding its way into her relationship with her love, and might otherwise have to be abandoned (in the other sense). In this sense her interest in leaving could be understood as a perfectly straightforward defense against the pain of loss (if she were not in analysis, her fantasies and longings would no longer be subject to interpretation).

The COUPLE is at risk to the PAIR who is or feels itself to be at risk to the GROUP. Insofar as the analyst becomes identified with the GROUP, as he always must, he is a danger in the PAIR and a deeper frustration in the nascent COUPLE than he will be when in the emerged COUPLE. For this reason it has always seemed to me foolish to imagine the analyst as a blank screen: Analytic work is full of risks, even for those who work only with "analyzable" patients, which patients alive with envy barely are, and patients who feel themselves to be at risk are bound to push beyond these to see where our troubles lie—to get to where we are at risk. Only when they have penetrated to the center of our dis-ease, can patients feel safe enough to trust us. (I think this is true from our vantage point as well.) I think it quite wrong for the analyst to reveal his dis-ease—as I have already said, the problem is that we ask that we be discovered too soon—but not to be transparent and to be opaque are two quite different matters. The patient must be allowed to gauge his risk, it is only common sense that he would want to—and indeed, the worry is that too often, armed with the arrogance of omnipotent fantasy, the patient is indifferent to his risk. (We are inclined to think, and who can blame us, that it makes perfect sense for a patient to come and spend his time and treasure with us after investigations of our competence and reputation that can only be called negligent, but at least we shake our heads when they display the same diligence in choosing one of our weaker colleagues.)

At the door, P. was asking this question: Can you stand for me to go? What will happen to you and to me if and when I do?

That we can stand for our patients to leave us at any time, in any condition, is a minimal condition for being in practice. P. elected to stay with her analyst until termination. Her termination, fortunately, was taken slowly.

Time, isn't always experienced as linear—it is sometimes felt to be circular or to have shrunk to a flickering dot like the last image on the TV screen before it goes blank. But when it is experienced as time's → arrow, it provides a dimension in which things can happen. When things don't go well—foiled again!—there is an "again" there. Time is one part of a dimensional experience, of which space is a second. Space is in important ways reserved for the COUPLE: it describes degrees of proximity, of closeness, contact and intimacy. The epigram for this might be, "Together, at last!" but the live-wire word is "together." When time becomes foreshortened, it is like accordion-pleating the arrow: This develops an additional dimension: a Matisse line drawing becomes a Pollock becomes a Stella construction and so on. The once-simple arrow must now be thought of as a balloon which, when squeezed in some portion, expands proportionately in another. In psychological terms this dimension turns out to be depth. As time, or the belief in time, or the belief in time as a friend (optimism), becomes foreshortened, time contracts, as if a mass condensing upon itself, and in this new gravitas there come to be different palettes of colors, increased intensities, shadings and chiaroscuro and new dimensions of meaning. Intimations become convictions, hints become voices barking orders: thus do the no-things replace the nothings when there is an intolerance of nothing. These pockmark the smooth bland surface of what is so and infuse it with significance, meaning, implication, and staying power. The depressions that mark where what was supposed to be but is not is one example, the questions to which the answer of anorexia points are another. As Kellman and Spelke's (1983) work shows experimentally, it is as we have always known psychoanalytically: infants arrive at age three or four months with a highly evolved set of preconceptions and expectations as to how things are or should be. The two little cylinders protruding beyond either side of a screen are or should be ends of a dowel that lies hidden behind the screen: they are not two little blocks—they are *related*.

After termination P. married, moved to another city with her husband, and, returning briefly to the city for a visit, had some sessions in respect to her tensions about becoming pregnant. In these tensions was a mild resurgence of the possibility of baleful magic. Insofar as randomness, accident, chance, meaninglessnes cannot be tolerated, they cannot properly be converted into nothing, mourned and relinquished. They remain no-things, and as nothings, menace the self with the dire regalia of foreshadowings and forebodings, portents and omens, with which most of us (knock wood) are familiar only through folklore, and for which the usual cure involves elements of prophecy, ritual, propitiation, and counter-magic.[4]

That these same measures also are used in the white magic we practice to make our hopes come true shows the role of hope in resisting the conversion of no-things into nothings. It is hope, after all, that furnishes the idea that anything is possible. And it is hope that drives the substitution of no-things for nothing. This sleight of mind provides us our world of preconceptions and premonitions, at whose heed we pass so much of our lives. In the top drawer of the hope chest are a legion of woulds and coulds —the clauses for a world of contracts, according to which, since we do our parts, we know others will do theirs.[5] In the deeper drawers are the architectural plotlines for our life, the schemes by which we move from here to over there, schemes often rationalized by our belief that we have devised a plan or are following one provided by society or someone else. In a planless, contractless, analysis, such premonitory designs—unseen hands—become visible and thereby open to consideration. As P. showed, these plotlines reach beyond one generation to the next.

NOTES

1. For years the psychoanalytic literature on homosexuality could only contemplate active and passive or male and female homosexual orientations, as if these reductionistic positions were inherent and not themselves an envious perversion of what people do together.
2. Kahn (1974) stresses the need to bear in mind that "one of the most important nutrients is the right dosage of positive aggression and even hate by the analyst" (Khan, quoted in Eckstaedt, p. 92).
3. In recounting his work at Northfield, Bion (1961) provides a detailed description of what it means to display evidence for one's findings—as opposed to asserting one's conclusions, which he also does. Briefly, he encourages the patients in the psychiatry facility to air every complaint they have concerning how their treatment keeps them from getting well and returning to the front. One by one he takes these obstacles and helps to remedy them. Finally there is but one left—the 20 percent of the men the others find to be out-and-out malingerers. Bion asserts that there are those 20 percenters everywhere, and that, now all else being remedied, the 80 percenters are using them as points of resistance. Though this is an assertion, it follows upon a careful and systematic demonstration that despite what they devoutly wish, the difficulty was not in the obstacles, now fixed, but in the men. The men are able to accept this, and form into the self-study groups that Bion later was to reestablish at Tavistock.
4. In our culture, litigation, suits, and counter-suits, often seem to have something of this function.
5. Clauses and *"clauses-belli"*: when others do them, all's right with the world, but when they don't we have every right, it seems to us, to feel betrayed and vengeful or depressed and filled with refusal or apathy.

REFERENCES

Abraham, K. (1919). A particular form of neurotic resistance against the psychoanalytic method. In *Selected Papers on Psychoanalysis*, chap. 15. London: Karnac Books.

Bion, W.R. (1957). On arrogance. In *Second Thoughts*. New York: J. Aronson, 1967.

—— (1961). *Experiences in Groups*. New York: Basic Books.

—— (1966). Book review: *Medical Orthodoxy and the Future of Psychoanalysis* by K.R. Eissler. *Int. J. Psycho-Anal.*, 47: 575-579.

—— (1970). *Attention and Interpretation*. New York: Basic Books.

Bollas, C. (1979). The transformational object. *Int. J. Psycho-Anal.*, 60(1): 97-107.

Calvino, I. (1985). *Mr. Palomar*. Translated by W. Weaver. San Diego, CA: Harcourt Brace Jovanovich.

Calvino, I. (1988). *Six Memos for the Next Millennium*. Translated by P. Creagh. Cambridge, MA: Harvard University Press.

Eckstaedt, A. (1989). Ego-syntonic object manipulation. *Int. J. Psycho-Anal.*, 70: 499-512.

Eissler, K.R. (1953). The effect of structure of the ego on psychoanalytic technique. *J. Amer. Psychoanal. Assn.*, 1: 104-143.

—— (1965). *Medical Orthodoxy and the Future of Psychoanalysis*. New York: International Universities Press.

Etchegoyen, R.H. (1991). *The Fundamentals of Psychoanalytic Technique*. London: Karnac Books.

Freud, S. (1914). Remembering, repeating and working through. *SE*, 12: 147-173. In J. Strachey (Ed.), *Standard Edition of the Complete Psychological Works of Sigmund Freud*, 24 volumes. London: Hogarth Press and The Institute of Psycho-Analysis, 1953-1974.

—— (1923). *The Ego and the Id. SE*, 19: 12-66.

—— (1924). The economic problem of masochism. *SE*, 19: 159-170.

Homer. *The Complete Works of Homer*. Translated by A. Land, W. Leaf, E. Myers, and S. Butcher. New York: Modern Library.

Kellman, P.J. and Spelke, E. (1983). Perception of partly occluded objects in infancy. *Cognitive Psychol.*, 15: 483-524.

Khan, M.M.R. (1974). *The Privacy of the Self*. London: Hogarth Press.

Lacan, J. (1949). The mirror stage as formative of the I. In *Écrits*. New York: Norton, 1977.

Meltzer, D. (1967). *The Psycho-Analytical Process*. London: Heinemann.

Mitrani, J. (1993). On "Adhesive pseudo-object relations" as illustrated in *Perfume*. Unpublished ms. [Subsequently published in *Contemp. Psychoanal.*, 1994, 30(2): 348-366, and 1995, 31(1): 140-165.]

Phillips, A. (1993). *On Kissing, Tickling, and Being Bored: Psychoanalytic Essays of the Unexamined Life*. Cambridge, MA: Harvard University Press.

Rivière, J. (1936). A contribution to the analysis of the negative therapeutic reaction. In Hughes, A. (Ed.), *The Inner World and Joan Rivière: Collected Papers 1920-1958*. London: Karnac Books, 1991.

Sacks, O. (1985). *The Man Who Mistook His Wife for a Hat*. New York: Summit.

Tustin, F. (1981). *Autistic States in Children*. London: Routledge and Kegan Paul.

Winnicott, W.W. (1962). The aims of psychoanalytic treatment. In *The Maturational Processes and the Facilitating Environment*. New York: International Universities Press, 1965, pp. 166-170.

AMERICAN IMAGO

Studies in Psychoanalysis & Culture

Martin J. Gliserman, *Editor*
Louise J. Kaplan & Donald Moss, *Coeditors*

Founded in 1939 by Sigmund Freud and Hanns Sachs, ***American Imago*** explores the important role that psychoanalysis plays in contemporary cultural, literary, and social theory. *Published quarterly in March, June, September, and December.*

WINTER 1997 (VOLUME 54, NUMBER 1)

- On the Fetishization of "Creativity"; Towards a General Theory of Work / DONALD MOSS
- Paranoia and the Delusion of the Total System / CYNDY HENDERSHOT
- Re-Writing the Myth, Rereading the Life: The Universalizing Game in Pier Paolo Pasolini's *Edipo Re* / NIKOLA PETKOVIC
- The Song of Rolland: An Interpretation of Freud's "A Disturbance of Memory on the Acropolis" / DEBORAH STEINBERGER
- Against Vanishing: Winnicott and the Modern Poetry of Nothing / LEE ZIMMERMAN

Prepayment is required. **Annual Subscription:** $31.00, individuals; $75.00, institutions. **Foreign postage:** $3.00, Canada & Mexico; $6.25, outside North America. **Single-issue price:** $8.00, individuals; $19.00, institutions. **Double-issue price:** $12.00, individuals; $29.00, institutions. Payment must be drawn on a U.S. bank in U.S. dollars or made by international money order. MD residents add 5% sales tax. For orders shipped to Canada add 7% GST (#124004946RT).

Send orders to: **The Johns Hopkins University Press,** P.O. Box 19966, Baltimore, MD 21211-0966, U.S.A.

To place an order using Visa or MasterCard, call toll-free 1-800-548-1784, FAX us at (410) 516-6968, or send Visa/MasterCard orders to this E-mail address: jlorder@jhunix.hcf.jhu.edu

 PUBLISHED BY THE JOHNS HOPKINS UNIVERSITY PRESS

MNEMOSYNE: DEATH, MEMORY, AND MOURNING[1]

Edward Emery

Death is *the Other*, understood to be both the alien within (the unconscious) and the stranger who beckons through enigmatic desire. The dead cross the threshold of the beyond (the invisible) and link to the here (the visible) through incorporation. The biography of mourning does not cohere into a univocal event. A distinction is made between mourning through the idol and mourning through the icon. The former is a mourning in which the Other is incorporated within me as part of me, no longer Other. One who incorporates "death" and elevates it to the status of idol cannot bear difference. Envy of existence is the handmaid of one who mourns through the idol. Mourning through the icon, in contrast, is a type of mourning in which the incorporated Other retains their distinctive otherness and so renders closure on the work of mourning impossible. Death as the alien within who is not collapsed through mimesis into derivatives of the death drive supports being at one with "O." Iconic mourning gives rise to the post-depressive position —to an "it is good" beyond the ambivalence of good and bad.

KEY WORDS: Mourning; Death; Memory; Remembrance; Incorporation; Crypt; Ghost; the Other; Density; Envy; Persecution; Horror; Post-depressive position; Grace; "O"; and Jacques Derrida.

> Remembering one departed, once,
> On the steep path, a Wanderer advances
> Moved by his distal premonition
> Of the other—but what is this?
> (Holderlin, "Mnemosyne").

> . . . singled out within the unerring arms of death closing in, one finds one's own forces of existing, one finds a compass of elemental possibilities corresponding to oneself alone, awaiting immemorially for oneself alone. . . .

> Death which has no front lines cannot be confronted. It cannot fix a direction; the groping hand of life touches it everywhere, just beneath the apparent support of all surfaces that rest and that phosphoresce in their places (Lingis, "Sensation: Intelligibility in Sensibility").

There is a thickness to memory, a density. Memory is never transparent or lucid. Memory is always more than consciousness can grasp, is in excess of the mind's want to comprehend. Memory is made up of sedimentations —of depth and history, and affects—woven, for the sake of cohesion, into story. The density of memory further thickens when the one who is recalled is rendered past through death. When death is the aporia in which all anxieties terminate, the story line memory writes is a labyrinth of shadow and question not easily cured or worked through.

When story must contain this most radical of border crossings, memory amplifies the particularities of person and events recalled into mythopoetic traces, story lines of sovereign excess. The stories of life, of one's living, the lived topographies of intention, act, gesture, and expressive will do not accommodate this excess. The unsignifiable of death turns the antecedent of life, when recollected, into more than the sum of its acts and ways of being. Life in parentheses grows into myth (the story of feeling in action) and thus cannot easily be encountered freshly, with the rapt openness of wonder. Yet, there is something of wonder and rapture and mystery in this passing of a life for death is a sovereign excess, an unspeakable numinosum. Death in its most nude, raw, and unbidden arrival breaches all contact barriers, flooding into memory an angst that further introduces into the container that memory is an effraction, a breach.

How does memory contain representations of one whose very recall alters how memory contains? When the one who has died is both an other and becomes, in death, also the Other, their recollection can only be contained in memory in a way that perturbs memory's function as container. What pours forth through the breach of death alters the containing function and transposes the economy of forces that structure memory. Death refigures the economy of investments and expenditures. The economies of life organize around the bond, binding relationships, building out of these links dialectical systems of production and regulation (the family, the group, the state). The economies of these relationships form around and out of a "third" that grows through conservation, control, continuities, preservation. This conservational "third" that structures the economies of life works according to the principle of more of the same in the face of difference.

Death, on the other hand, is a "third" of another order who, as Eliot said, walks beside, hooded, in brown mantle. It is the radical difference that deconstructs the same. It is the difference that tolerates no difference, that overrides the negative at work in life and destructs all dialectics of growth. Death "can no longer," writes Jacques Derrida (1978), "*collaborate* with the continuous linking-up of meaning. . . because it literally no longer *labors*". Beyond the productive engendering of labor, death is an irreversible expenditure without reserve. At once sovereign, excessive, and beyond repair, the expenditure of death is an example of what George Bataille (1989) calls a general economy, a transgressive event that counters in the sense of going beyond the restricted economy of exchange in which meaning is bound, like libido, in acts that build toward future and across generations.

Is death nothing less than the most radical curtailment of what a restricted economy intends? Is death nothing less than the squandering nothingness of a general economy? Is it nothing less than the point of excess demarcating the limma of life in its generative productivity of educating, caring, repairing, building toward the good? Is it anything less that the caesura that gestates absence and revolutionizes the lacks (the scarcity of goods, as in money and milk) inscribed in a restricted economy? Is death not, as Derrida (1993) also suggests, a crossing of a border, a trespass, an overstepping, a transgression? Is it not a certain *pas*—at once a "step" and "not?" Is this step that is not the echo chamber in which the silence of abyss reverberates? Or, as one patient put it in speaking of her mother's death, is death not a hole in the ozone layer?

"To the one who has asked so many questions, death comes softly as the lost question," writes Maurice Blanchot (1992, p. 66) in *The Step Not Beyond* (*Le pas au-delà*). The lost question is also the question that puts into question the question of loss. The lost question: the question of loss. Both are beyond answer as both, once linked as in a pair, form the caesura that moves what we call, for want of a more fluid name, self beyond all borders and that undoes the demarcations of this same self's tensions between difference and identity. The lost question harbors, as in a crypt, the question of loss. What is present in such loss when this loss is beyond mourning is, as both Bion and Boris remind us, unmitigated absence. Beyond mourning, this absence is also beyond repair and the agencies of depressive concern. It is an absence that presences as radical dislocation, marking where one is not and where one will never again be.

This mark, further, can only be rendered as a grave step: a negation beyond all negativity whose trace is like ash dispersed in wind. Who still speaks here at the mouth of this furnace and amidst this whirlwind? And with what voice? Possibly, the one beyond all naming. Possibly, the still, small voice, the one who speaks as through a silence beyond syntax and phoneme. The one who speaks prophetically in and through silence speaks of the Other, now given to us as enigma and as the mysterious lost question. The beyond of death transforms the one who was other to me, my familiar even intimate other, into an other of another order: *the Other*.

The ontological plenitude of the Other plays between existential registers of otherness. Jean Laplanche (1997) reminds us of the play of difference between the Other as an intrapsychic presence and the Other as the enigmatic intentionality of desire one who is other to me incites. The unconscious, he suggests, is *Das Andere*, the Other-thing in us, the alien in us who never domesticates and so never is less than an alien, uncanny. In relation to the alien in us who is the Other-thing, there is always a foreboding intimation of being haunted. The Other-thing is the ghost within. The Other who is other to me is *Der Andere*, the other person who is stranger to me but who, even in their familiarity and their factual remembrance, never becomes circumscribed in the closure of knowing. The unconscious, it is said, cannot represent death even though it is the site and space of the deepest drives, including the drive toward death. Perhaps, death is not a signifier but the space of signification. Perhaps death is the unconscious in the sense that the unconscious is the alien in me. This, I think, is what Lacan (1979) meant when he said that God is not dead, just unconscious—in other words, the wholly Other is the Other-thing. A related view also can be found in Matte-Blanco (1988) who emphasizes an equation between the deepest unconscious indivisible mode of being where the no space-time of symmetry equates to death. This Other-thing is that which "disturbs" and "scars." Like death, it cannot be cured or domesticated through the rationalities of cause and effect or the paradoxical discharges of projective identification (both linking and splitting ones).

The Other-thing is a specter, a haunting alterity that scars as it incites memory as its medium. It is, as a site, the "beyond" internalized. The guarantee of this alien-in-me, Laplanche (1997) emphasizes, is the message or sign that addresses me from the one who is an excess with respect to the insistent narcissistic wish to appropriate. Through death, the one who in their otherness awakened me, pained me, excited me further structures, in their place, a radical otherness in me—an alien who never tires of conveying messages that are never other than heterogenous, enigmatic and for which there is no exhaustive hermeneutic. We always want to re-integrate, personalize, mark with the signature of "I-ness" this Other in me. The wish is that through the dividing line of the domestic (repression) death as the "beyond" in me is befriended, made companionable for the ego. Now present through the real as the alien-in-me, the death of the other is an evocative chill, a shudder of the uncanny that won't cease. The Other now speaks in the gap, from the abyss, in whispers of nothingness. Not in the storm, not in the cloud but in a presence that speaks a vastation of silence. The Other who I knew and with whom I found meaning through a lived commerce is now, as the Other, an exorbitant and transgressive silence. The Other punctures all signs, gives urgent poignancy to all significations. Like the silence of a Charterhouse, the silence of the Other is grand, round, full, dense. The one who I knew as an other now become the Other issues a silence of magnificent bigness that overflows and further renders diminutive the limited space in life a personality, even a big one, occupies.

The silence of the Other is the silence of the general economy. More than the productive pauses in the flow of signs, the silence of death is the inassimilable but co-present voice of the unnameable Other. It speaks through the most enigmatic of unconscious registers, one that Freud (1915, 1920, 1923) alternatively spoke of as the non-repressed unconscious and as the "third" unconscious. The silence of the Other speaks as the whisper next to us (the "third" who, as Eliot said, walks beside us) but as from the other side, beyond the dialogic threshold through which the one lost becomes, for us who still question, the lost question.

The intersection between question, loss, and transgression shape something like an epistemophilic concern. When not in denial, or its perverse cousin disavowal, we still want to know. Who goes now? Where? With what voice? As a ghost? Or guiding light? These rumblings bring us, as all inevitably do, back to Freud and his speculations on the beyond. For he is the one for whom the "beyond" is beyond both mourning in the sense of grief resolved, and beyond pleasure in the sense of a resolutely driven decentering excitation. Linked through a haunting silence, death is, as Freud said, the drive toward zero that works in silence. There is, I think, an uncanny resonance between this drive that scandalizes life and the step toward "not." *The Step Not Beyond* conjoins with the ironic thematics of play, repetition, and death in *Beyond the Pleasure Principle* as its further, more disturbing Nietzschean realization. At the core of this "beyond" is a symmetrical equation between desire and death. "Dead desire: desire immutably changed into desire through death and death as an adjective" (Blanchot, 1992, p. 86). Death as drive returns the organism to thermodynamic equilibrium. It is through the agency of this leveling difference that the energetics of death meet the ontological uncanniness of the person before the nonrelational breakthrough of death: exposed, vulnerable, raw, naked.

Death as ontological authentication makes immanent the itinerary of our ownmost possibilities even if it leaves open as a question how one's ontology in its characterologic specificity assigns thermodynamic pertuberance to the wish for simple cohesion, for unity, for oneness of purpose. Death itself cannot be written yet it is through writing that we hope to at least circumambulate the space of absence that is the haunting alien otherness of death. Writing, like the unconscious, is death's other-thing, medium and channel of its near impossible interiorization. We latch onto words as landmarks and anchors against a background groundlessness that is ever waiting and that, with shock, breaks through to bring to silence all commemorative repetitions—both of angst and of mastery. The word, however, is not the bastion against the nudity of death or the whisper of its upheaval. Again, Blanchot (1992):

> From where does it come, this power of uprooting, of destruction or change, in the first words written facing the sky, in the solitude of the sky, words by themselves without prospect or pretense: "it—the sea," is written. . . that somewhere the possibility of a radical transformation is inscribed, be it for a single one—the possibility, that is, of its suppression as a personal existence. . . . Do not draw any consequences from the words written one day. . . . Do not hope, if there lies your hope—and one must suspect it—to unify your existence, to introduce into it, in the past, some coherence, by way of the writing that disunifies (pp. 1-2).

In writing, in eulogizing there is the want to unify, to make one in the sense of an essence that is whole, essential, substantial. Writing death wants to enflesh through the mark of words the body now forever gone. In writing death—and is there, truly, any other writing?— there is the want to harken back to a past ripped apart from the present. We want to seek unity through remembrance. We want to get down the facts in order to undo the gap of otherness inscribed in the commemorative excess of memory. Words knit stories out of the fabric of wishes. Even as they recollect and so gather together, words, once they are the supplement of the wish, suggest the pretence of cohesion, of unity, of resolute being, of what we like to think of as the "true" self. In this nomination of self, it is all too easy to idealize representation and to repress that truth is, in its root sense *alētheia*, saturated with what Freud called the antithetical meaning of primal words. The "true" self is at once a revealing and a concealing, a disclosure and a covering over, a condensation and a displacement, an authentication and a dissimulation.

One cannot help but think at this cross-road between the wish for reflections of at-one-ment and the radical disjunction of the Other (as the "beyond" and the "Other-thing") of that writer for whom writing was both a symptom and model of the mind as he wrestled with the whole catastrophe of psyche—both in its sexual and deadly nature. One year before his daughter's death, Freud writes in *Beyond the Pleasure Principle*, in the context of death's drive, of his grandson (the son of this very daughter) playing with such determination the spool game of Fort/Da, of gone/there, of death and the magical mastery of return. Ernst plays with the question of loss in the arc that locates loss in an action that poses as a question the "that" and the "what" which is present to him now as gone in the fateful step beyond—present now as the lost question, otherwise personified and named mother. What Ernst could intimate and turn, for dis-easeful solace, into a game Freud, not tricked by hope and its promise of ontological cohesion in the face of disaster, could not. The grandfather felt only the raw unbidden agony of the gone. He felt its shock, its astonishing horror, its dissociating presence. Freud was to write to the minister Pfister less than a week after his daughter Sophie's death that she is dead "as if she had never been" (letter of January 27).

"As if she had never been." In so saying Freud engages the agon of the impossible: the step *Not*, beyond. "As if she had never been." This declaration echos endlessly back on itself. How do we comprehend this event of stilling absence in which the one lost is lost beyond all registers of representation—beyond memory, beyond recall, beyond the elegiac of commemoration? It is as if she were liquidated, without a trace, without a word that could stand for her, gone beyond representation, lost behind the veils of concealment, absorbed as in a black hole or a vacuum or the matrix of primal repression. This "never been" points surely to a disorientation akin to the ghostly presentations of the uncanny. All ghosts return as ghost is in its nature the one who returns (*le revenant*) and so it is for Sophie. The beloved daughter now dead comes back as "never been." She haunts through the grand silence that infects all auditory signatures of receiving and taking in the Other. What in one moment was so familiar, so much an extension of "mineness" and of ego topography became, instantly, faster than a blink or a thought, jettisoned to the other side of a threshold whose un-homely otherness could not, through acts of mind, be crossed or trespassed. This sudden and irreversible shift of worlds is breath-taking, asthma-making. Like an empty mouth for which what comes is never the right fit, what looms large in the dizzying stillness of the "never been" is an un-fillable empty space.

Mrs. Klein, in writing about art as reparation, describes a woman whose depression attunes her to a blank wall as this attunement inspires a want to fill that grows into marks, gestures of hand and color, a painting. And paint she does, so well that this expression of self fills the blank with a work admirable enough for exhibition, for the collective approving and critical gaze. What Freud describes, however, is a blankness of another order: a blankness beyond repair and so also beyond memory and desire. The blankness of "never been" is a blankness without boundary. It is one that cannot be contained in the representations of a projective geometry. The loss Freud describes is a blankness of less than two dimensions. It is more like a hole in space than a space of absence to be filled. This is the space of the "never been." In a world whose topography is so shaped, there is "nothing" to mourn. How does one mourn a hole in the ozone layer?

Horror abounds in this world of dismantling vacuum. It tends to saturate all difference. It introduces stupor in place of mind. As if this is not enough, there is for one so horror bound a pull first to feel and then to become a most malignant form of envy, what Bion (1965) alluded to as envy of existence. Envy of existence is the cold uncanny derealization of all life and living. This is an envy that wants more than what the other has or wants. Its want is a hatred of wanting. Its greatest spites are growth, time, alterity. Envy of existence turns a malicious righteous hate toward all difference and all otherness (especially the Other-thing). Under the gaze of the eye that envies existence, life itself becomes an abomination, an insult, a mockery. Seen through the lens of this envious eye, one so envied preserves being through protest, in the life assertive announcement of their otherness. And it is precisely this gesture that becomes suspect for the gaze that envies existence. The other is then vigilantly scanned for defect—which then becomes the "truth"— in order to puncture signs of difference. Envy of existence possesses through an invasive and righteous outrage over discovered "badness." The mating of horror with envy of existence fuels an insistent hypertrophy of the immoral conscience—that "SUPERego" which is ruthlessly and murderously righteous, all the while thinking it is in "the right" and "the know" as it uses omniscience to cancel the space of inquiry and potential discovery.

When horror is contained in an envy of existence, what grows in place of inquiry is a field of confusion linked to persecution. This emotional field gives rise, as Meltzer (1978) has suggested, to a terror of dead objects. Here, confusional states do not hold open to uncertainty but solidify into objects that first look good but harbor, it is feared, malignant intentions. Haunted by terror of the dead, those who envy existence harbor an envy that functions like a dense object (Emery, 1992) or malignant tumor. The vision of cure such persons hold involves a combination of adhesive identification (sticking on to all surfaces—the body, wall, and especially glass) so as to level difference (whether through implosion or explosion, it matters little) and eradicate "the Other-thing." Envy of existence is also envy of the Other's "Other-thing." This often takes the form of preoccupation with the Other's "Other-thing"—its intactness, its "truthfulness," its "health." All of this concern masks an underlying belief: cure or a semblance of living depends on depositing horror and deadness in the Other who is seen in their strategies of otherness as cold, hateful, deceptive, sneaky, malicious, brutal. If envy of existence does not mate with horror, something other than murderous stasis becomes possibe. A gap can be tolerated. There is then room for the alterity of "the Other-thing." The alien in me is then not a space invader. What almost imperceptibly follows is a kind of calm inside of which eventually something like a reverence for the beyond begins to form. There still is shock and horror and numbness, and agony, but there is less insistent and invasive adhesiveness. In a manner that is not defensive, what can then be experienced is a subtle yet building quiet, a diffuse but pulsating stillness in which life begins to glimmer and a glow with its "this-ness" and "that-ness," with what Buddhists call "such-ness."

Black holes also give rise to big bangs, to new worlds (Smolin, 1997). The more black holes, theorizes Smolin, the more new creations take shape within the holes themselves. Black holes give rise to multiple worlds, each of whose laws are distinctive and evolving. What is compelling in this view is that states of collapse not only destroy, they also make room. Psychically, the condition for this possibility is one in which "black hole" modes of existence are relatively free from the envy of the immoral conscience. Then, collapse is kin to crucifixation. Breakdown and tearing apart become breaking open and breakthrough. This was no doubt the case for Freud and for Klein, and Bion and Boris.

On a less grand scale, one can also see this in the pain of ordinary life. Often, there is a kind of intergenerational yoking between the heterogenesis growth effects and death-driven envy of existence. However, when the deadening projective identifications of invidious wishes to obliterate do not effect a proliferating unconscious parasitism, black holes can make room for big bang ontogenesis. Not yet "knowing" of her mother's imminent death yet intimating it, a daughter gets pregnant, shadowing the child to be with the grandmother's non-being yet also assuming through fecundity a distinctive re-working of the maternal position. Another mother looks at a sonagram, sees in photographic grey her granddaughter to be in utero, and, with insidious speed, psychosomatically opts out, preferring the negation of the "beyond" to the resented fate of replacement. Certainly, a collapsing envy of existence implanted in the Other can work like a time bomb of deferred action, though in these examples something other than envy—at least initially— has the last word. Envious negations that fail in establishing a reign of murderous omnipotent control ironically open a conduit toward conception of new life and hope for another chance. Even though the possessive wish for the same dies hard, in these examples the residuum of envy present through the ghostly effect of repetition tends toward dilution rather than concentration.

Something like this fecundity within the destructive implosion of black holes also is at work in death itself. There is in the pain of dissolution and breakdown often a subtle, quiet, almost unnoticed space whose presence is at first flooded over with terror and with the body's proteolytic action toward itself. Despite the wrenching spasms of breakdown into the elementals of stardust, a quiet still small voice also grows in the pause between labored breaths into an ineffable spaciousness, what the poet Gerard Manley Hopkins called, in other contexts, a vastation. This expanse within collapse envelops and pulls the one dying into an interiority intimated by those still in life as an "elsewhere-ness." Presence of the "elsewhere" thickens into multidimensional expanse as it takes the place the person and personality previously occupied. What I am wanting now to describe, however tentatively, is a building spaciousness that simplifies will, that is beyond drive, its agonies of fracture and the reparative intention. In dying, this fading from presence is a pull toward the beyond.

The pull toward the beyond through death also can be, for the one who is dying and for those who care for them, more than the non-relational nothingness of death. It also can be an epiphany. The "elsewhere-ness" that opens up in the midst of agony and breakdown, and dissolution shapes something like a post-depressive position. At work in this organization of experience is less what Bion, following St. John of the Cross, called faith as antidote to catastrophe than grace. By grace, I mean a gratuitous moment in the face of catastrophe in which there is breakthrough toward a blank envelope of expanding non-dual unities. Releasment into this state of expansion does not cancel out the catastrophic nor does it defend against breakdown. Grace holds co-present in awareness both catastrophe and breakthrough to a non-ordinary dimension of awareness and being.

At the borderline of life and in the raw denudation of pain that cannot be borne, there opens an opening to a plenitude of depth beyond measure. Matte-Blanco (1988) spoke of this dimension of the beyond as the no space-time indivisible mode of being. Breakthrough to this dimension is privileged at the borderline of "lifedeath." I imagine post-depressive grace as the vehicle for this breakthrough. In post-depressive grace, there is a spacious reorganization of being from its containment in the constrictive shell of personality toward an endless never-receding vanishing point. This that I imagine as an approaching vanishing point envelops the person, now without personality but with awareness, in something like a holosphere. The post-depressive position is a generative hyperspace. in which abides an enveloping surround of infinite depth, an incommunicable something gentle, a fourth dimensional buoyant softness beyond good and bad, gain and loss.

In this expanding and interpenetrating spatial manifold ramifying through and between the here and the beyond, there is a radiant Good beyond the good that can be spoilt, damaged, lost, turned bad. Expansive releasment into the beyond opens to a Good about which one can only say "it is done" in the sense of "it is good." The flesh-leaving that is at one with breakthrough to encounter with this ravishing, terrifying radiant Good either can be an agonizing slide or sudden slippage into the hyperspace of approaching death. For one who witnesses this most remarkable and unexpressible of events, there is in the surround a thickening presence that elicits awe, that stills and softens the tension arc between hope and despair into something like mutual but differential releasment toward an invisible whose abiding becomes what for the constitution of the ego is scandal: "the gift of death" (Derrida, 1995). For one who has loved passionately and been devoted and borne the pain of disillusion and ambivalence, and who has in love also suffered for and with their now dying loved one, they also are witness to something astonishing:

> Her skin was translucent, her eyes clear as the spring skies, a smile floated continually on her. . . . The rasping gulps in her throat pounded at the thick and surging night. Her face was radiant, her eyes opened wide, immobilized on her, her face was transfixed with awe (Lingis, 1994, pp. 242-43).

Writing on the space of "the between," the philosopher William Desmond (1995) speaks of the "astonishing middle." This is the space of radiance, of opening to the Open, to *the Other*, to wonder, to awe. Through the awesome tearing and ripping of loss and destitution, and abandonment that wounds in extremis ego identifications and their nutriment, the event of death is an annihilating opening to the unfathomable. In this cleaving and heaving and wrenching there opens "the astonishing middle." Desmond (1995) writes:

> The astonishing middle comes before us and stuns by its sheer beauty. There is a sheer elemental pleasure in its irreducible otherness. This elemental pleasure is appreciation, where appreciation marvels in the goodness of the showing of being as good for itself. It is precious; it is prized; it is prized for itself with a value beyond all price. . . we are in the neighborhood of the primal "it is good" and we hear something of its music. There is given to us ontological joy (p. 201).

"Her eyes opened wide. . . her face was transfixed with awe." What I am thinking of as post-depressive grace moves the one who is dying into further and further reaches of an interiority beyond all defensive and reparative identifications. In this pull that releases, concern for loved ones can function as impediment and intensify agony until resolution and last minute repair is reached. Post-depressive concern breaks through the depressive anxieties, and feared damage over integration between "good" and "bad" into the spaciousness of the "it is good." This "it is good" is like a deep sinking floating.

A mother who is dying and in near coma labors heavily in her breathing as heart and kidneys begin to fail. Barely able to speak, she appeals to her son who is bedside with urgent demand. Her last words: "What does mother want?" The son, scanning memory in the midst of panic, recalls the twisted and tortured guilty symbiosis between he and her and between his mother and hers. All, it feels, is on the line. No easy answer, no denial. In the radical poignancy of this moment in which intermingling biographies reach the fruition of an essential truth, he says, "she wants you to rest in her arms." With this, the mother drinks deep from the cup of life. She sighs a voluminous round, seemingly endless silent sigh. Her chest stops shaking. She sinks to quiet; her breath no longer labored. The mother, for once, listens and finds release into the "elsewhere" from which she never returns. Upon hearing her wish blessed and her need confirmed, this willful near-anorexic woman ceases to struggle and oppose. For once, in the final moments, not less but more is more. She says yes to the Good. Her face again appears downy and supple. Her caved in cheeks appear to bulge round, almost full. She takes in. She enters the endless depth of the astonishing middle. And yet, there remains, despite the miraculous grace of this moment full with epiphany, an unshakable dislocation can adhere to the survivor. Freud's remark upon his daughter's death again echoes: "as if she had never been." Freud reminds us that there is, for us still on this side of the border, an unassimilable shock, a tearing away at narcissistic identifications. Death inserts into life an ontological rupture that registers in awareness and attention as frozen time.

For the one who is left on this side of the beyond, there can be a split between the almost mystical fecundity of post-depressive grace and the splintering effects of the residual vacuum. Alternately suspended and oscillating between the two, the mind in mourning can seek something like a compensatory pseudo-softness by descent into spinning numbness (whose variants range from the oceanic mental reverie of a "philosophic" acquiescence to psychosomatic shock) or, alternately, can spin off into the soothing reverie of speculation. One version of this wish for mastery is thinking about through the speculum of writing. As Freud was reported to have said to Joan Rivière, "write it out!" For Freud, writing as an act and model of mind links up with speculation in his work on the death drive, for it is there that he emphasizes speculation as a mode of imaginative repetition. In the aftermath of the transfigurational event of death, the mind's labor works at once on and against mourning.

The transfiguration of death effects both an authentic and humbling awe before the expanding rapture of mystery, and a shock that can petrify both states of mind and of time. If the pain of loss does not split the self into dissociated fragments of envy, immoral conscience, encapsulation, and autistic adhesion, one can find palliative and even generative dispersal through a partially defensive oceanic at-one-ment or through mourning raised to the sublime of speculation. There can be a figurative (in the sense of giving shape to) lining inside the doubly disoriented mind as it both whirls in the peace of the event and works to manage the agony of the gone. The poignancy of the "there is" becomes through mournful thought reworked into the illusionist's performative "as if," as in "as if she had never been." It is at this junction between what we might think of as post-depressional grace and pre-schizoid autistic grief that memory also must do double duty. There is, as Derrida (1989) suggests, no accidental conjunction between memory, memorial, memorandum, memoirs and mourning. What remains in the face of this excess and exorbitant breakthrough of the beyond that renders nothing one loved is their memory—bequeathed, as Derrida also reminds us, *"to me"* and *"to us"* and *"to the memory"* as nothing now no longer comes from the other to the present.

Yet, what this interiorization "in us" as memory is in fact, is far from clear or at least univocal. Memory is handmaiden to mourning for through memory mourning labors. Yet, the form mourning takes with respect to memory is in part determined by the status of this interiorization "in us" within the register of memory. There is a difference between a mourning that is possible and one that is impossible. On this point or, rather, on the point that is the impossibility of mourning we can hear between Blanchot and Derrida the cadence of reveberating echo:

> Loss is impossible—It passes through the impossible—It is in this that it is really loss, loss of thought, never compensated—Loss is demand, it demands of thought that it be un-thought, loss of loss (without annulment of return): only repeating, falling due (luck that does not fall due) of the neuter" (Blanchot, 1992, p. 68).

> Is the most distressing, or even the most deadly infidelity that of a *possible mourning* which would interiorize within us the image or idol or ideal of the other who is dead and lives on in us? Or is it that of the impossible mourning, which, leaving the other his alterity, respecting thus his infinite remove, either refuses to take or is incapable of taking the other within oneself, as in the tomb or the vault of some narcissism? (Derrida, 1989 p. 6).

Possible mourning inscribes the other as ideal and idol within the space of the "within me." There, the dead one now lives, both idealized and idolized. Impossible mourning: loss without compensation. Impossible mourning preserves the otherness of the Other in place as "the Other-thing." For impossible mourning, there is no idol. Impossible mourning inscribes the Other, now dead, as present "within me" in their alterity, in an otherness that remains not-me and more than me. The incorporative and inscriptive alterity of impossible mourning is beyond me even if it is housed as other within me. Memory of the loved one now deceased has two mournful biographies: a mourning that is idolatrous and a mourning that is the idol's opposite, that works on us through a presence akin to an icon's giving of itself.

The first mourning—the possible mourning of the idol—has its itinerary, its course in time, its connection to biography, to internal object dramas, to the background stage of repressed phantasy. At the onset of mourning through the idol an end with foreclosure can be sighted. There is in possible mourning prefigurative closure. In mourning through the idol, the alterity of the alien within me is the interiorized "third" in triangular tension with the swoon between self and idol. Mourning through the idol seeks to solve the problem of want. I now no longer want anything from the dead because they are symmetrically inserted within me as more of the same. But what of mourning that preserves the alien within me as alien? This is a mourning that is both not possible yet is. It is mourning beyond possibility. Connected to the beyond, impossible mourning is beyond closure. It shapes the future's becoming. Mourning that is not possible goes on and on—not necessarily toward melancholia—but toward a limitless if unbearable course: toward a "beyond" in the here and now where there is no horizon or vanishing point. How can one mourn, through the circuits of cathexis and de-cathexis to the lost object, within a bearable and finite temporality if the one mourned is assigned in memory status other than idol? How does one mourn one who is present within me in a manner other than as the fixed ideality of an idol? How does one mourn the other in their incorporative alterity? How does one mourn an icon?

Jean-Luc Marion (1991) contrasts idol with icon. Idol, he suggests, freezes the gaze, concretizes it. In an idolatrous relation, the gaze petrifies in its beholding the idol. The idol functions in Marion's words, as an "*invisable* mirror," one that blocks access to the invisible. When the gaze freezes on the idol its aim disappears as does the not-aimed at. The brilliant light that surrounds the idol as fascinating halo or aura reflects in the eye of the beholder an experience of self that is lost to the mirror of the visible. The dead one as idol "within me" opens up within-ness in a manner that fails to open beyond the self-object relation of co-extensive self-completion. Mourning through the idol, the other now dead is co-heir of and with my self-experience (here, the dead one is my double with difference begrudgingly acknowledged) and present as the reductive finite summation of the other's in assimilable excess. Idolized mourning mourns enviously, possessively. As idol, the mourned dead never exceeds my gaze, never is in excess of the tyrannizing adhesiveness of the look. Idolized mourning enshrines the refusal of the "beyond," of radical Otherness and of "the Other-thing" as alien in me. Mourning through the idol substitutes, in the place of the Other-thing, the insistent specular glow of a constituted presence. Within the idolizing attitude, memory becomes saturated with remembrances that fixate on the materiality of recollection.

Mourning through the idol exploits the incarnational history in the recollective gathering of one who is now dead. One who was known not only through their thought but also through the word's immanent embodiment —this shape, that face with those playful pained eyes—and in the lush sublimity of their expression—ironic, witty, compassionate, tragic, errant, razor sharp—is now no more enfleshed but no less, in their dis-incarnation, present. That hand frequently shaken, that gentle laugh, those times sitting together musing, conversing, joking are now forever past. They are, I would add, forever past in a past tense that is a radical past-ness akin to the disjunction Freud, in the case of the Wolf Man, spoke of as "pre-history" and to what, in the case of his daughter deceased, he described with honesty: "as if she had never been."

The smooth curvature that the visible follows into the invisible is, after death, a path now reversed. For one who has died, their being as visible folds over into the invisible. Now relating to the other in their death, we must do the near impossible: we must track the visible back through the curvature of the invisible. Thus, a mourning that does not enshrine or fetishize the Other is an impossible mourning. Memory is the conduit through which the chiasm linking the visible with the invisible channels from the invisible back toward the visible. For memory makes use of image as its currency and converts this economy into a sensibility that contains ghost-lines of flesh and word. Through a hologram of identifications, a loved one now dead again takes shape, their sensibility re-represented. The departed, no longer embodied now transubstantiates within and from the beyond. Interiorization incorporates the ghost of the other, recalling again that ghost or phantom is also *le revenant*, one who returns. Special acts of memory are required to recall and commemorate one who has passed on. Memory that can approach the event of death without collapsing the past (the before death) into empiric documentation is a memory that muses, that wanders, that moves between temporalities and tensions of consciousness. To muse on and around the specter of one who has passed on may, with fortune, bring forth their image (*eidolon*). Not to be confused with the deadening voyeurism idols compel, image as *eidolon* configures a density that points toward the beyond. Musing conducive to the iconography of image-building is first cousin to the work of mind Bion called reverie, a function that turns raw emotional unpleasure into digestible phantasy and dream-able thought. As Bion well knew, the muse of reverie also has its gadfly. For Socrates, in the *Theaetetus* (191b), image is the gift memory—but not remembrance—inscribed on the wax tablet both Freud and Socrates thought of as mind. The loss of one whose shadow (ghost or specter) haunts the kingdom of the "I" requires a kind of fluid memorialization that converts phantom into image, and so transforms idol into icon. Only then can memory function as recollection in the root sense of *legein*: to assemble, to lay out an account. The way toward remembrance of one who has past beyond all past tenses passes through the assembling gathering of recollection.

At these multiply interwoven crossroads of the visible and invisible, of phantom and image, of memory as recollection and memory as remembrance, tension between idol and icon builds. Mourning through the idol gathers together the other as a palpable but interior "visability," a specular guiding light, a fascinating phantom. Mourning the Other installed within as idol occurs at the level of the other's materiality, the thing-ness of their lived being. Through these objects, this favorite book, the restaurant where we last talked, the other is remembered, again located, inscribed within the visible and equated with the spectral density of object and place. Within these signifying fields and through the thick memorable this-ness of things and places, the Other comes back as a haunting phosphorescence that seals over the gap of the "Other-thing," the alien in me. The Other as idol fascinates, seduces, excite, filling absence with figurative presence.

Icons, in contrast, exceed the limits of the visible. They open the look to something like a transfiguring invisibility that shines forth through the Other, now dead, in their alterity. As icon, there is an ungraspable and unlocatable luminosity to the way the other is present to me. As icon, the other is, more than ever, a phenomenon—a shining light that shines forth from the clearing of absence. This phenomenal iconology of the Other recollects the now departed one through a distinct mode of memory: through traces of a past that were, as history, never present in the sense of being bound to the actual, to the visible, to happenings rendered literal. Mourning through the icon honors the undecipherable enigma of the Other. Death, said Derrida, also is a "gift" in the sense that it comes free and unbidden. Mourning through the icon opens to receipt of this gift, one that, within the limits of the possible, cannot be resolved. The "gift of death" gives through memory an otherness whose advent announces the yet-to-come:

> The memory we are considering here is not essentially oriented toward the past, toward a past present deemed to have really and previously existed. Memory stays with traces, in order to "preserve" them, but traces of a past that has never been present, traces which themselves never occupy the form of presence and always remain, as it were, to

come—come from the future, from the *to come*. Resurrection. . . does not resuscitate a past which had been present; it engages the future (Derrida, 1989, p. 58).

The Other present within as iconostasis moves me beyond the closures of their givenness toward foreshadowings of post-depressive grace. What I am imaging as a "post-depressive position" mourns through the Other interiorized as icon. The post-depressive position greets the world with wonder over what is to come, over what is yet to come from the undefinable unknown beyond. When the alterity of the other is mourned through iconic consciousness, one remains attuned to the alien in me as a blessed "elsewhere-ness" whose present tense breaks through constant conjunctions. Mourning through the icon approximates a post-depressive position. It opens the one who survives to a depth goodness whose radical difference can only be described by word that sounds stuffy to modern ears: glory. In excess of all conceptions and preconceptions of who the Other was, an iconostasis of the Other institutes a celebratory if impossible mourning. Here, the depth of the visible opens to the beyond of the invisible.

"The only concept," writes Marion (1991), "that can serve as an intelligible medium for the icon is one that lets itself be measured by the excessiveness of the invisible that enters into visibility through infinite depth, hence that itself speaks or promises to speak this infinite depth, where the visible and the invisible become acquainted" (p. 23). In an iconic object relation, union grows through the distinctions of alterity. Mourning that takes into account this excessiveness of the invisible is not a finite work of a limited and encrypting narcissism but an ever-deepening cross-fertilization between the lived one I remember (the visible) and the one memory interiorizes (the invisible). Memory is shaped by this excessiveness of the invisible. So shaped, it contains the death of the Other as enigma. Yet, it too must take in the day residue of the visible. There is, then, a bipolarity in memory: one profile incorporates the Other in their in assimilable otherness (as icon); the other profile seeks through the register of the visible a symbiotic appropriation in which me and other are conjoined, and then suspended in the inviolate remove of a psychic crypt or secret vault (as idol).

The clandestine insistence, repetitious adhesions, and displaced often violent masks of mourning through the idol expresses the raw pain of impossible mourning—namely, that there is in me who survives and in relation to the Other, now dead, as alien in me an ineffable and terrible solitude for which the tyranny of stasis is a pseudo-solace. It is this radical, breath-taking solitude Freud spoke to in the shocked afterglow of his daughter's death: "as if she had never been."

This solitude is not an abiding quiet against a spacious and glowing background presence. Nor is it the solitude of being with "the Other thing" or with a friend, as my Other, in silent repose. It is, rather, a desolate solitude in relation to which crypt and claustrum (Meltzer, 1982) function as havens. Melanie Klein (1963 [in 1976]) touched the irredeemable destitution of this solitude in her last paper "On the Sense of Loneliness":

> However much integration proceeds, it cannot do away with the feeling that certain components of the self are not available because they are split off and cannot be regained... the lost parts, too, are felt to be lonely (p. 302).

Incorporation of the dead one is also incorporation of death. To massively identify with the dead one is to incorporate not only "their" death but also death. One who incorporates "death" and elevates it to the status of idol cannot bear difference. They handle the problem of the alterity of the dead beloved and of death itself by canceling out any otherness that is outside of control. Toward this end, envy of existence is their handmaid. To the solitude of Freud and Klein we can add the voice of Derrida (1989) for whom self-reflexive incorporation of the Other is a central problematic:

> The "within me" and the "within us" acquire their sense and their bearing only by carrying within themselves the death and the memory of the other; of an other who is greater than them, greater than what they or we can bear, carry, or comprehend, since we then lament being no more than "memory"... this mimetic interiorization is not fictive; it is the origin of fiction, of apocryphal figuration (pp. 33-34).

Mimetic interiorization works counter to envious appropriation (I want what you want) as a solution to solitude. It, rather, supports the figurative functions of the alien in me: signification and metaphorization. Envy, in contrast, collapses all tropologies of representation and all elegiac story lines of the "within me" as it turns the Other into a dominating ghost with privilege.

Mimetic interiorization, if successful, however must not be complete. Otherwise, this representational function turns mimesis into an envious parasitism whose intention is to eradicate both mourning and interiority. Mimetic interiorization must not cover over the abyss of solitude through totalizations that reduce the Other to a "figure" within me. Mimetic interiorization must, if successful, also fail:

> ... faithful interiorization bears the other and constitutes him in me (in us), at once living and dead. It makes the other *a part* of us, between us— and then the other no longer quite seems to be the other, because we grieve for him and bear him *in us*, like an unborn child... an aborted

interiorization is at the same time a respect for the other as other, a sort of tender rejection, a movement of renunciation which leaves the other alone, outside, over there, in his death, outside of us (*ibid*, p. 35).

Only through an aborted interiorization not subverted through envy can mind grow toward contact with what Bion named "O"—which we might here translate as the being-ness of the Other. Death as the alien within who is not collapsed through mimesis into derivatives of the death drive supports being at one with "O." We might also think of "O" as both *Das Andere* and *Der Andere*. "O," further, can be thought of as the ecstatic and untransformed abysmal presence of the sublime Other at the chiasm between what is intimated as gone and what remains, still there.

Death of one loved opens us to raw epiphanies of "O." This presentation of "O" at the contact barrier with the Other (now the alien within) beckons and builds a haunting background to the shifting tenses of consciousness, and to the realizations of "O"'s intimations. "O" as death is the non-repressed "third," the one who walks beside, made manifest through the exorbitant middle and given through the nutriment of contact with "the Other-thing." The aborted interiorization of death keeps "O" ever raw, fresh, still to come, linked to the beyond. Contact with "O" is only possible through a mourning that is impossible. "O" is given in grace. An epiphany, it can shock, flood, seize. We can, however, always seek solace from its call to be through reducing the iconostasis of mourning into idols of mimetic desire. But to do so is to miss that the alterity of the Other within is, in the solitude of their strange otherness, also the gift of a Goodness that is more than the ambivalences of good and bad. It is here, at the contact barrier with this Goodness, that "O" graces the personality with an impossible mourning: the "gift" of death:

> Graceful vicissitude, like day and night
> Light issues forth, and at the other door
> Obsequious darkness enters, till her hour
> To veil the Heav'n, though darkness there might well
> Seem twilight here; and now went forth the morn
> Such as in highest Heav'n, arrayed in gold
> Empyreal: from before her vanished night,
> Shot through with orient beams: when all the plain
> Covered with thick embattled squadrons bright. . . .
> Reflecting blaze on blaze, first met his view. . . .
> (John Milton, *Paradise Lost*, Book VI).

NOTE

1. This paper is offered in memory of Harold Boris, a wise good friend.

REFERENCES

Bion, W. (1965). *Transformations*. Northvale, NJ: Jason Aronson, 1983.
Blanchot, M. (1992). *The Step Not Beyond*. Albany, NY: State University of New York Press.
Derrida, J. (1989). *Memoires for Paul de Man*. New York: Columbia University Press.
—— (1995). *The Gift of Death*. Chicago: The University of Chicago Press.
Desmond, W. (1995). *Being and the Between*. Albany, NY: State University of New York Press.
Emery, E. (1992). On dreaming of one's patient: Dense objects and intrapsychic isomorphism, *Psychoanal. Rev.*, 79: 509-535.
Freud, S. (1915). *The Unconscious. SE*, 14: 161-215. In. J. Stratchey (Ed.) *Standard Edition of the Complete Psychological Works of Sigmund Freud*, 24 volumes, London: Hogarth Press and The Institute of Psycho-Analysis, 1953-1974.
—— (1920). *Beyond the Pleasure Principle. SE*, 18: 7-64.
—— (1923). *The Ego and the Id. SE*, 19: 3-66.
Klein, M. (1976). *Envy and Gratitude*. London: Hogarth Press.
Lacan, J. (1978). *Four Fundamental Concepts of Psychoanalysis*. New York: Norton.
Laplanche, J. (1977) The theory of seduction and the problem of the other. *Int. J. Psycho-Anal.*, 78(4), in press.
Lingis, A. (1994). *Abuses*. Los Angeles, CA: University of California Press.
Marion, J.L. (1991). *God Without Being*. Chicago: University of Chicago Press.
Matte-Blanco, I. (1988). *Feeling, Thinking, Being*. London: Routledge.
Meltzer, D. (1978). *The Kleinian Development*. Perthshire, Scotland: Clunie Press.
—— (1992). *The Claustrum*. Perthshire, Scotland: Clunie Press.
Smolin, L. (1997). *The Life of the Cosmos*. New York: Oxford University Press.

15 Brewster Court
Northampton MA 01060
USA

SOME NOTES ON THE ORIGIN OF DESPAIR AND ITS RELATIONSHIP TO DESTRUCTIVE ENVY[1]

Richard P. Alexander

Psychoanalytic research has alerted the author to the prevalence of a certain type of early emotional trauma which leads to the development of a despairing type of infantile depression. This paper is based on a study carried out over the past several years consisting of analyses conducted by the author as well as from certain cases under his supervision. In the intrapsychic situation, the infant in relinquishing its expectations of gain from the primal object, acquires the unconscious belief that help in the real world does not exist and, thereby, becomes a player in a pathological narcissistic defense system. The paper also aims to show how destructive envy develops as an incipient outgrowth of the ensuing survival mentality that takes form, the basic aim of which is to undermine hope. An approach toward resolution is described, aided by a clinical case designed to illustrate how the original damaged links to the primal object may be repaired.

KEY WORDS: Disappointment; Desperation; Survival mentality; Hopelessness; Negative personality; Vengeance; Destructive envy; Secondary personality; Emerging personality; Containment; Renewed hope; Narcissistic defenses; Projective identification; Kleinian theory; and W. R. Bion.

In her last paper, "On the sense of loneliness," delivered at the Copenhagen Congress, in 1959, Melanie Klein (1963) stated that she understood the roots of the "inner sense of loneliness to emanate from the infant's yearning for the unattainable, perfect internal state." Klein felt this painful, lonely state to be inevitable, attributing it to the loss of the earliest close contact between the baby's unconscious and that of the mother on the preverbal level, which constituted, she felt, "the foundation for the most complete experience of being understood." Regardless of the later satisfactions attained through one's ability to put thoughts and feelings into words, Klein believed that there would remain "an unsatisfied longing for this original understanding without words," thereby indicating the extent to which she felt that normal development and integration itself would be the main contributor to the production and maintenance of this painful feeling state.

It is of some interest from a historical point of view that two years earlier Bion, at the Paris Congress, introduced his concept of "normal projective identification," the very process through which the infant could gain the kind of understanding which Klein felt, due to development, would be irretrievably lost. The discovery and formulation of this concept came about through Bion's (1957) analytic experience with a particular patient where he found that breakdown of this earliest interchange between mother and infant resulted in what he called a *primitive psychic disaster*. Later (1962a, 1962b), Bion expanded upon and deepened the meaning and significance of this finding by establishing it as the foundation for his container-contained (♀♂) theory. This work emphasized how the mother's inability to function as an adequate receptor to her infant's distress, communicated via normal projective identification, could bring about serious damage to the earliest linking processes. In the clinical setting this concept has become a valuable tool in helping the analyst to make distinctions between projective identification as a primitive form of communication from its use by the patient as a weapon of attack, an important issue that has been investigated by Rosenfeld (1971b) and B. Joseph (1982) and which will be further discussed in this paper in terms of the relationship of its pathological form to vengeance.

I would now like to make a connection between this contribution of Bion's, obtained through clinical research, with more recent findings by D. Stern (1985) gained by infant studies, and utilize these as a backdrop for furthering our understanding with regard to this presentation. Certain of Stern's observations, e.g., point to the extent to which the infant, in an effort to keep the relationship to the mother intact, will be noted to make accommodations to her idiosyncratic behavior which, I feel, may constitute the earliest instance of the relinquishment of mental development in the service of insuring one's survival. In this compromised interchange, it might be said that the infant sacrifices its evolving self and, instead, indulges the needs and beliefs of the mother upon whom its existence so depends. A later version of such indulgence is epitomized, e.g., by a patient in my series who recalled capitulating to the admonitions of his overly anxious mother who, during the so-called medication ritual, would often exclaim, "take the medicine or you'll make me sick." A resultant of this dynamic and its import was, furthermore, observed by way of Bion's *Experiences in Groups* (1961) wherein the Basic Assumption group mind, desperately involved with concerns of its survival, operates to prevent what is experienced as the threatening effects of the effort of the individual to achieve growth. Stern (1985) felt that he could ascertain, by way of his infant observations, instances in which the baby would evidence "a loosening of its center of gravity" as it "shift(ed) its interest from inside to outside," and felt that this alteration of focus could interfere with identity development and encourage instead the formation of a "false personality."

By contrast, the patients under investigation in this paper, based on six analysands of my own, in addition to four from supervisees over the past several years, have been more seriously affected and are closer to the "primitive disaster" configuration, although "false self" features are not uncommonly present here, as well. The data with these patients indicate that a more disturbing traumatic effect has taken form, in which the infant develops a sense of "non existence" as a result of experiences with an emotionally absent mother, i.e., where the organism develops a sense of its not being held or contained in the mother's mind. A significant consequence of this early sense of loss, and one which will constitute a major thrust of this paper, is the early development of a destructively envious attitude that gets directed against the existence of a two-party presence and, in particular, the possibilities that this reality brings forward.

In developing his concept of "hyperbole," Bion (1965) describes a situation where the infant's normal projective nonverbal communication as a result of its not being adequately received or rejected by the mother, will set in motion an even more vigorous attempt to be recognized. Ultimately, its efforts remaining unanswered, the infant will become exhausted and withdraw from its reality. It can be understood that the time of life in which this impasse occurs will be quite crucial. Klein (1952), for example, postulated a period, which she called the paranoid-schizoid period, in which the ego is indeed in a state of existence but lacking cohesion and, thus, is quite vulnerable. Clearly, a hyperbolic experience taking place during this time of life would, in all likelihood, be more catastrophic than one occurring in later infancy. My clinical findings suggest that the misfortune taking place at this earlier period brings with it a state of ego fragmentation. However, I feel that this type of disruption does not take place directly but secondarily, resulting from the too-early idealization of the primal object, constructed in an effort to maintain an illusion of its goodness. Disruption of the ego would thus take place when the forces of reality finally break through this defensive structure—the stuff that in the extreme case may give rise to the formation of psychogenic autistic states. With the exception of two or three patients in my series (one of which, for comparing and contrasting purposes, will be later commented on) the patients under study here, I feel, succumbed to the trauma at a later period of their infant development, resulting in a different dynamic configuration.

These patients have been able to advance a greater distance without meeting up with undue harm to their emotional growth, but have run into trouble at the point that Stern (1985) has conceptualized as the "core self" stage of development. Here, he particularizes a time between seven and nine months, when the infant gradually comes upon the momentous realization that there is another mind out there as well as his/her own, and that this intersubjective experience, "the subject matter of the mind," is potentially sharable with some else's, i.e., a crucial development of a greater awareness that self and other have separate minds that can interface. He considers this phase to be a "quantum leap" forward in the infant's mental growth, a shift that provides it with a new sense of "presence and social feel" which is matched by that of the parents who now experience their infant differently. Analytic work with the cases under study here suggests that the mothers or parents, due to difficulties of their own, were unable to respond with sufficient interest or enthusiasm to this all-important mental advance of their offspring.

In these cases, the ego has been strong enough to "give up" on the primal object itself, leading to the development of a belief that no good object or reality ever existed for them in the first place. Thus, these cases, rather than paying the price of the too early idealization of the object, are operating instead from an aggrieved and vengeful position, as if following a motto somewhat along the lines of "Okay, I don't exist for you (as a reality I once wanted), then you don't exist for me." The double meaning of the word "disappoint" is pertinent here where the mother in disappointing the expectation of her baby has now herself been dis-appointed by her offspring. This configuration is also captured in the famed "sour grapes" fable of Aesop where the original desire for the object along with the object itself becomes devalued and rejected. As a result of this lost contact with the primal "good object," where no memories of good experiences remain in the mind of the (future) patient, it can be understood that the analyst's task can be quite daunting and one which requires, as was so well-stated by Winnicott (1963), of the analyst to "help the patient to reach back through the transference to the state of affairs that obtained before the original trauma."

Paramount to bringing about this achievement will be the task of helping the patient make room for the early mental pain that became intolerable and was thus impossible to "suffer" (Bion, 1970), and which has been continuously rejected through excessive and violent projective identification. While aiding the patient effect this change, by way of functioning as an adequate container for this pain, success here will also depend on being able to help the patient cope with the sense of uncertainty that was originally overwhelming to the point that the fear of dying had deteriorated, in its state of despair, into a wish to die. Here it can be seen that the unavailability of an adequate containing object required to keep the infant's uncertainty within tolerable limits had been sadly lacking.

As previously indicated, my suspicion is that the mothers of these patients were "good enough" up to the time that the infant was able to achieve the "quantum leap" forward so as to be able to enjoy its differentness and separateness, a reality that the mother was unresponsive to or perhaps became hostile to as it failed, to coincide with her preconceived or rigidly established mind set as to how her baby *should* be or act. In further relating this type of problem to the failure of the mother to adequately respond to her infant's normal projective identification, Boris (1994) points out that these individuals "have their jobs cut out for them if they are to bounce back rather than forthwith begin the job of dying." This so-called "dying," in my view, constitutes the death of hope and thus of retaining interest in the primal object, as well as in the healthy remnants of the self which, though quite fragile, continue to reach out for contact.

Bibring (1951), in this regard, originally described what he called "the basic mechanism of depression," an "intersystemic" condition in which the ego, in becoming overwhelmed, is no longer capable of gratifying itself, leading to a state where emotional strivings lose their significance. But it was Erickson (1968) who emphasized the significance of *hope, per se,* and the essential factors necessary within the family to insure its health, stressing the importance of the mother being able to provide a "psychosocial protection and stimulation" so as to give the infant the conviction that she is trustworthy enough to satisfy and regulate its needs and expectations; and that it is the very advent of the infant that acts to inspire hope in the mother or parents and makes her/them want to give hope, thus "awakening in them a strength (which is) confirmed in the experience of care." More recently Meltzer (1988), in developing his concept of the *aesthetic conflict*, has also emphasized the importance of the mother's reciprocal response to her offspring's wish to know her (Bion's K link), where the satisfaction of this quest saves the infant from developing undue suspicion and distrust. Meltzer likens failure here to Othello's dilemma, i.e., the vulnerability to loss of trust due to the unbridled uncertainty.

My findings suggest that the failure of the birth to inspire hope in the mother and become the impetus to reciprocate by giving hope to her infant, may come about when the mother herself has been unduly effected by a deep sense of deprivation, which evokes, in turn, an expression of hostile envy, and is thus prevented from experiencing a sense of gratitude in response to giving birth. Sandell (1993), in this regard, has drawn attention to the connection between hope and the capacity for healthy, admiring type of envy and contrasts this state of mind with that which produces hostile envy and operates instead within an inner atmosphere of hopelessness. In my view, this latter condition is part and parcel to states of narcissistic withdrawal, which in the clinical setting can give rise to considerable instability. Here again, healthy hope, in its precarious state, can easily be undone by the effect and unconscious meaning of the week-end break.

For example, after a constructive session in which the analyst is experienced as being quite helpful and valuable, the patient may again lose contact with the "good" object of the infantile transference, as the unbearable feelings of loneliness and abandonment are reactivated and all sense of the existence of goodwill has again been lost. This sequence can be most dramatic and impressive upon the return of the patient to the analysis on the Monday where he/she now experiences the analyst as being a distant and uncaring stranger—a potential danger to be on guard against. This inability to retain contact with the good reality can be understood to accrue from two sources: (1) a time when the necessary work to keep the good object in mind became too arduous and was relinquished, giving rise out of desperation, to a survival mentality; and, (2) a reactivation of an internal destructive and cynical effort within the negative narcissistic side of the personality, the aim of which is to destroy the effects of the previous gain and thus undermine hope.

This extremely tenuous hold on the relationship to the "good" object is typical of these patients, where a characteristic finding is that of the absence of any satisfying or endearing memories in relationship to the primal object, often described in terms of a lack of genuine caring capacity on the mother or parents' part, along with references to the mother being "depressed," "overanxious" and/or "detached—not there." These descriptions, which are consistent with the outgrowth of an infantile despairing type of depression, in combination with faulty internal solutions can be understood to contribute to a characteristic developmental arrest, manifestation of which includes marked disturbance in the capacity for intimacy with self and object and an inhibition of the two-party (hetero) sexual desire. In view of the fact that with these patients, the part of the self which remains in hope and holds out in favor of life forces is quite weak, a wide split will soon develop within the personality. And the inequality of this split is apt to be so great as to be practically indistinguishable from it being understood as merely constituting a split off part. On the surface, however, this situation may not be so apparent, so well is the true nature of things concealed by what I have come to refer to as "the secondary personality," a point which will be taken up more fully in a latter section. I wish instead, at this point, to consider the importance of this split itself.

Trauma and Narcissism

In carrying out this investigation, it is important to emphasize that in the cases under discussion here, the effect of the trauma is so much operating solely on a deep emotional level, that any sense of abuse may remain quite buried and only make its appearance rather late in the analysis. Thus, a definite distinction can be made between these cases and those described by Shengold in *Soul Murder* (1989). While in both instances, references to "broken heart" or "damaged spirit" are applicable, his study pertains to children of three years onward who were subjected to physical and/or sexual abuse, or deprivation which is not the case here. On the other hand, the emotional impact did not occur so early or in such a manner as to bring about extreme pathology, i.e., gross borderline/psychotic or autistic symptomatology. Therefore, the cases in this investigation may also be contrasted with those described by Spitz (1946), Tustin (1981), or Bowlby (1980), although his study is pertinent here by way of his dispelling the prior view that very young children lack the capacity to experience these very painful emotions and suffer their sequelae. It should also be added that Tustin (1986), in abandoning her earlier idea of normal autism, later formulated the concept of autistic enclaves operating in less disturbed patients, which is pertinent to this investigation.

Research on early development suggests that the infant is "an excellent tester of its reality" (Stern, 1985), which Begoin (1995) has suggested may potentiate the earliest form of "learning from experience." Therefore, the infant's capacity to recognize the emotional insufficiency and inadequacy of the mother, e.g., the sense of not being held in the mother's mind, can stimulate an overpowering fear of dying and a subsequent urge to deny this perceived danger by escaping into a state of illusion. This retreat from reality may take various forms of reinventing of one's story, including those of idealization, ascribing blame to one's self (Fairbairn's [1944] "moral defense"), or believing one has the power to change the mother into a more appealing person, etc. The following vignette may be illustrative in this regard.

Dr. S., a thirty-five-year-old psychiatrist, entered analysis with complaints of "depressed moods" which would alternate with excessive anger and harmful self-destructive actions. In the course of our work he was able to recover an early pain of loneliness and a sensitivity to feelings of being "unwanted" and "devalued." In addition, he would sometimes experience a sense of great mental exhaustion which we discovered was related to early efforts to gain reassurance by getting the mother's attention and altering her dissatisfied facial expression, failure of which would give rise to states of survival anxiety and ultimate psychic withdrawal into an imaginary world. It was quite striking how this early struggle in relation to the mother would get played out in his work with certain types of uncooperative patients where a compelling countertransference need to change the nature of the patient's resistance could be seen to be operating. In this setting, my analysand felt obligated to relieve his patient of her presenting dissatisfaction and would experience vicissitudes of a deep-seated fear and anger when these efforts would go for naught.

This kind of faulty solution, manifesting the infant's desperate effort to maintain a connection to the mother (so as to ward off the early anxiety and pain related to the threat of loss) can be particularly harmful when it leads to an excessive idealization of the object and a further depreciation of the self. Beneath this defensive maneuver, however, and stemming from the effects of the psychic withdrawal, lies the development of a most dangerous configuration, possessing pernicious qualities. I am referring here to the potential for malignant growth, a development which can take hold when the uncontained ($-♀♂$) excessive distress and anger turn into a rage of murderously irrational proportions. The feelings of helplessness and hopelessness which are now prominent foster, as well, a "sour grapes" with a vengeance attitude toward the primal object and toward reality itself, giving rise to a profound contempt for life. In my view, the omnipotent state of mind that now develops, previously described by Rosenfeld (1971a) in terms of the idealization of destructiveness, gives rise to an envy of murderous proportions.

The extreme nature of this dynamic has been well-illustrated in the fictional works of Ukio Mishima (1963),[2] particularly in his novella, *The Sailor Who Fell From Grace With The Sea*, wherein the love capacity of the main character, Noburo, becomes so eroded that he becomes a participant in the underground activity of the murderously vengeful and envious adolescent gang. This narrative skillfully points out the degree to which the early failed efforts to maintain the healthy connection to the primal object (Bion's L, H and K links) has resulted in an undermining of emotional capacity, leading to an ego insufficiency and to being swept up into a highly destructive, narcissistic system. Thus, the original painful emotional experience remains uncontained ($-♀♂$) and in a condition of disgorgement through violent projective identification, reinforcing thereby the state of withdrawal which prevents, in its wake, any chance of re-establishing the connection to the original, but too brief, "good" reality. It is this devolution, I feel, that potentiates the development of an organized anti-growth motive, which I will now refer to as the "negative personality." Meltzer (1978), in referencing this destructive system, identifies it "as a rival organization for creating lies," consistent with "big brother" in Orwell's *1984*. This "lie," in the patients under discussion here, is one that gives rise to and reinforces a cynical point of view of life, including the belief that no genuine help or goodness exists or has ever existed.

The Negative Personality and Its Relationship to Hostile Envy

Klein, in utilizing Freud's (1920) original idea regarding the presence of a death instinct, developed it into the foundation block of her theory of infantile personality. Here, she felt, in keeping with the emphasis placed on constitutional factors, that the death instinct was an inborn force which threatened the infant with a basic fear of annihilation. This survival fear was dealt with, she theorized, in part by projection, giving rise to persecutory anxiety, but also by converting it into its own aggression. This latter idea of primary hostility was further developed in *Envy and Gratitude* (1957), in terms of the infant's inborn impulse to possess the breast out of love and through its recognition of the breast as being the source of all good things. Failure of the fulfillment of these possessive claims explained, she felt, the destructively motivated attacks which, in turn, could also function to defend against envy by way of spoiling or devaluing the object, understood, as well, to be the stuff of the negative therapeutic reaction.

It is my position, by contrast, that destructive envy having devolved from a breakdown of the two-party interactive system is, by its very nature, devaluing of the object. Destructive envy of this kind emanates not from love of the object but from the loss of that love and in response to the unbearable disappointment that is part and parcel to this loss. Here, as well, inadequate containment of the primitive fears and needs gives rise to an overwhelming survival anxiety, hostility, and, ultimately to despair. It is this kind of breakdown that brings forth an all-important change in the nature and direction of the infant's epistemophilic impulse, constituting a shift from wanting to know the mother (Bion's K link) to a desperate need (related to its survival anxiety), to possess and appropriate the breast/mother. This latter condition is no longer conducive to promoting growth within the two-party interactive system, but to promoting of collusion and to developmental arrest. In addition, I feel that the failure to distinguish between these two forms of the epistemophilic impulse has lead to some confusion regarding distinctions between two party/one party systems. This problem, that became more pronounced following the publication of *Envy and Gratitude*, where envy was felt to arise solely from a primary source, can be noted in Rosenfeld's (1971a) paper. He describes the violence of the envy embodied in the wish to destroy the analyst, an impulse that makes its appearance after the analysand begins to emerge from the pathological narcissistic state and is now confronted with the recognition of the existence of and significance of a two party situation.

The nature of the violence here, I feel, is not adequately understood due to there being an insufficient appreciation of the essential threat and challenge to the belief system of the patient when he/she emerges from this narcissistic state; the belief, inherent to this pathology, being that one has the power to produce or reproduce oneself. In addition, this lack of clarity appears to have been compounded as a result of the tendency to think of the envious attack as being directed against the anatomical object itself, prototype being the breast, rather than the emotion that links objects and gives to them their sense of reality (Bion's L, H and K). Therefore, it can be understood that the hostility that is operative here resides within that part of the personality which feels itself to have been cheated of the mother-infant growth-enhancing two-party experience and is, due to this (secondary) envy, opposed to this linking process. This oppositional personality, caught in the lie and the cynical view, is not then an entity that is independent of the pathological narcissistic state but is part and parcel to it, albeit existing in a latent or protomental form. Therefore, it is the patient's newly developed capacity for cooperation, evidenced by being able to emerge from the closed one-party system (Fairbairn, 1958) or the claustrum (Meltzer, 1992) that so stimulates and flushes out the violence of the destructive envy. It is this hostile, narcissistic side, with its belief of possessing these omnipotent powers, which I wish to refer to as *the negative personality*, a system which can also be understood to bring about a negative therapeutic reaction.

Segal (1983) also describes a clinical situation in which her patient, in emerging from this narcissistic state, is compelled to want to spoil the beauty and richness of the analysis and its two-party reality. By way of this vignette she is suggesting that destructive narcissism and hostile envy may actually function like two sides of the same coin, an idea closer to my view where destructive envy is perceived as a secondary phenomenon, operating within the realm of despair. This meeting of minds again becomes contradicted, however, by way of the tie Segal maintains between this form of envy and the idea of a primary death instinct. Here, in her 1966 paper and again in 1992 she attempts to make use of the suicide scene in the Jack London novel *Martin Eden*, to demonstrate the existence of a death instinct that acts to overpower the will to live. The material in the novel that she uses, however, has been taken out of context from the totality of the story which, highly autobiographical, supports the very position that the hero's wish to die, rather than emanating from some primary source, stems instead from his inability to bear the pain of the loss of the primal object which has been reactivated by the breakup of a present-day love affair. The despair that follows, brings with it the characteristic massive loss of hope and of interest in the life of one's emotions. The crucial point in this narrative occurs when Ruth, Martin's previous love, asks for forgiveness for having rejected and abandoned their love in favor of remaining steadfast to her bourgeois, establishment values—material values put ahead of what Martin calls "sacred love." The psychodynamics of this sequence is quite consistent with the great deal that is known about London's early life (well-documented, for example, in Irving Stone's [1969] excellent biography) where, before birth, he was literally rejected and deserted by his father and, soon after his birth, emotionally abandoned by his mother.

Consistent with the patient in my series, the true explanation for the self-destruction lays within the ashes of the unresolved infantile trauma and while London, consistent with patients in my series, was able to achieve considerable success by determination and dint of hard work, he was never able to resolve the psychic scarring that formed as a result of his very humble beginnings. This creative work emanated from an unconscious depth that even London himself was unable to comprehend, similar to a person who can only have but surface understanding of the meaning of his dream. In the crucial scene before his suicide, Martin, in turning away from the original pain that is being reactivated by his present disappointment, suddenly experiences a massive loss of interest in self and object which has permeated life itself, exclaiming, "I care for nothing—it is too late now, something has gone out of me—I have always been unafraid of life but I never dreamed of being sated with life—empty of desire for everything." Here, he has been overtaken by the unresolved early despair, similar to the analysand who expresses him/herself as being "fed up with life." But, behind this contempt for life, issuing forth from the negative personality, lies the deeply buried unresolved anxiety and pain associated with the original loss and trauma. In his real life, the despairing side of London's personality, by contrast, took a chronic form by way of self-destructive alcoholism.

Vengeance as the Linchpin of the Negative Personality

As previously indicated, in commenting on the life and works of Mishima, a malignant process may take form when despair, now under the sway of a murderous envy, combines with the idealization of destructiveness. Here, the primal object that was once an object of love and desire has now, from the position of the negative personality, become an object of hate, as have the emotions themselves which have become too painful to bear. But now, even hate has become intolerable as this emotion is felt to be too closely related to the original trauma of the lost love.

It is in this context that Bion's (1962b) concept of the minus links (–L, H and K) is most meaningful, where hatred of emotion itself becomes the overriding principle. In addition, that part of the self that has been able to retain, albeit in a damaged form, its original dependent longings for the primal "good" object will have become similarly hated and kept at bay. This state of affairs which gives rise to the deep split within the personality previously referred to, will result in a basic incapacity to experience care or to value help. Although, for a time, this deficit may be well-covered over by the "secondary personality" (see *infra*), the dominant personality of these people have long ago given up on any idea of benefiting from cooperative effort and have come to operate instead from a position of ruthless self-interest.

Socarides (1966), in his seminal paper "On vengeance," emphasized the significance of this emotional response in terms of one's urge to "get even." Implicit here is the notion that these patients, deep down, are operating from a sense of having been victims of emotional abuse and from a belief of feeling quite entitled to retaliate in kind. On the micro level, however, this vengeful action takes the form of ridding the psyche of feelings that were once, and continue to be, too painful to bear. Therefore, this vengeful action constitutes an attack on the mind, particularly that aspect of mind responsible for conscious awareness; and thus, the close relationship between vengeance and the mechanism of projective identification as a means of ridding the psyche of unwanted mental pain can be seen. Furthermore, since projective identification operates as an omnipotent mental mechanism, its use in excess furthers the unconscious belief that emotions are to be used as weapons of power, and provide the very means by which one *can* "get even."

Vengeance, therefore, assiduously directs itself against the linking process and the emotions which serve to link objects. In studying the dynamic interplay of emotions within the negative side of the personality, it can be recognized that while vengeance provides the *means* (via projective identification) through which the internal and external relationship can be destroyed or omnipotently controlled, it is the envy that constitutes the *motive* for the attack, i.e., that another should have or gain access to valuables that one was originally denied or deprived of.

In this state of vengeance, however, one has given up on and ultimately lost contact with the existence of possibilities, i.e., the chance for new growth and constructive change. These people, therefore, are incapable of thinking in terms of the "glass (being) half full" and instead remain peculiarly limited to a pessimistic view in their confinement to the process of "getting even." Since the subject is unable to advance, envy is further stimulated by and directed against those who can. In the clinical setting, the emerging self, with its capacity to value the advantages of work accomplished by the analytic couple, will be resented and *hope*, in particular, envied. Progress of this kind will, in turn, bring about a negative therapeutic response as the healthy but still weaker side continues to be overwhelmed. Greed will also become quite active since, any possibility of "better" has been rendered inoperative and only efforts in the direction of "more and more" will be able to preside. Boris (1990) has shown how greed may overpower the possibility for gratitude by way of a (projective) "identification with a vengeance," operating out of envy to deny the analyst a separate existence and thereby prevent the possibility of his being experienced as a true source of goodness. A fourth emotion that operates in the realm of the negative side which also resides in hopelessness and compliments vengeance, envy, and greed, is that of a deep-seated and most ungenerous grudging attitude. This impulse is directed against any sense of goodwill, accomplishment, or gain from being admitted into or maintained in conscious awareness and, thus, available to the mind so as to facilitate further advance.

When these destructive efforts can be laid bare, enabling the patient to recognize the advantages that mental growth provides, then it will be possible to demonstrate the nature and action of the internal conflict (Bion, 1965), i.e., that the difficulty lies within one's own personality and is not based on a problem between patient and analyst. Until this is accomplished there can be no possibility of the envy being experienced as ego dystonic and, thus, the analysand will continue to function in an "impenitent" manner, attempting, in a state of entitlement, to justify his/her grievances, often in a perverse manner, at the expense of the analysis—an important issue previously noted by Spillius (1993).

It is these emotions then, spearheaded in particular by hostile envy, that are in operation to bring about a negative therapeutic reaction, a response which is operative due to the split between the frail but healthy and the dominant destructive side. While this dynamic is characteristic of the majority of patients in my series, as indicated earlier, I would like to present a so-called special case, for comparing and contrasting purposes, to show that in instances where progress in the analysis remains quite minimal, the usual form of the negative therapeutic reaction will not be noted. In this situation, the prevention of advance is carried out both by stealth and clever manipulation of the patient-analyst relationship, and it may take some time before this deviousness becomes clear. I have in mind here the patient who is adept at "reversal of perspective" (see Bion, *Elements of Psychoanalysis*, pp. 50-60), an action that suspends emotional contact and keeps the analyst's expectations in this regard forever unfulfilled.

One patient in my series, who was particularly adroit at this maneuver, had early in the analysis revealed, through the aid of a series of fragmented "dreams," that his internal world existed in a state of considerable disruption. Soon, further material gave me reason to suspect that he had been so emotionally traumatized in early life as to leave him totally sensitive to his own pain and equally insensitive to the pain of others. The exquisite nature of his own responsiveness was such that the slightest alteration in the analytic situation, e.g., change in the tone of my voice or physical movement in my chair was experienced by him as being equivalent to an upheaval of major proportions. Such experiences would be either denied by him outright or at best responded to by a most superficial, "Well, maybe you're right," when, with the aid of the next hour's "dream," it was possible to show him the nature and extent of his response. This resistance to direct insight plus his adeptness at covering over his considerable dis-ease by a quite polished debonair manner, enabled me in time to realize that in all likelihood we could not make progress by the usual analytic method. This appraisal was also furthered by my recognition of the extent to which he was operating by way of massive projective identification, the result of which was that any problems that I thought I could see to be operative in him quickly became those of his wife (or his analyst).

Matters being what they were, I began to feel that, in an effort to "make the best of a difficult situation," I would have to modify the usual interpretive approach and follow, instead, one that was closer to a "corrective emotional" method. Involved here was the necessity to relinquish any direct effort on my part to be *helpful* by way of offering insight, to one in which I would not be experienced by him as being *harmful*. My inner acceptance of our situation soon had a salutary effect on my mood, and I suspect that it was this intersubjective assent that the patient was unconsciously able to respond to and before long he indicated that "things" were better at home and at work, when previously there had been frequent references to "divorce" and "need to change the job." Clearly absent, however, was any indication of gratitude or that this improvement could have anything to do with our meetings and, before long, references to termination were in the offing. The abrupt and arbitrary nature of this decision, based on travel distance and expense, proved to be too much for me and, in returning to my usual interpretive mode, I suggested that while the reason he was giving for wanting to end the analysis were certainly valid ones, there might be something deeper operating that he was not aware of, having to do with "taking the next step," that was stimulating anxiety. This interpretation was visibly disturbing to the patient and quickly side-stepped by a quick denial, the sternness of which had not previously been seen, and the hour ended. The next session began in a manner that was reminiscent of the earlier period, i.e., before the modification of technique, in which the patient would report a "dream" that would indicate the extent to which he felt my behavior to have been reckless, insensitive, and dangerous; but now the dream revealed, as well, a sense of extreme internal danger that had been activated by my suggestion that there might be a "next step" for us to attempt to traverse. This dream made it quite clear that the very idea of the existence of a "next step," placing value on direct human effort for mutual benefit, was entirely forbidden—Orwell's *Big Brother* in its most blatant form. In the dream, fear produced by this prohibition acted to drive the patient into hiding within an underground retreat, and it was apparent that this felt danger emanated from a violent and malignant form of envy, represented here as being an invading and infiltrating military force, which quickly acts to disallow direct emotional contact and thus put a stop to any vestige of hope. It can thus be seen that in this more disturbed "special" case, where mental growth is so slight (in contrast to those in my series where the conflict between the two opposing sides can eventually take form and thus give rise to the possibility of advancement beyond the survival state of mind), a negative therapeutic reaction has no opportunity to develop.

In making distinctions between the different forms of envy along the malignant→destructive→admiring→continuum it may be further useful to comment on what can be considered as normal envy of the infant or young child, beginning with its relative helplessness and proceeding to the recognition of the differences between itself and the "big people" that populate its world. It is this natural vulnerability of the small organism which behooves the caretaker to want to protect it from projections emanating from their own unsolved problems—inadequacies enacted that might serve to stimulate undue envy in their offspring. Contemporary Kleinians (e.g., Britton [1989] and Feldman [1992]) have recognized and described the unfortunate effects of this kind of breakdown in the parent-child interchange, a variety of which will be addressed in the case example to follow. The analyst can be alerted to the effect that this type of early impingement has had by way of references to "incompetence" and "inadequacy," not always referred to by name, as these feelings make their way into the infantile transference and become further illuminated through the inner conflict between the opposing sides of the personality. Mitrani (1993) has pointed out how the acquisition of this kind of understanding may require the analyst to exercise "negative capability" and resist, in the presence of mounting uncertainty, the temptation of seeking reassurance by finding refuge in familiar theories.

Technical Considerations and Illustrative Case

A consistent finding noted in the analysands under discussion here is the presentation of a personality structure that is designed to cover over the severity of a basic problem which dates back to the original trauma—a structure which I refer to as the *secondary personality*. The function of this organization is to defend against acquiring knowledge of the primitive psychological disaster, a structure which has similarities to what has been previously referred to by Deutch (1942), Winnicott (1960), Meltzer (1966), and Bick (1968) in terms of "as if personality," "false self," "pseudo-mature," and "second skin," respectively; but in addition, in the patients under discussion here, the secondary personality is specifically designed to keep at bay awareness of the deep unresolved disappointment that had given rise to an unbearable sense of loneliness, the loneliness without hope. In addition, this spurious aspect of personality also operates to keep hidden the destructive, murderous trends that have developed within the negative side.

A more superficial layer of "cover up" may also manifest itself in certain cases by way of a display of (false) optimism which will sooner or later give way to a pessimistic and cynical point of view since, on a deep level of mind, hope has long also been relinquished. Thus, as analysis deepens, the façade will give way and expose an underlying, generally suspicious and unfriendly state of mind, and while exposure of this despair is crucial to the advancement of the analysis, the lack of genuine good feelings and the distrust that come forward will put considerable strain on the working relationship and give rise to critical moments.

The analysand, at this point, may also be only too willing to concede that the problem is "inborn" and thus unresolvable, in keeping with the belief (lie) that help or goodwill is nonexistent. An important part of the work, at this juncture, will be to clarify the origin and nature of this misconception in terms of the early giving up (of hope) on the holding environment. Thus, a major step will have been achieved when the patient is able to consider that his or her long-standing narcissistic self-protective stance, which has functioned to ward off possible re-exposure to the once unbearable psychic pain and terror may constitute a wrong choice. This advance, though it may bring forward the pain of deep regret, will usher in the all-important possibility of the "next step."

Included here will be the opportunity to show the patient, in more minute detail, how their grudging and vengeful attitude is operating to prevent internal change, notably by keeping the advantages present and available in today's reality confused with the deprivation of early life. Helping the analysand make these distinctions provides another means by which the "conflict within" can become better identified. Progress here will expose pockets of deep envy operating within enclaves which act to deny the existence of two-party mutuality, and the benefits inherent in taking the "next step." Included in this progress will be the uncovering of previously "unmentionable" hidden murderous impulses, consistent with a very early feeling that one has been cheated or stolen from. This latter discovery extends the nature of a dynamic which now must include the split between the so-called split off parts themselves, i.e., the one in which, in spite of the damage done, continues to yearn for the primal object; the other where, because of the damage done, harbors deep-seated murderous urges that remain hidden due to primitive fears of discovery. As pointed out by Steiner

(1993), the analyst's ability to recognize and successfully help the patient expose these emotions will be instrumental in facilitating release from his/her *psychic retreat*. I have found, as well, that this freeing effect will be instrumental in shifting the balance in favor of the healthy emerging side of the personality, thus rendering the negative therapeutic reaction more manageable. The following example from the consultation room may be useful in illustrating some of these points.

Mrs. X, from very early childhood, had been severely traumatized as a result of her exposure to an extended family feud which, in particular, involved bitter fighting between her parents. The mother's over-involvement in this rivalry with the father and his family left her daughter emotionally uncared for. As the patient's story unfolded, it was revealed that she, referred to here as Mrs. X, attempted to cope with the terror that this sense of abandonment gave rise to by pushing her body against and into a corner of the living room wall in a desperate effort to gain some semblance of support. It was later revealed that this section of wall became like an idealized mother through which an illusion of the existence of a perfect union and sense of oneness could be gained.

During approximately the first year and a half of the analysis it was difficult to discern evidence of progress due to the patient's excessive compliant and pseudo-cooperative behavior which would, at times, briefly alternate with violent bouts of defiant behavior. It could be understood that an enactment of the relationship to the "bad" idealized mother who was secretly hated were issuing forth, but interpretations along these lines made in an effort to clarify this situation failed to be of benefit, and it soon became apparent that the early breakdown had left the patient with a greatly impaired capacity for genuine participation. Matters, therefore, appeared rather bleak for us until around the end of the second year of the analysis when, after its resumption following the summer break, Mrs. X reported a dream which now more clearly revealed the nature and extent of the psychic damage and which ushered in the beginning of an important turning point.

In the dream, a polar bear is seen lying on an expanse of arctic ice. Kneeling down beside it, the patient sees that the bear has only the strength to partially turn its head in her direction and open one eye so as to give the slightest show of recognition. Mrs. X understood the pun implied by this image, i.e., (bear)ly alive, and thus could appreciate the more superficial meaning, but our further work was helpful in revealing its deeper significance, i.e., evidence of the existence of an emotionally damaged real self that yearned for the good primal object, but whose hope and interest in this pursuit was in serious danger of being extinguished.

While the recovery, through the dream, of this severely traumatized primitive self was important in improving her ability to cooperate, the fragile nature of the healthy interest, as noted in the dream, was no match for the considerable resistance to progress that continuously dogged us every inch of the way. Nevertheless, it was this change for the better that led to the recovery of the aforementioned frightening memories of the parental fighting and her escape into the make-believe illusory world of the perfect union; and it was later revealed that this turning to the world of imagination would follow failed attempts to change the mother's scowl or frown into a smile. This recovery also gave deeper meaning to the patient's attempts to please the analyst, stimulated in part, when the analytic procedure itself was felt to be too exacting and was confused with mother's sternness.

As our work continued and the omnipotence of the illusion of perfect one(ness) began to lose some of its power, a new symptom in the form of troubled sleep now appeared. I soon understood this disturbance to be explainable by way of the efforts of the emerging infantile self that now, more strongly, was wanting to make contact and have its wishes responded to, i.e., to be picked up and gain benefit from the sense of being held in the (mother's) mind. This desire, though bolder, was still ineffective in exercising much control over the destructive side, so that these healthy yearnings were more or less limited to breaking through into awareness at night, when her defenses were less active, to interrupt her sleep. At the same time, our work on this problem further revealed the extent to which Mrs. X functioned as a divided self which, in turn, was instrumental in exposing the cruel and perverse nature of the vengeance. Here, Mrs. X was able to recognize the satisfaction she experienced by frustrating and disappointing the analyst, at the expense of the analytic couple. Soon thereafter, a critical point was reached when the patient, evidencing the effect of being unduly stressed by the effect of these conflicting forces, quite spontaneously expressed a deep hatred of her desire "to be held" as well as for the feelings of sorrow and fear of abandonment that were related to this wish.

While the awareness of this powerful hatred of her healthy self which yearned for good contact was quite painful, it enabled her, for the first time, to recognize that she was no longer limited or restricted to the survival→despair→omnipotent mentality; but had arrived at a point where she could consider the possibility of choice, i.e., to act on the hatred of her pain and reject the emerging self or to want to find a means through which she could gain help for this aspect of her personality. The struggle between seeking the comfort of escape or facing up to the fear of going forward was well-documented by a dream she presented in the second session of the following week.

In the first part of the dream, which she emphasized as being very frustrating, she is looking at a beautiful ceramic tile molding but is quite dissatisfied with its appearance, feeling that too much grout is showing between the tiles. She attempts to deal with this felt problem by placing a larger tile, displaying a flamingo design, over the grouted area, but feels that this does not look right either. Then the scene shift and she finds herself in a beautiful home, the owner of which is a pretty, dark-haired woman who shows her through the house. On the tour, she sees that there are three swimming pools in each of three large rooms. When she recognizes her desire to go for a swim, the owner is not around to give permission, but she decides to dive in anyway and finds it quite satisfying.

Her associations plus benefits gleaned from our prior work made it possible to show Mrs. X that her efforts to cover over the grout between the tiles represented her long-standing attempt to escape from the too painful and hated reality of the existence of two(ness); an experience which she had so early felt cheated of, but which she continued to deprive herself of as a result of the strength of the "lie," the denial that help existed and could be depended upon. This part of the dream was also saying that, due to her improved reality sense, the familiar escape into the illusion of perfect oneness was no longer so satisfying. That it was beginning to be experienced as too restrictive, appeared to be confirmed by her association of having recently watched a National Geographic documentary that showed that "flamingo birds don't fly very well" and are limited to wading in shallow water. By contrast, the second part expressed a new-found interest in the realm of possibilities and a willingness to confront risk, both of which revealed a dimension of mind not previously noted.

Involved here was a new-found ability to keep the goodness of the analyst/mother in mind and thus remain attentive to the reality of the moment so that she might retain the capacity to interact with her infantile self. Through this achievement, she could begin to give genuine consideration to the interpretation (in contrast to her previous compelling tendency to avoid contact) indicating that she was now able to have and keep open a mental space to think in; an advance which, in turn, made it possible for her to develop a true regard for psychic pain and an interest in the discovery of her truth. In addition, this part of the dream gave indication of her developing ability to experience the beauty of the analytic process itself.

My further interpretation was to point out that she apparently had become able to recognize the advantage of this new approach, where the three swimming pools within the beautiful house might represent the possibilities she now could feel were available in the present session and the two remaining hours of the current week. Toward confirming this interpretation, Mrs. X added that on the night of the dream she had attended a theatrical performance. Worrisome thoughts about present-day business problems had prevented her from concentrating during the first act, but during the intermission, in thinking about some of the things we had discussed in the afternoon session, she was "somehow able to enjoy the second half."

This advance, revealed in the second part of the dream, coincided with Mrs. X now showing visible signs of softening along with the recovery of some childhood memories of contact with "good" objects—persons in her life whom she had had positive feelings toward and who she felt had loved her, in particular the paternal grandmother from whom she had received helpful comfort. This progress provided her with sufficient strength and courage for us to uncover frank murderous feelings toward the mother which, from very early times, had been felt to have been too frightening to admit to her mind. The opportunity to now experience an acknowledgment and acceptance of these heretofore forbidden and unthinkable feelings provided a means by which her mind could be further strengthened and thus be better positioned to counter the destructive action from the negative side. Failure to maintain this gain, however, could give rise to the reappearance of the "worrisome thoughts" previously mentioned, expressions of very early feelings of abandonment and attendant survival fears, which, when they lose the benefit of containment, can get misplaced by becoming attached to problems in present day reality. The resurgence of this symptom, brought forward by her inability to maintain the connection to her distressed infantile self and maintain the capacity to value the giving and receiving of help, can be understood in terms of the murderous hatred losing its containment and again turning vengeful. The process of this breakdown, as it made its appearance in the moment of session, made it possible to more clearly show Mrs. X this negative side at work, in particular, the perverse satisfactions she was again experiencing through her efforts to frustrate and disappoint the analyst. This insight, while embarrassingly painful, enabled her to more sincerely want to maintain the connection to her working (mind) self. Through the intimate nature of this work, I have also come to recognize that the development of harmful countertransference reactions that can get stimulated by this kind of uncooperative response can be avoided by being able to keep in mind that it took root at a time when the patient, in hopelessness, gave up interest in the primal object and in valuing the benefits of the working relationship. The following, more recent material, may shed further light.

Following a brief break in the analysis, Mrs. X began the session in an admittedly angry (but more courageous mood) stating, quite openly, that for all the effort she was expending she was "getting little back." Our prior work enabled me to recognize this state of mind as being related to that early time of life when the mental work involved in maintaining a connection to the inadequate mother becomes too arduous and gave rise to a state of mind bordering on feelings that all goodness in the world was lost and had vanished. At the same time, the analyst was also alerted to the underlying presence of a perversely motivated attitude aimed at disturbing my peace of mind, i.e., "getting even." But as the session proceeded it was possible to help Mrs. X to see that giving over her mind to these urges left her with little more than the tendency to "find fault" or "ascribe blame," forms of escape which would soon leave her feeling more frustrated and angry, and with a greater sense of helplessness to find a way out. This interpretation, at this moment in time, proved to be enough to allow her to recognize and understand the way in which her mind was dysfunctioning, which, in turn, brought about an abrupt change in the atmosphere of the room. And, as we proceeded, Mrs. X gave evidence of again being able to appreciate the advantage of the "give and take" interaction between two minds working together. The extent of this achievement provided her with sufficient courage and trust to regain contact with herself on the primitive level, an advance made additionally clear by way of her final statement of the hour: "I('m aware of) want(ing) to be held—so it must be close to the end of the session—I realize I owe a lot to you and need you" (want and value a psychoanalysis)....

This representative case example, I feel, illuminates some aspects of the importance of helping the patient develop an even greater capacity to "suffer" mental pain, an achievement through which regaining contact with the "good" primal object and a resolution of the trauma can become possible. The patient's recognition and appreciation of the nature of the inadequacy that has taken form within and leads to the faulty and harmful solutions, will go a long way toward helping the patient develop an understanding and acceptance of the inadequacy of the original object, a learning that can only take place through the analytic experience.

NOTES

1. Expanded version of a presentation made at the "Conference on Envy" held at the Psychoanalytic Center of California, Los Angeles, September 21, 1996.
2. Mishima's works are particularly pertinent here in view of his own disastrous early childhood, in which he was literally kidnaped soon after his birth by a highly emotionally disturbed grandmother within the house of ineffectual and intimidated parents. His sense of abandonment and idealization of martyrdom was not only reflected in his creative writings, but also in his death at age forty-five carried out by ritual seppuku.

REFERENCES

Begoin, J. (1995). Review of *Sincerity and Other Works. Collected Papers of Donald Meltzer*. Edited by Alberto Hahn. London: Karnac Books, 1994. *Int. J. Psycho-Anal.*, 5: 1049-1053.

Bibring, E. (1951). The mechanism of depression. Presented at the Annual Meeting of the American Psychoanalytic Association, May, 1951.

Bick, E. (1968). The experience of the skin in early object relations. *Int. J. Psycho-Anal.*, 49: 484-486.

Bion, W.R. (1957). On arrogance. In *Second Thoughts*. New Jersey/London: Aronson.

—— (1961). *Experiences in Groups*. London: Tavistock Publications.

—— (1962a). A theory of thinking. In *Second Thoughts*. New Jersey/London: Aronson.

—— (1962b). *Learning From Experience*. New York: Basic Books.

—— (1963). *Elements of Psychoanalysis*. New York: Basic Books.

—— (1965). *Transformations*. New York: Basic Books.

—— (1970). *Attention and Interpretation*. New York: Basic Books.

Boris, H.N. (1990). Identification with a vengeance. *Int. J. Psycho-Anal.*, 1: 127-140.

—— (1994). *Envy*. New Jersey: Aronson.

Bowlby, J. (1980). *Loss: Sadness and Depression*. New York: Basic Books.

Britton, R. (1989). The missing link: Parental sexuality in the Oedipus complex. In Steiner, J. (Ed.), *The Oedipus Complex Today*. London: Karnac, pp. 83-101.

Deutch, H. (1942). Some forms of emotional disturbance and their relationship to schizophrenia. *Psychoanal. Q.* 11: 301-321.

Fairbairn, W.R.D. (1944). Endopsychic structure considered in terms of object-relations. In *An Object-Relations Theory of the Personality*. New York: Basic Books, 1954, pp. 82-136.

—— (1958). On the nature and aims of psycho-analytical treatment. *Int. J. Psycho-Anal.*, 39: 374-385.

Erickson, E.H. (1968). The human life cycle. In *A Way of Looking at Things*, ed. Stephen Schlein. New York: Norton.

Feldman, M. (1992). Splitting and projective identification. In *Clinical Lectures on Klein and Bion*. London and New York: Tavistock/Routledge.

Freud, S. (1920). *Beyond the Pleasure Principle. SE*, 18: 7-64. In J. Strachey (Ed.), *Standard Edition of the Complete Psychological Works of Sigmund Freud*, 24 volumes. London: The Hogarth Press and the Institute of Psycho-Analysis, 1953-1974.

Joseph, B. (1982). Addiction to near death. *Int. J. Psycho-Anal.*, 63: 449-456.

Klein, M. (1933). The early development of conscience in the child. In *Love, Guilt and Reparation & Other Works, 1921-1945*. New York: Delta.

Klein, M. (1952). Origins of transference. In *Envy and Gratitude & Other Works, 1946-1963*. New York: Delta.
—— (1957). Envy and gratitude. In *Envy and Gratitude & Other Works, 1946-1963*. New York: Delta.
—— (1963). On the sense of loneliness. In *Envy and Gratitude & Other Works, 1946-1963*. New York: Delta.
London, J. (1967). *Martin Eden*. London: Arcol and Penguin.
Meltzer, D. (1966). The relation of anal masturbation to projective identification. *Int. J. Psycho-Anal.*, 47: 335-342.
—— (1978). *The Kleinien Development, Part III, The Clinical Significance of the Work of Bion*. Scotland: Clunie Press.
—— (1988). The aesthetic conflict: Its place in the developmental process. In *The Apprehension of Beauty*. Scotland: Clunie Press, pp. 7-33.
—— (1992). *The Claustrum*. Oxford: Clunie Press.
Mishima, Y. (1963). *The Sailor Who Fell From Grace With The Sea*. New York: Knopf.
Mitrani, J.L. (1993). Deficiency and envy: some factors impacting the analytic mind from listening to interpretation. *Int. J. Psycho-Anal.*, 4: 689-704.
Rosenfeld, H.A. (1971a). A clinical approach to the psychoanalytic theory of life and death instincts: An investigation into the aggressive aspects of narcissism. *Int. J. Psycho-Anal.*, 45: 332-337.
—— (1971b). Contributions to the psychopathology of psychotic states: The importance of projective identification in the ego structure and object relations of the psychotic patient. In Doucet, P and Laurin, C. (Eds.), *Problems of Psychosis*. Vol. 1, The Hague: Excepta Medica, pp. 115-128.
Sandell, R. (1993). Envy and admiration. *Int. J. Psycho-Anal.* 6: 1213-1232.
Segal, H. (1966). Discussion of "From Gravida to the death instinct" by Law rence J. Friedman. *Psychoanal. Forum*, 1: 55-58.
—— (1983). Some clinical implications of Melanie Klein's work: Emergence from narcissism. *Int. J. Psycho-Anal.*, 64: 269-276.
—— (1993). On the clinical usefulness of the death instinct. *Int. J. Psycho-Anal.*, 74: 55-61.
Shengold, L. (1989). *Soul Murder: The Effects of Childhood Abuse and Deprivation*. New York: Fawcet Columbine.
Socarides, C.W. (1966). On vengeance. *J. Amer. Psychoanal. Assn.*, 14: 356-375.
Spillius, E.B. (1993). Varieties of envious experiences. *Int. J. Psycho-Anal.* 6: 1199-1212.
Spitz, R. (1946). Analytic depression. *Psychoanal. Study Child*, 2: 313-342.
Steiner, J. (1993). *Psychic Retreats: Pathological Organizations in Psychotic, Neurotic, and Borderline Patients*. London and New York: Routledge.
Stern, D.N. (1985). *The Interpersonal World of the Infant: A View from Psychoanalysis and Developmental Psychology*. New York: Basic Books.

Stokes, H.S. (1974). *The Life and Death of Yukio Mishima*. New York: Farrar, Strauss and Giroux.
Stone, I. (1969). *Jack London, Sailor on Horseback*. New York: Signet.
Tustin, F. (1981). *Autistic States in Children*. London: Routledge and Kegan
Tustin, F. (1986). *Autistic Barriers in Neurotic Patients*. London: Karnac.
Winnicott, D.W. (1960). Ego distortion in terms of the true and false self. In *The Maturational Process and the Facilitating Environment*. London: Hogarth.
—— (1963). From dependence toward independence in the development of the individual. In *The Maturational Process and the Facilitating Environment*. London: Hogarth.

436 N. Roxbury Drive
Suite 216
Beverly Hills, CA 90210
USA

The Grammar of the Unconscious
The Conceptual Foundations of Psychoanalysis
CHARLES R. ELDER

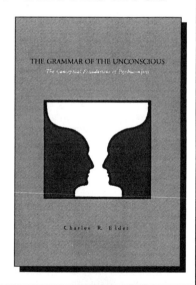

An inquiry into the distinctive features and conditions of the language of psychoanalysis, using Wittgenstein's method of grammar.

"Clearly an important contribution to our understanding of what Freud was doing in the development of psychoanalysis and to the ongoing debates about the scientific status of Freud's project and the nature of psychoanalytic work itself."—*Psychoanalytic Books*

270 pages $16.95 paper

 PENN STATE UNIVERSITY PRESS
USB 1, Suite C • University Park, PA 16802-1003 • Orders: **1-800-326-9180**

Before We Were Young
by
Michael Ian Paul, M.D.

Before We Were Young

An Exploration of Primordial States of Mind

Michael Ian Paul

esf

The reader of this work will certainly come to realize that its content is anything but prosaic. It belongs to the cutting-edge of psychoanalytic exploration and is unique in its oeuvre. Seldom does one find so many strands from such a variegated and gifted background coupled with an additional gift for innovative thinking and "imaginative conjecture" that speaks so credibly and immediately to the inner life of "every patient."

James S. Grotstein, M.D.

Before We Were Young. An Exploration of Primordial States of Mind by Michael Ian Paul, MD. Binghamton, NY: *Esf* Publishers, 224pp. $35.95. Hard cover, smythe sewn, printed on typographer's antique paper. ISBN 1-883881-24-2.

Table of Contents

Forward by J.S. Grotstein
1. Introduction
2. The Sense of Strangeness
3. A Contribution to the Study of Dimension
4. A Mental Atlas of the Process of Psychological Birth
5. Primordial Development of the Penitential Transference
6. Phenomenology of Mental Pressure
7. Practical Psychoanalytic Epistemology
8. Intonational Elements as Communication in Psychoanalysis
9. On the Imitation of Human Speech
10. Transformational Aspects of Phantasy in Relation to Dyadic Communication under the Influence of Marijuana

References, Index

ALL ORDERS TO BE SENT TO:
Esf Publishers, 1 Marine Midland Plaza, East Tower–Fourth Floor, Binghamton, NY 13901, USA.
Fax: **(607) 723–1401** E–mail your order: **jmkor97@aol.com**

Name _____
Address _____
_____

METHODS OF PAYMENT
☐ I enclose a check (made payable to *Esf* Publishers) for:

☐ Yes! I like to order *Before We Were Young* for $35.95 plus $3.00 (USA and Canada) or $7.00 (outside USA and Canada) s/h charges.*

☐ Please invoice my credit card
  ☐ Master Card   ☐ Visa
for the amount of _____

☐ Yes! I am a subscriber/I want to subscribe to the *Journal of Melanie Klein & Object Relations*, and receive *30% off the list price* for Dr. Paul's book.

Card No. (16 digits): _____

Expiration Date:_____ (month/year)

☐ Yes! I want to subscribe to *EINAI. An Annual* (see inside back cover in this issue), and receive *30% off the list price* for Dr. Paul's book

Signature_____
Date:_____

☐ Please send me information about other publications.

*Residents of New York State please add applicable sale tax.

IT PAYS TO SUBSCRIBE!

On Hallucination, Intuition, and the Becoming of "O"
by
Eric Rhode

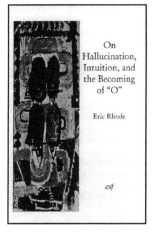

On Hallucination, Intuition, and the Becoming of "O"

Eric Rhode

esf

TABLE OF CONTENTS
Forward by Gilead Nachmani, Ph.D.
Part One. **The Caesura as Transparent Mirror: W. R. Bion and the Contact Barrier**
1. The Definitions of Mind and Body. 2. "A System that Continues to Function However Damaged it May Be." 3. "The Powerful Inanity of Events." 4. The Relationship of the Beta Screen to the Theory of Catastrophic Change. 5. Bion and Lévi-Strauss.

Part Two. **Optic Glass: The Nipple-Tongue as Preconception**
6. The Role of Hallucination in an Infant Observation. 7. "The Cosmos is a Mirror in which Everything is Reflected." 8. The Disappearing Tennis-Net. 9. From a Paternal to a Maternal Conception of Transference. 10. The Paranoid-Schizoid Version of the Imaginary Twin. 11. Transition Concepts.

Part Three. **Transformation in Hallucinosis and the Institution of Divine Kingship**
12. Annihilation and Transformation in Hallucinosis. 13. Catastrophic Fusions: Kings and Diviners Among the Moundag of Chad. 14. The Dread of Verticality that Underlies a World of Space and Time. 15. The Body as Cosmic Impress. 16. The Divine King and the Macrocosm of Destruction. 17. The Divine King as Microcosm of Creation. 18. The Double Labyrinth. 19. The Duration of the Body and the Reverberation of the Image. 20. The Fetish as Replacement for the Organ of Psychical Perception.

Part Four. **The Play Shakespeare Did Not Write**
21. The Gifts of the Saturnalian King. 22. The Opening and Closing of Shutters on a Window. 23. The Hidden God. 24. The Relationship of Swallowing and the Prehensive Object. 25. Absence of Breath and Cordelia's Mirror. 26. The World's Deep Midnight. *List of References. Index.*

On Hallucination, Intuition, and the Becoming of "O" by Eric Rhode. Binghamton: *Esf* Publishers, 224 pp. Soft cover, smythe sewn, printed on typographer's antique, acid-free paper. ISBN 1-883881-26-9. $24.95.

ALL ORDERS TO BE SENT TO:
Esf Publishers, 1 Marine Midland Plaza, East Tower–Fourth Floor, Binghamton, NY 13901, USA.
Fax: **(607) 723–1401**   E-mail your order: **jmkor97@aol.com**

Name_____
Address_____
_____

METHODS OF PAYMENT
☐ I enclose a check (made payable to *Esf* Publishers)
for: ☐

☐ Yes! I like to order *On Hallucination, Intuition, and the Becoming of "O"* by Eric Rhode, $24.95 plus $3.00 (USA and Canada) and $7.00 (outside USA and Canada) s/h charges.*

☐ Please invoice my credit card
   ☐ Master Card   ☐ Visa
for the amount of _____

☐ Yes! I am a subscriber/I want to subscribe to the *Journal of Melanie Klein and Object Relations*, and receive *30% off the list price* for Eric Rhode's book..

Card No. (16 digits):_____

Expiration Date:_____ (month/year)

☐ Yes! I want to subscribe to *EINAI. An Annual* (see inside back cover in this issue), and receive *30% off the list price* for Eric Rhode's book.

Signature_____

Date:_____

☐ Please send me information about other publications.
* Residents of New York State please add applicable sale tax.

IT PAYS TO SUBSCRIBE!

WOMB ENVY

Joseph H. Berke

The purpose of this paper is to explore the intense hostility that female potency, and the central organ associated with it, the womb, can attract from men, as well as other women. The hatred of female creativity, womb envy, is a basic feature of Western, as well as other cultures. It may be more prevalent than penis envy, a concept which I think could more appropriately be termed penis desire or penis greed. In considering womb envy I shall trace the history of the hatred of the womb, and then focus on four major areas of womb function: menstruation, fertility, pregnancy and childbirth.

KEY WORDS: Breast; Castration complex; Couvade; Dreaded womb; Envious anger; Envious rivalry; Female creativity; Female fears; Female potency; Greedy womb; Grenvy; Hatred; Jealous rivalry; Masculine dread; Penis envy; Penis greed; Phallus; Projective identification; Sadism; *Vagina dentata*; and Womb envy.

The womb is the core of female potency. It is a part of the body that can create and produce concretely what men (and some women) can only make metaphorically. It is an organ which has long been idealized and envied for its capacity for feeding and breeding, for loving and being made love to.

Although the womb is such an intense focus of feelings, in psychoanalytic studies, the male organ, the penis has usually been the center of analytic investigation. Such preoccupations with the penis extend from the anatomical organ to far reaching concerns about strength, power, authority, virility, ambition, energy and enterprise, which account for Carl Jung's trenchant remark, "the penis is only a phallic symbol" (Rycroft, 1972).

The longing for male qualities, functions and status, *the phallus*, features in many cultures, but in this century Freud (1932) drew special attention to phallic wishes during the course of describing the development of female sexuality. He observed that at a certain stage in their lives the physical interests of children shift away from the mouth and anus to the genitals. Then the little girl discovers what she lacks and passionately desires the missing part: "The discovery that she is castrated is a turning-point in a girl's growth.... Her self-love is mortified by the comparison with the boy's far superior equipment" (p. 126).

Freud called the sudden shocking awareness of absent maleness and the wish to overcome it, *penis envy*. Related to the *castration complex* or the *masculine complex*, this term (and attendant assumptions) has achieved a prominent place in the psychological literature and popular parlance. But I believe it is a misnomer, and as generally used, perpetuates several misconceptions.

The classical concept of *penis envy* has little to do with envy. On the contrary it conveys intense admiration, emulation and identification for all things masculine. It is a wish, first for a penis, then for a penis in intercourse, and finally for a penis substitute, such as, a baby.

An admixture of resentful, raging, spiteful, spoiling, begrudging, belittling attitudes and actions towards men, maleness and male organs certainly does exist. This is appropriately called *penis envy* and can be expressed by the penis as well as towards it. However, this was not an essential part of Freud's initial formulations. It is more correct to say that Freud was referring to what might be better termed, *penis greed*, an insatiable desire for the male member and all the perks and privileges that seem to accompany it (Berke, 1989).

The early analysts also believed that *penis envy*, or what I call, *penis greed*, was essentially a biologically determined feature of females which condemns them to spend much of their life trying to regain something they had been born without. Karl Abraham (1932) stated confidently that most women want to be men:

> ... we come across this wish in all products of the unconscious, especially in dreams and neurotic symptoms. The extraordinary frequency of these observations suggests that the wish is one common to and occurring in all women (p. 338).

In my view what most women want is to be women. And they want to be women in spite of the intense hostility that female potency, and the central organ associated with it, can attract from men, as well as other women. The point of this paper is to explore the parameters of such hatreds and to redress the balance of analytic thinking about what has been inappropriately termed *penis envy* and what may be more appropriately recognized as *womb envy*.

The womb has long been considered to be an extremely dangerous organ. Around 400 B.C. the philosopher Democritus advised Hippocrates that "... the womb was the origin of six hundred evils and innumerable catastrophes" (Hunter and Macalpine, 1963, p. 223).

This view has permeated civilized thought right down to modern times. The famous Persian physician, Haly Abbas (?-994 A.D.), compared the womb to a "wild animal longing for semen" (Veith, 1965, p. 95) and the sixteenth century French writer, Jean Liebaut (1597) declared:

> The uterus has naturally an incredible desire to conceive and to procreate. Thus it is anxious to have virile semen, desirous of taking it, drawing it in, sucking it, and retaining it (p. 529).

By "womb" the doctor might well have added the labia, the clitoris and the vagina—the entrance, the signal and the passageway to the dark interior of a woman's body which, together with the breasts, comprise the essentials of feminine endowment. Variously called a center of creativity or a furnace of carnality, a biological powerhouse or a suffocating mother, the womb is the focus of both dread and desire. The latter, like a lilting Lorelei, urges a return to the beginnings of life, to a state of weightless warmth and blissful envelopment. Wilhelm Tell narrated these feelings in, "Song of the Fisherboy." There a voice from the depth of a "clear smiling lake" calls forth:

> With me thou must go,
> I charm the young shepherd,
> I lure him below (Horney [in Ruitenbeek, 1966, p. 84]).

Tell's poem refers to a shepherd, or boy, but the wishes might equally apply to a shepherdess, or girl. They concern everyone who recalls the delights of the breast and seeks, with varying degrees of desperation, to discover and rediscover the entrance and passageway to Mother's body. Therefore, the initial conception of the womb is a magical interior, a conjunction of body and breast which carries the expectation of continuous, effortless pleasure experienced as warmth, softness, fullness and satisfaction.

Unlike the breast, however, the womb cannot be seen or grasped, nor can its goods be felt or tasted. It is an infolding rather than an out folding of the body, something dark and secret, readily transformed by the mind into a trap, a lure, whose siren-call is a "hiss from the abyss" threatening to drain and devour, dissolve and destroy whomever or whatever might enter. This dreaded tomb is a greedy womb, a creature imbued with the very cravings that have been directed towards it. Just as the bosom can appear like a cornucopia or a crocodile, depending on mood, and circumstances, the depths of a woman can seem like a cavern of contentment or a chamber of horrors. Such a fathomless hell contains hideous perils, as Tell also described in another ballad, "The Diver":

> Salamander–snake–dragon–vast reptiles that dwell

In the deep, coil'd about the grim jaws of their hell (*ibid*, p. 88).

These lines convey universal fears that the womb/woman is not only hungry for semen, the male fluid, but also for the penis, the male member. Lizards, snakes and reptiles represent maleness, the male members which have been bitten off and captured. Such phantasies lay the basis for intense anxieties that either the penis has been devoured and digested, or that it has been trapped and incorporated so the womb becomes a cave filled with the organs of any man with whom the woman has had a relationship. There they lurk, sinister guardians of the treasures within.

Such greed sustains the impression that the vagina/womb/woman can never be satisfied. This includes the actual greed of a mother, for example, who never gets enough because she rarely gives enough, and the projected greed of infants and children of either sex who invade their parents with screaming mouths and flailing arms. Rebuff arouses revenge followed by "the perils of the deep." As Karen Horney (1966) has pointed out:

> I think it is probable that the masculine dread of the woman (mother) or of the female genital is more deep-seated, weighs more heavily and is usually more energetically repressed than the dread of the man (father). .. (p. 88).

The dangers encompass both rapaciousness and oblivion. Rapaciousness leads to a terror of being torn apart, as by sharks in the sea. Oblivion conjures forth fears of falling apart, of dissolving in intrauterine waters as might occur during a period of regressive withdrawal. The accompanying experience of ego-loss or loss of identity has been commonly compared to "mental castration," a view echoed by Ruth and Theodor Lidz (1977) in their paper on "male menstruation":

> Horney's (1923) belief that men's fear of women and dread of the vulva derive from the boy's fear of loss of self-esteem because his penis is not large enough to satisfy his mother and his subsequent fear as a man of being sucked in or engulfed during intercourse should not be taken too literally, but rather in terms of the pull of the wish-fear for reunion with the mother and re-engulfment by her (p. 27).

The wish to return to the womb is only one of the hundreds of "evils and catastrophes" that have been attributed to it. Generally these dangers comprise disease, dementia and demonic possession. They reflect a litany of fear and hatred of "the mysterious capacity that woman's bodies have of creating babies out of food and what men give them" (Rivière, 1937, p. 32).

Melanie Klein (1957) demonstrated that the womb, as does the penis, tends to receive a lot of the ardor and anger that may be initially directed to the breast (which helps to explain the oral origins of genital passions), the womb is not a passive organ (p. 195). However, in recent decades, old epithets like "furnace" or "powerhouse of carnality" have gained new meanings as sex research reveals that woman have a great capacity for orgasms, and feminist writers like Kate Millett proclaim that the sexual performance of woman are naturally stronger than men.

So we are faced with a situation where modish myths of female dominance and newborn enmities about womb power echo ancient fears and begin to erode the previously preeminent "dangers of male supremacy." Marmor (1968) conjectures that as women become more valued and privileged in Western society, they will become more hated, and ". . . unconscious manifestations of penis envy will begin to diminish, and those of women envy will begin to increase" (p. 230).

Related to this hatred, many peoples have believed that the womb has a will, even a life of its own. It can be lustful or rejecting, angry or depressed. It can decide to reside in the pelvis or the belly or the throat, or sometimes outside of the body altogether. In other words, it can be a separate animate creature that happens to be housed inside a woman.

Globus hystericus, or inability to swallow, was often ascribed to the uterus rising to the throat. To overcome the problem women were advised to repeat, "Womb high, womb low, get back to the old place that God sent you. In the name of God, the Father, the Son. . ." and to make the sign of the cross three times (Shorter, 1982, p. 287).

Three thousand years ago the Egyptians blamed the womb or uterus for a vast array of complaints ranging from physical illnesses to hysteria. The term "hysteria" comes from the Greek word *hystera* meaning uterus. The Egyptians thought that the emotional excesses and bizarre physical manifestations of hysteria were solely a disorder of women, a view that persisted, with a few notable exceptions, until the 1600's, when the English and French physicians, Edward Jordon and Carolus Piso respectively, affirmed that hysteria was caused by perturbations of the brain and could afflict men as well as women (Veith, 1965, pp. 120-129).

During the Greco-Roman period hysteria was considered to be a constriction, a *suffocation of the womb* or *suffocation of the mother* (*ibid.*, p. 22). But theories about the womb and the role of women changed radically with the writing of St. Augustine and other Christian theologians. They affirmed that female maladies, in particular hysteria, were caused by an "alliance with unholy powers," typically, "seduction by the devil," and hysterical women were equated with witches. However, the organized persecution of them did not begin in earnest until the ninth century when Charlemagne, emperor of the Holy Roman Empire, decreed the death penalty for

> . . . all who in any way evoked the devil, compounded love-philters, afflicted either man or woman with barrenness, troubled the atmosphere, excited tempests, destroyed the fruits of the earth, dried up the milk of cows, or tormented their fellow-creatures with sores and diseases (in Garinet, 1818, p. 29).

Charlemagne's decree signifies an abhorrence and hostility towards woman's powers, their bodies, their functions, their products and their pleasures that culminated in 1494 with the publication of *Malleus Maleficarum* also known as *The Witches Hammer* (H. Kramer and J. Sprenger, 1951 edition). The impact of this work was immediate and long lasting. It became an international "best seller" and an established authority by which untold numbers of women were tortured and executed *ad majorem Dei gloriam* over the next couple of centuries.

The book purports to define witchcraft, to describe witches and their methods, and then to detail the steps to be taken in prosecuting them. It contends that women are greedy for sex and they can only be gratified by copulating with the devil. Lust is their hallmark and if thwarted in any way, they will "deprive man of his virile member."

The *Malleus* indicts women for being deceptive and carnal, castrating and evil. It argues that their intelligence is poor, their memories are weak and their passions are inordinate. Their chief symptoms are envy and jealousy.

> What else is woman but a foe to friendship, an unescapable punishment, a necessary evil, a natural temptation, a desirable calamity, a domestic danger, a delectable detriment, an evil of nature, painted with fair colours! (in Veith, 1965, p. 63).

This picture is the mirror image of age old antagonisms towards women and their powers of production and reproduction that continue to surface via religious fundamentalism, radical puritanism and kindred public and private attitudes. It reflects intense desires to disparage and debunk that "vessel which bears all things," including its capacity to receive, to conceive, to delight, to suffer and to bear fruit. It expresses the spirit of malice insinuated within the body of another.

Why was the *Malleus* so influential? As an exposé, it was part of a widespread reaction to the rebirth of science and the renewal of art and literature that occurred during the Renaissance. Many people were trapped between their hunger for knowledge and beauty (exemplified by the female form) and theological condemnation. They could only admit these hungers, aside from act upon them, at the price of burning guilt. Consequently, they perceived the object of their desires, particularly women, as provocative and extremely dangerous. The *Malleus* helped men (and women) to deny their own guilt ridden impulses and relocate them elsewhere—in the vagina and uterus seen as "lousy with lust." The devils were disembodied desires which could indeed bedevil by arousing intolerable anguish. Therefore, because of this process of projective identification, the private parts of women became what people feared most in themselves.

But the *Malleus* did more than absolve guilt. It was a basic text in attacking women unleashed by the church in its struggle with the forces of the Renaissance. The tome illuminates a thousand year history of envious and jealous rivalry with femininity, barely held in check by the capacity of the (male) church to "elevate spiritual motherhood" and "devalue real motherhood" (Chesler, quoted by Chase-Marshall, 1978, p. 55). The tract remains of interest because it exploded on the world like a volcano through which the deepest detestations that men harbor towards women were able to flow.

Heinrich Kramer and James Sprenger were the Dominican monks who had been commissioned by Pope Innocent VIII to write the book and strike out at "deluded souls." The alleged delusions ("many persons of both sexes. . . have abandoned themselves to devils, incubi and succubi") were metaphors meaning that many persons began to believe that goodness resides in women, that they are life renewing and ecstatic and are desirable in their own right (Veith, 1965, p. 59). These beliefs conflicted with dogmas that the church was the source of goodness and light, the fountainhead of spiritual and temporal truth, the urobolic union of male and female, big, embracing and all sustaining.

The challenge, akin to that of Galileo in the next century, called forth massive envious retribution. Perhaps the most sinister result was that women's minds and bodies were undermined by constant attributions of evil—envious attacks which transformed them from victims to victimizers.

The most vicious onslaughts were aimed at their genitalia, said to be in league with the devil. The accusations operated like Bacon's poisonous "ejaculations and irradiations." No wonder the vagina and uterus became dreaded objects! They were treated as combined evil eyes and envious mouths, organs infected by the deviltry of their accusers. I refer here, of course, to the operation of projective identification and the ways that the envied object can appear as the envier, the persecuted person as persecuting. Old women were favorite objects for this because, like Gericault's painting, "A Mad Woman with the Mania of Envy," they appeared to embody the life begrudging spite of their accusers. It is likely that in many instances the accused women were bitter and bizarre, which made it all the easier for them to become the focus of others' malevolent projections.

The idea of the vagina as a malevolent mouth, a genital Khorba, Khobee (evil mouth creatures, northeast India), did not arise with Pope Innocent

VIII or the authors of the *Malleus*. Institutionalized hatreds simply allowed them to give vent to their own simmering suspicions. Countless boys and men are shocked to discover that women do not possess a penis, but others are more upset to learn that women have an extra orifice which enables them to take things in and get extra satisfactions. As a thirty-year-old male patient of Felix Boehm (1966) once remarked, "It vexes me that women have two openings in the lower part of their bodies, while men have only one. I envy them that" (p. 128).

For children and adults who remain preoccupied with oral issues, this lack of a third passageway is a great disappointment, and a source of enmity which heralds various attempts to abuse, spoil, stuff up, mutilate or otherwise destroy the organ, or its equivalents, just as happened during the Inquisition.

It must be said, however, vagina envy is not limited to men. It is a powerful impulse in girls and women who fear that their genitals are too small and inadequate. Great anxiety and rage follows comparisons and conclusions that they will not be able to get or give food and love to the same extent as others.

Jealous rivalry also contributes to the ill will. Wife versus mistress, mother versus daughter, it is hardly necessary to detail the bad tempered, vituperative behavior that can be aroused by third party threats to love and emotional preeminence. The third party may be perceived as a sex organ. On a large scale this took place during the late middle ages. The Mother church identified the Renaissance with sensuality and seemed to treat non-virgins as debased vaginas, temporal competitors to its own spiritual openings and openness.

Certainly the *Malleus* and subsequent mania were frequently used by women to persecute other women. In England Elizabeth I made witchcraft a capital crime in 1562. A year later Mary Queen of Scots did the same. By the late 1600's this public savagery had crossed the Atlantic, although it had begun to ease in Europe. Women were prominently accused, as well as accusers in the New England witch trials. These currents continue today in divers forms such as "Satanic Ritual Abuse" and "Alien Abduction," which are a few of the examples that Elaine Showalter (1997) has detailed in *Hystories: Hysterical Epidemics and Modern Culture*.

While the vocabulary has changed, "pollution," "abuse," and "alien" having replaced "devils" and "succubi," the intention is similar, to define and denigrate women as wicked walking wombs. The men and women who instigate these actions might conceal their envies and jealousies, but they would agree with many of the views I have cited, that the womb is/has:

— *an experience*: choking, constricting and dissolving;

- *a part of the body*: an evil eye, an envious mouth, a dark, castrating interior;
- *an animate or inanimate thing*: a wild animal, a frog, a furnace;
- *a place or setting*: a trap, a tomb, an abyss, a well, the sea, the deepest depths;
- *qualities, capacities and characteristics*: draining, devouring, lustful, hysterical, poisonous, sinful and inciting; and
- *a mythical or real woman*: a siren, a Salome, a witch or a prostitute.

In all this, women are a center of mystery and a keeper of mysteries which men spend their lives trying to discover, debunk, emulate and prove worthy of knowing.

Margaret Mead (1950) has described several South Seas tribal societies in which men have appropriated mystery and claim, through the playing of the sacred flute, to guard the secrets of life. The essential activities of the tribe revolve around the making, learning and ceremonial playing of the flute, tasks from which women are excluded. This allows the men to compensate themselves for a basic inferiority within a tribe that reveres fertility, and to overcome feelings that their real roles are uncertain, ill-defined, and possibly unnecessary.

This attitude and the underlying implications are remarkably similar to that of the United States Marine Corps. It also claims to take boys and make men of them. In Mead's tribes a crocodile figure "represents the men's group and (the initiates) come out new-born at the other end" (*ibid*, p. 103). In the Marines, boot camp is the magic crocodile or incubator which turns raw recruits into warriors.

Soldiers and military matters are the direct rivals of peace, procreation and motherhood. They not only transform boys to men, but creation to destruction. This envious spoiling of creativity, and usurping of female functions, have been well portrayed by many writers, especially John Milton in *Paradise Lost*, where Satan envies God. He wants to spoil Heaven and take it over, but he fails. Then Satan and all the other fallen angels decide to construct Hell as a rival to Heaven. They assume the powers of death in lieu of the forces of life and forever seek to destroy what God has created.

Mead, the Marines, Satan, they all demonstrate various attempts to emulate, control and take over female functions and products, a project motivated by envy and awe. Male pride is very much an issue here, to do with the constant sense of having to prove oneself in the face of women "who only have to be themselves for things to grow naturally inside them." The "ensuing anything you can do I can do better attitude" in conjunction with spiteful putdowns or physical threats is a "manic assault" on female prowess. It conveys contempt; triumph over the need for care or for sex; and greedy control over powerful but frightening forces.

Nonetheless, men also dress and behave like women for non-malicious reasons, to avoid loss and make good real or imagined damage done to them. But, in a male oriented, competitive culture this is not an easy task and the opportunity to emulate women may be totally proscribed or limited to a few ceremonial occasions. The result may be a resurgence of vengeful rage for all the pain suffered in trying to be feminine.

The experience of women is not dissimilar. They have a sense of biological and social insecurity heightened by envious and jealous rivalries with mother, sisters and familial surrogates. But they are innately closer to the figures whom they wish to harm as well as emulate. Therefore, the pattern of violence is different, more likely to be inner rather than outer directed. As in sterility, this leads to the negation of function. Seemingly an attack on the self, it inevitably embraces a vicious onslaught on an "internalized other." For one patient of mine this "other" was her mother. She used to gloat: "I may be barren, but so is the woman my mother wanted to be when she decided to live inside me."

She also liked to provoke strangers to beat her up. They were her wrath. She was her mother. The masochism was a chimera. She hated the power of women. In the rest of the paper I shall trace the ambivalent intentions of boys and girls, men and women, towards four major areas of female potency: menstruation, fertility, pregnancy and childbirth.

Menstruation

There are records of male horror and fascination with menstruation in practically every society. Albertus Magnus, a thirteenth century medical scholar, noted in his book, *The Secrets of Women*: "Menstruating women carried with them a poison that could kill an infant in its cradle" (Quoted by Shorter, 1982, p. 287).

More recent observers have asserted that menstrual blood can "turn wine into vinegar," "cause mayonnaise to curdle" and make "the very flowers in the fields lose their aroma," aside from doing terrible things to the male member (*ibid*, p. 287). Many restrictions and taboos on menstruating women confirm these fears and the basic ideas that menstruation is dirty, damaging, contaminating, castrating and a sign of castration as well as a punishment for sin (Lidz and Lidz, 1977, pp. 23-25).

Yet, men have maintained the deepest interest in womb-blood as a life giving magical potion and the essence of female reproductive power. They admire and begrudge the fact that girls have a clear-cut signal of biological maturity and a natural means of self-purification.

In Australia the male members of various aboriginal tribes go to extraordinary lengths to replicate menstruation at puberty. They practice ritual subincision. This involves cutting a slit along the entire under surface of the penis and leaving an opening called a "vulva," "vagina" or "penis-womb." The vital issue is not simply the original wound, but subsequent reopenings of it to produce blood called "woman" or "milk." This represents menstruation and fertility. It is used to ritually anoint and paint the body in the rainbow-serpent ceremony when "a vaginal father replaces the phallic mother" (Roheim, 1945, p. 165).

The Indians of New Guinea have different methods of inducing male menstruation. They stuff a razor sharp leaf up and down the nostril, or scrape the tongue with it (Lidz and Lidz, 1977, p. 18). These activities are an important means of self-purification and an essential precursor to playing the sacred flute, a secret rite which embodies creativity and fertility. Interestingly, most of the women know all about the secrets, but they pretend to know otherwise, "The women take the attitude that as they have everything of importance—the babies, the pigs, the gardens—they will let the men have their flutes and their ceremonies if it makes them feel satisfied" (*ibid*, p. 20).

Although overt displays of male menstruation are uncommon in Western society, Bruno Bettelheim (1955) has described the intense desire of teenage boys to possess female features and to mimic the menses. One small group of boys and girls at the Orthogenic School decided that "The boys would cut their index fingers every month and mix their blood with that of the menses" (p. 30).

I could cite other examples where boys and men have wounded themselves or covertly suffered recurrent accidents or internal hemorrhages for the same purpose. It is possible that these practices are much more frequent than is generally realized (Boehm, 1966, p. 128).

Women share traditional beliefs that they are unclean and contaminating during the menses. In popular parlance they often refer to the menstrual period as "the curse," a term which implies much more than "a nuisance." Such convictions undoubtedly contribute to the emotional distress and physical pain that can accompany the menses. They also contribute to modern preoccupations with pads, tampons, medications and other means to soak up, clean up or stop the menstrual flow.

"Evil," "dirty," "bad," "unhealthy" are concepts which hark back to the *Malleus* and long before. They reflect fear, ignorance, superstition, observation and malicious insinuation, but from another angle, it maybe that these attitudes persist so tenaciously because women find them useful as a defense to protect themselves against envy of their biological potency and pride. In this sense women may consciously or unconsciously try to convince others that their tangible evidence of fertility and reproductive power is really disgusting and dangerous. The hope is that men (and female rivals) will be less inclined to take it over and attack it. The difficulty occurs when women forget that they are using a ruse, and become the object of their own loathing, as Joseph Reingold (1964) points out in his work, *The Fear of Being Woman: A Theory of Maternal Destructiveness.*

Fertility

The eye filled with greed and envy (grenvy) does not threaten one biological function, rather the entire capacity to bring forth bread from the earth, babies from the body or ideas from the mind. Together they represent the good, creative breast and womb which give and sustain life. In agrarian societies these activities are so highly prized that they may be given divine status, to which men wholly aspire.

Man the creator painted caves, built huts and made myths. Collectively the myths are "spiritual storehouses." They insure against spiritual starvation while the priests and shamans who service them play the same role with the soul as women perform with the body. Both renew and give birth to life.

The earliest habitations followed the female form, while the earliest paintings had to do with food and fertility. These are often found in caves that can only be approached with the greatest difficulty, down "long, narrow, slippery corridors," or "through a manhole below which a river runs" (G. R. Levy [in Bettelheim, 1955, p. 147]). Bettelheim suggests that the artists deliberately picked womb-like interiors. In this way they not only depicted the animals, and showed where they came into being, but also made themselves and their fellow tribesmen experience the process of procreation and birth (*ibid*, 147).

In the progression from agrarian to industrial to post-industrial cultures the same impulses to recreate procreation and its setting remain very strong, but expressed with increasing degrees of abstraction. Magic leads to myth to religion to science to cosmic speculation, the big bang. Cave figures lead to representational art to abstract expressionism, black on black.

This trend is not universally satisfying. While the symbolic expression of womb dramas pervades art, literature and other disciplines, people crave their literal re-enactment. Visitors to the futuristic Israel Museum in Jerusalem return and may be reborn as they pass through a long corridor before entering the central chamber containing the Torah scroll and other treasures. Users of the curved passageways of the TWA terminal at Kennedy airport in New York have a similar opportunity.

In contrast, the films of Stephen Spielberg allow onlookers to relive and relieve their horror of the female interior by identifying with the hero, Indiana Jones. In *Raiders of the Lost Ark* he hacks his way through the jungle (pubic hair), negotiates a secret tunnel (vagina) and discovers the treasure room (womb). In *Indiana Jones and the Temple of Doom* the mise en scene is the villain's palace. A comparable sequence occurs. Only Jones can overcome the terrible dangers spears, darts, poison, pitfalls, tarantulas, crushing stones, and so forth.

The "passage with knives" or "passage with biting insects" represents the dreaded *vagina dentata* or vagina with teeth, representing the projective identification of greedy, malicious impulses in and onto the woman's body, initially the breast, then her inner organs. This is one of the earliest and most tenacious phantasies of a woman's insides and accounts for untold incidents of male and female impotency. Many men won't enter a woman, or even come near one, for fear that their penises will be chewed, mangled or poisoned by an envied/envious vagina/womb. Julia Segal (1979), among others, has explored this idea in, "Mother, Sex and Envy in a Children's Story," about the work of the storyteller, Roald Dalh. Segal demonstrates the connection between Dalh's "dreaded wood" and the "dreaded womb" of children's nightmares.

Besides male terrors, however, many women won't let men enter them, because they also fear their bodies are damaging, and if intercourse took place, they would be left with an intolerable sense of guilt. One reasons for the immense popularity of Spielberg's films is that they demonstrate the possibility of complete invulnerability to the vagina with teeth, indeed, to the bad, retaliating womb.

Ceremonies of the sacred flute, cave paintings, astronomical speculation or entertaining movies may celebrate fertility, or not, depending on whether they respect female prowess or debase it. The aggressive response, indicating envy instead of awe, is overtly and covertly destructive to a woman's body, abilities, pride, social position or life-opportunities. As in a manic attack, it doesn't just seek to emulate women, but to control and triumph over them.

Spielberg's films do not enhance femininity. They treat women as mildly inconvenient sexual toys or frightening, hateful objects. The overbearing arrogance of the hero more than compensates for feared female or male inferiorities. No doubt this is another reason why the films have been so successful. However, there is a change in *Indiana Jones*. The hero depends on his female accomplice to escape from the dangerous chamber with mangling spikes and walls. She partially portrays the good helpful womb. At least Spielberg hints that such an entity exists.

Since the sixties, there have also been useful changes in the psychological literature. Previously female capacities and accomplishments were rarely taken seriously. Women were seen as extensions of men. The wish to emulate them was frequently interpreted as "a defense against oedipal wishes," or "a sign of inadequate masculinity" or "an urge to obtain a superior penis," rather than as a positive desire in its own right (Jaffe, 1968). With certain individuals these views may or may not be correct. When applied indiscriminately, they are begrudging and disparaging, and, as far as women are concerned, confirm the need for a wary eye towards others' interest in their minds and bodies.

The traditional safeguards include amulets and talismans and occasional visits to a priest, rabbi, shaman or doctor. Among oriental Jews it is still fashionable to wear amulets in order to promote fertility, ensure pregnancy, assist delivery and generally avert the evil eye. Distinguished Kabbalists used to write special handbooks on amulet making. For a childless woman, for example, suitable texts would include: "There shall not be male or female barren" (*Deuteronomy*, 7, 14), "And the Lord remembered Sarah... And Sarah conceived" (*Genesis*, 21, 1-2) (Mindel, 1979, p. 55; Berke, 1996, pp. 859-860).

The magic is a protection against the ill will of female friends and relatives, not just men. These hostilities are especially dangerous because they have a nasty tendency to boomerang back against the perpetrators. The Argentine psychoanalyst, Marie Langer (1958) points out that women who simmer with envious anger towards their own fertile mothers are likely candidates for sterility. Projective processes lead them to feel that their own insides have been attacked and laid waste by extremely hostile internal and external figures, the proverbial "evil witch," which are said to cause sterility, abortion, and to steal, kill or eat newborn babies (Lomas, 1966, p. 210). Moreover, "the fear resulting from hatred of the fertile mother" prevents them from having good creative persons to take after. No wonder that spasms or anaesthesia of the entire genital apparatus may precede or accompany sterility. Yet, the malicious glee that spiteful daughters derive from preventing their parents from becoming grandparents barely compensates for the self-inflicted emotional and physical damage. Langer adds:

> ... the sterile or infertile woman sets up different barriers against the incorporation of the penis, semen or foetus, and defends herself by different means according to her personality structure. The understanding of paranoid and depressive anxieties, together with the concept of envy as the central factor, enables us to grasp the meaning and the psychosomatic mechanisms of many fertility disorders (*ibid*, p. 140).

Langer discusses a young girl who was able to overcome the fear and hatred that centered on her envied mother. Before beginning analysis, the girl had had several abortions and had twice tried to kill herself, first by taking poison and later by drowning. She had been terrified that her mother was trying to poison her. During the course of the treatment she tried to become pregnant and eventually succeeded. Just after the conception she had a dream,

> *She is in the cellar of her childhood home. Everything is full of dust and there are dead cockroaches hanging from the ceiling. One falls down. It disgusts but does not horrify her. She calmly starts cleaning the place (ibid, p. 140).*

The dream depicts a daughter who feels capable of restoring her own and her mother's womb (the cellar), and the children she had killed inside her mother and her self (the dead roaches, the abortions). Langer adds that by doing this she is able to overcome her guilt and fear of the past, and prepare her womb for a new and fruitful pregnancy.

Pregnancy

The worst fear that can afflict a woman is that her insides will be robbed and destroyed (Klein, 1932a, pp. 194-195). This is the female equivalent of castration anxiety. It is a deep sense of dread that encompasses the breast, the body, the womb and all the babies contained therein, past, present and future. They represent food, parents, life and the continuity of life.

Children at play demonstrate these fears and the wishes that lay behind them. Hanna Segal (1975) has described one little girl who was "preoccupied with pregnancies" (pp. 28-29). During one session she started to smear glue on the floor. This turned out to be her "sick" or vomit by which she hoped to spoil Segal's insides and prevent her from having new babies. Later she was frightened to come back because the same might happen to her.

In the same vein Melanie Klein (1924) narrated the story of "Erna," a six-year-old who was obsessed by brutal phantasies of cutting, tearing and burning. These led to an extraordinary inhibition of learning whereby "arithmetic and writing symbolized violent sadistic attacks on her mother's body and her father's penis," as well as the babies contained therein. Klein continued:

> In her unconscious these activities were equated with tearing, cutting up or burning her mother's body, together with the children it contained, and castrating her father. Reading, too, in consequence of the symbolic equation of her mother's body with books, had come to mean a violent removal of substances, children, etc. from the insides of her mother (pp. 56-57).

Simple observation of children's activities confirm such intentions. Girls and boys do treat their "Cindys," houses, cars, trains, and now, male dolls, with unbearable cruelty. As most parents can attest, a new toy may only last a few minutes before it is soiled and broken. On the other hand, gentle play harbors loving, reparative feelings. A near inconsolable grief may ensue if a favorite play thing is damaged. Klein (1932b) further comments:

> ... beneath the little girl's ever recurring desire for dolls there lies a need for consolation and reassurance. The possession of her dolls is a proof that she had not been robbed of her children by her mother, that she has not had her body destroyed by her and that she is able to have children (p. 182).

Attacks on the pregnant body extend to caves, houses and any life-filled interior structure up to and including the mind. That is why we react with particular horror when a malicious man or woman desecrates a house or cuts up pictures in a museum.

In my previous book, *The Tyranny of Malice* (1988), I discussed two patients who systematically interfered with my mental life (pp. 87-88, 95-96). They loathed my thoughts, to them, mental babies as well as psychic food, and the mind womb which carried them. These persons repeatedly refused me the time and space to develop my ideas. They engaged in a variety of anxiety provoking activities designed to abort my creative processes. Consequently, I noticed that my interpretations rarely grew to term. Either I would blurt them out prematurely (suffer a psychic miscarriage) or remain unheeded (be a bearer of stillborn messages). Their attacks illustrate another dimension of "the negative therapeutic reaction."

Psychotherapy involves hard labor, as does most creative endeavor that must emerge from a dark internal space. Artists and writers often remark that they feel like a woman making a child. Their finished product only comes forth after a prolonged confinement and difficult delivery, as Joan Rivière (1937) considers in "Hate, Greed and Aggression":

> Men's desire for female functions comes openly to expression in painters and writers, who feel they give birth to their works like a woman in labor after a long pregnancy. All artists in whatever medium work through the feminine side of their personalities; this is because works of art are essentially formed and created inside the mind of the maker, and are hardly at all dependent on external circumstances (p. 32).

Thus, in his *Diaries* the director, Peter Hall (1983), refers to a conversation with Harold Pinter. He was trying to beget a new work. Pinter told him, "I think I might be pregnant." Hall chuckled to himself, "This is great news. A play is on the way" (p. 113).

Few artists do not suffer long labors. But Mozart, however, could create whole symphonies in his head and transcribe them note perfect onto paper (Shaffer, 1980, pp. 65-67). This casts further light on Salieri's mischief. He hated Mozart with a passion perhaps only equaled by a woman who produces deformed or stillborn babies while her sister or neighbor gives birth to child after healthy child.

Aggressive onslaughts on the pregnant person and the child-to-be are commonplace, and include neglect, assault and malicious rivalry. As Kato van Leewen (1966) points out, "Marital difficulties, abortion wishes, mutilation fantasies, and criticism of the childless woman are amongst the manifestations of pregnancy envy" (p. 323). The competitive element is clear in *couvade*, the custom and ritual by which the father-to-be takes over the dress, activities and physical symptoms of his pregnant wife. Originally conceptualized in the mid 1800's to denote primitive tribal practices, couvade appears to be a general phenomenon (Lomas, 1966, pp. 208-209).

Based on a study of one hundred English fathers, Brian Jackson (1984) asserts that approximately one half went through couvade. In America he suggests the figure is even higher (p. 56). Jackson has described a cluster of couvade signals, the most prominent of which are a heightened interest in pets and physical fitness. For example, he observed one man who became obsessed with a newly purchased dog, "He was continually kissing it on the nose, nursing it, holding it close and staring into its eyes. He spoke to it in baby talk, and kept telling it, 'You're such a baby'" (*ibid*, p. 55).

Another man joined a health club and was forever weighing himself and sipping carrot juice. He used to explain that he was keeping fit for the baby. On the other hand, several men related a variety of physical symptoms including abdominal pain, back pain, "a feeling of fullness in my stomach," broken sleep patterns, strange cravings for food and drink and marked weight gain, "I've put on three quarters of a stone since Sally got pregnant. I'm keeping up with her all right" (*ibid*, p. 55).

Cuddling canines has a distinctly malicious edge when it detracts from the varied needs of the pregnant woman and puts her and the baby at a disadvantage to a dog. The envious father resents both his wife's condition and the special care and attention she requires. To him the pregnancy is a narcissistic wound which arouses strong desires to steal the limelight and ruin her health and happiness. Simultaneously he may feel intensely jealous of the fetus for seeming to appropriate his rightful love and pleasures. As one father put it "It's not a bun in the oven she's got. We've got a bloody Christmas turkey" (*ibid*, p. 57).

This turkey was an unwelcome intruder who came between the man and his mate as well as the idea of a great greedy feast from which he had been and would continue to be excluded. Far from sharing in a joyous occasion, the predominance of envy and jealousy alienated him from his future child. It is not too farfetched to think that in using words like "bloody Christmas turkey," he wanted to bludgeon the baby and eat it, a spiteful deed that incorporates the regressive wish to become the infant-inside-mother and regain all his "lost" real or and imagined comforts (Leff, 1985, pp. 176-78).

Childbirth

The alternative to being the baby is having the baby. Couvade demonstrates the extraordinary lengths to which many fathers may go to capture attention and foster phantasies of impregnation. But this holds true for other men as well, heterosexual and homosexual. Anal intercourse, fellatio, constipation, abdominal distention and ruminations about intestinal tumors have all preceded or accompanied strong desires for anal or umbilical births. A patient of Felix Boehm (1966), who was tortured by fears of colon cancer made such a connection during the course of his analysis:

> Recently it has occurred to me that possibly these difficulties are connected with an unconscious idea of anal birth. Perhaps my attitude to my other symptoms is like that of a woman during gestation (p. 135).

Test tube babies, cloning, gene splicing and robotics are further indications that female fears about the race of males taking over their generative powers cannot be taken lightly. As Phyllis Chesler (in Chase-Marshall, 1978) has remarked, "When you talk about cloning and babies in test tubes, you are talking about repressed male uterus envy" (p. 55).

As far back as 1818, Mary Shelley anticipated many of these same issues in *Frankenstein* (1897). She depicted a scientist who was obsessed with making life. He succeeded but created a monster and revealed a dilemma which has haunted us ever since. The monster has to do with a creature starved of love but imbued with the destructive impulses of its creator. The dilemma has to do with the ethics of imitating or interfering with natural processes. Procedures to redress sterility, produce drugs or automate hazardous and dehumanizing work may be developed with the best of intentions but still unleash terrible dangers. Fears about them underlie the longstanding debate about the "new science of conception" and several generations of monster and sci-fi films (Friedrich, 1984).

Doctors have not only tried to replicate life, but the womb as well. A former teacher of mine, Dr. Lewis Fraad, used to refer to the incubators in his premature baby unit as, "a womb with a view." He was a kind man who respected babies and their mothers. Indeed it would be unjust and incorrect to suggest that the scientific community has a malicious mentality. Whether a particular practice is harmful, or not, has to be judged within a multiplicity of contexts, social, historical, technological, psychological and so forth. Nowhere is this more true in the drama of childbirth, an event burdened by pain and flanked by benevolence and sadism. Until the late Victorian era, childbirth was a leading cause of death in women and few efforts were spared, no matter how gruesome, to save the life of the mother. Notable among these was the development of the use of forceps.

Forceps were especially useful in prolonged deliveries, when the infant got stuck in the pelvis. Prior to forceps the only recourse to losing the mother was to kill the child and pick it out of the womb piece by piece (Shorter, 1982, p. 84). But, a forceps delivery, especially without anaesthesia, was a fearsome business. The vagina and uterus were frequently torn by incompetent or impatient attendants and the resultant mortality rate was high. As late as 1920 certain urban practitioners were known as "forceps fiends" and their abuses led to restrictions on home deliveries (*ibid*, pp. 152-153).

Antisepsis became a major area of obstetrical concern in 1847 when Semmelweis published his momentous discovery that the simple use of disinfectants markedly reduced maternal infections. Previously both doctors and midwives barely thought of washing their hands. Few women would deliver without a transient fever (called "weed" or "milk fever") and many died from massive infection (the dreaded "childbed fever"). All too often a hospital confinement was akin to a death sentence (*ibid*, pp. 103-114). Yet Semmelweis was generally ignored and antisepsis did not begin in earnest until three decades later when the Germans and French obstetricians adopted Lister's work with carbolic acid (phenol). Subsequently a rigorous asepsis became the norm and septic deaths a rarity.

In current practice women in labor suffer from overscrupulous cleanliness. They are scrubbed, shaved and purged, a routine which many find upsetting and degrading. Yet, it is only the first part of a ritual by which their condition becomes medicalized and responsibility for their body and its function is more or less taken out of their hands. Peter Lomas (1966) points out that:

> Much that is done in the name of medical necessity has the consequence of preventing the mother from regarding herself as a mature human being, from participating actively and fully in the birth, from loving and caring for her baby, and from taking an uninhibited and triumphant joy in the occasion (p. 212).

Lomas adds that the convention of segregating the mother and transferring the significance of the procedures away from her is very similar to couvade. But in this instance it is the doctor who takes over rather than the husband. The directly destructive components of this control are manifest in excessive surgery, notably in episiotomy and hysterectomy.

Episiotomy is the cutting, usually with a pair of scissors, of the tissue at the base of the vagina during the second stage of labor. Originally described in 1742, it has become a popular means of avoiding vaginal tears, facilitating forceps deliveries and protecting the fetus from a prolonged labor. But many midwives and doctors question its validity (Shorter, 1982, pp. 171-173). Serious tears of any kind are infrequent and the operation itself carries significant risk of pain, scaring and fistula formation between the vagina and anus (Dansig, 1982, p. 12).

Two hundred years after its inception the suitability of this procedure still requires substantiation. Similar questions becloud the hysterectomy, the partial or total removal of the womb usually done later in a woman's life. Many practitioners also believe that this operation is performed far too frequently and with little consideration of the severe emotional sequelae. The general medical attitude seems to be that women should "be happy to have a potentially cancer-bearing organ removed" (Dickens, 1984, p. 355).

The loss of control, pain and humiliation that accompanies antisepsis, and the cutting, scaring and scooping out that occur during forceps, episiotomy and other surgical procedures come ominously close to fulfilling women's worst fears, that their bodies will be invaded, robbed and destroyed. In large measure this accounts for the dread that precedes childbirth and the depression that follows it.

The classical psychoanalytic view is that women equate childbirth with castration because it provides the penultimate proof that they are not male. On the contrary, childbirth is the climax of feminine biological achievement. If castration takes place, it results from the way that help becomes hurt during the hard work from conception to birth (Lomas, 1960, pp. 108-109).

I distinguish three major reasons for this negative transformation. The first is social and medical inertia. Traditions, no matter how damaging, die slowly. The second has to do with the traumatization of the attendants in the face of suffering and death. Doctors, midwives and relatives will go to almost any length to prevent the loss of mother and child, and avoid their own horrific fear and guilt if they cannot to do so. The third factor is envy of female creativity, happiness, active accomplishment and last, but not least, her suffering. This leads me to consider that procedures like episiotomy, which remain questionable, but are nevertheless, widely performed, are likely to be highly structured defenses against guilt as well as the manifestation of institutionalized envy. By this I mean that spiteful, begrudging, destructive wishes towards women are hidden within respected societal practices that allow sadism to be indulged with a minimum of personal responsibility.

Deep rooted, non-medical, social and religious customs also express comparable antagonisms. Among many tribes and cultures women are treated like pariahs, instead of celebrated, after childbirth. Churching was widely practiced among Anglicans and Catholics until the twentieth century. It is a form of religious decontamination that gave a woman permission to reenter society. But it also conveyed the view that a new mother is "unclean" and a source of evil. In Germany, for example, people used to believe that a new mother could contaminate a well, or cause a house to burn down, if she entered it before the churching ceremony had taken place (Shorter, 1982, p. 289).

With noteworthy exceptions, women generally tend to accept the treatment meted out to them during pregnancy and childbirth in a detached, stoical, long suffering, almost masochistic manner. Given the extent of their physical and emotional vulnerability, this stance is hardly remarkable. It is a stratagem of self-sacrifice designed to protect themselves and their forthcoming child from external dangers and internal conflict. The latter may surface as a puerperal breakdown when dread of internal enviers, experienced as condemning, attacking mother and sister figures, becomes overwhelming, especially if it coincides with actual rejection or damage (Lomas, 1960). Then all the complicated propitiation gestures, the shaving, the enemas, the anaesthesia, the exhausted if not meek compliance with doctors who cut her body and nurses who remove her baby go for naught and the woman is left with her own momentary but terrible fragility within a world that looks upon creativity, whether in art, science or females, with ambivalent fascination.

Childbirth, and the other major areas of female potency, indicate that the womb is more than a part of the body, a thing, a quality, an experience, or a person. The womb encompasses both the idea and actuality of a function, a product and universal reality.

Menstruation, fertility, pregnancy, childbirth and creativity are positive functions which contribute to the concept of the good womb.

War, ritual bleeding, sterility, couvade, and medical mania convey the opposite. They are negating, mutilating activities which signify the destroying and destroyed womb.

The products of the good womb include rich blood, healthy babies, books, plays, sculptures, symphonies and life-enhancing innovations.

While the foul womb yields bad blood, dead babies, deformities, monsters, roaches and robots.

Both wombs, fair and foul, connote universal realities ranging from the deepest depths to celestial abodes, from human consciousness to cosmic consciousness, from Heaven to Hell. Each bears some responsibility for the generative powers generally attributed to the womb, the uroboros, the origin of all things, which is neither entirely female nor entirely male.

At a time, however, when umbilical pregnancies and intelligent robots are a distinct possibility, it is worth recalling that the human species derives from the body of women, not the rib of Adam, nor the head of Zeus. Such myths contain the seeds of hubris, a distinct overstepping of bounds, to compensate for a feared inferior biology. As Zilboorg (1944) has observed:

> It was man who perceived himself biologically inferior, and it was this sense of inferiority and concomitant hostility that led to the phenomenon of couvade—neurotic, hostile identification with the mother. . . it is not penis-envy on the part of the woman, but woman-envy on the part of the man, that is psychologically older and therefore more fundamental (p. 290).

In contrast, Melanie Klein (1957), in *Envy and Gratitude*, has quoted a five-year- old boy who conveyed his acceptance and wondrous belief in the continuity of life. He hoped that his pregnant mother would give birth to a girl, and added, ". . . then she will have babies, and her babies will have babies, and then it goes on forever" (p. 203).

REFERENCES

Abraham, K. (1932).*Selected Papers on Psycho-Analysis*. London: The Hogarth Press, 1973.

Berke, J. H. (1988). *The Tyranny of Malice. Exploring the Dark Side of Character and Culture*. New York: Summit Books.

—— (1989). Penis greed. *Br. J. Psychother.*, 5(3): 423-429.

—— (1996). Psychoanalysis and Kabbalah. *Psychoanal. Rev.*, 83(6): 849-863.

Bettelheim, B. (1955). *Symbolic Wounds*. London: Thames & Hudson.

Boehm, F. (1966). The femininity complex in men. In: Ruitenbeek, H. (Ed.), *Psychoanalysis and Male Sexuality*. New Haven, CT: College and University Press, pp. 120-146.

Chase-Marshall, J. (1978). Who's afraid of Phyllis Chesler? *Human Behavior*, September 1988: pp. 52-57.

Chesler, P. (1952). *Women and Madness*. New York: Doubleday & Co.

Dansig, J. (1982). Scissor-happy? *The Times Health Supplement*, London, 29 January 1982, pp. 12-13.

Dickens, A. (1984). Uterline ligaments and the treatment of prolapse. *J. Royal Soc. Med.*, 77, May 1984: pp. 353-356.

Friedrich, O. (1984). The new origins of life. How the science of conception brings hope to childless couples. *Time*, 10 September 1984): 34-43.

Freud, S. (1932). Femininity. In *New Introductory Lectures on Psycho-Analysis, SE*, 22: 112-135, 1968. In J. Strachey (Ed.), *Standard Edition of the Complete Psychological Works of Sigmund Freud*, 24 volumes. London: The Hogarth Press and the Institute of Psycho-Analysis, 1953-1975.

Garinet, J. (1818). *Histoire de la magic en France*. Paris: Foulon.

Hall, P. (1983). *Peter Hall's Diaries*. Ed. Goodwin, J. London: Hamish Hamilton.

Horney, K. (1966). The dread of women. In: Ruitenbeek, R. (Ed.) *Psychoanalysis and Male Sexuality.* New Haven, CT: College & University Press, pp. 80-92.

Hunter, R. and McAlpine, I. Eds. (1963). *Three Hundred Years of Psychiatry 1535-1860.* London: Oxford University Press.

Jackson, B. (1984). *Fatherhood.* London: George Allen & Unwin.

Jaffe, D. (1968). The masculine envy of women's procreative function. *J. Amer. Psychoanal. Assn.*, 16: 521-548.

Klein, M. (1924). An obsessional neurosis in a six-year-old girl. *Collected Works (CW)*, Vol. 2: *The Psycho-Analysis of Children.* London: The Hogarth Press, 1975, pp. 35-57.

—— (1932a). The effects of early anxiety-situations on the the sexual development of the girl, *CW*, 2, 1975, pp. 194-239.

—— (1932b). The significance of early anxiety situations in the development of the ego. *CW*, 2, 1975, pp. 176-193.

—— (1957). *Envy and Gratitude,* InCollected Works, Vol. 3: *Envy and Gratitude and Other Works 1946-1963.* London: The Hogarth Press, 1975, pp. 176-235.

Kramer, H. and Sprenger, J. (1951). *Malleus Maleficarum.* Translated by Montague Summers. London: Pushkin Press.

Langer, M. (1958). Sterility and envy. *Int. J. Psycho-Anal.*, 39: 139-143.

Leff, J. R. (1985). Facilitators and regulators, participators and renouncers. Mothers' and fathers' orientations towards pregnancy and parenthood. *J. Psychosom. Obst. Gynecol.*, 4: 169-184.

Leibaut, Jean (1597). *Thresor des remedes secretes pour les maladies des femmes.* Paris.

Lidz, R. and T. (1977). Male menstruation. A ritual alternative to the Oedipal transition. *Int.J. Psycho-Anal.* 58: 17-29.

Lomas, P. (1960). Dread of envy as an aetiological factor in puerperal break down. *Brit. J. Med. Psychol.*, 33: 105-112.

—— (1966). Ritualistic elements in the management of childbirth. *Brit. J. Med. Psychol.*, 9: 207-213.

Marmor, J. (1968). Changing patterns of femininity. Psychoanalytic implications. In Baker Miller, J. (Ed.) *Psychoanalysis and Women,* 1974, pp. 221-239.

Mead, M. (1950). *Male and Female.* London: Victor Gollancz.

Mindel, L. (1979). May Heaven protect us. *Jewish Chronicle Magazine,* 8 June 1979.

Milton, J. (1975 edition) *Paradise Lost.* New York: W. W. Norton.

Rivière, J. (1937). Hate, greed and aggression. In Rivière, J. and Klein, M. *Love, Hate and Reparation.* London: The Hogarth Press, 1967, pp. 3-56.

Rheingold, J. (1964). *The Fear of Being a Woman. A Theory of Maternal Destructiveness.* New York: Grune & Stratton.

Roheim, G. (1945). *The Eternal Ones of the Dream.* New York: International

University Press.

Ruitenbeek, R. (Ed.) (1966). *Psychoanalysis and Male Sexuality*. New Haven, CT: College and University Press.

Rycroft, C.A. (1972). *A Critical Dictionary of Psychoanalysis*. London: Penguin Books.

Shaffer, P. (1980). *Amadeus*. London: Andre Deutsch.

Segal, H. (1975). *Introduction to the Work of Melanie Klein*. London: The Hogarth Press.

Segal, J. (1979). Mother, sex and envy in a children's story. *Int. Rev. Psycho-Anal.*, 6: 483-497.

Shelley, M. W. (1897). *Frankenstein*. London: Gibbings & Co.

Shorter, E. (1982). *A History of Women's Bodies*. London: Penguin Books.

Showalter, E. (1997). *Hystories, Hysterical Epidemics and Modern Culture*. New York: Columbia University Press.

van Leewen, K. (1966). Pregnancy envy in the male. *Int. J. Psycho-Anal.*, 47: 319-324.

Veith, I. (1965). *Hysteria. The History of a Disease*. Chicago:University of Chicago Press.

Zilboorg, G. (1944). Masculine and feminine. Some biological and cultural aspects. *Psychia.*, 7: 257-296.

5 Shepherd's Close
London N6 5AG
ENGLAND

INSIGHTS ON ENVY:
A KLEINIAN ANALYSIS OF SHAKESPEARE'S *OTHELLO*

Ronald E. Villejo

In this paper, the author utilizes Shakespeare's *Othello* and Kleinian theory to illuminate the dynamics of envy. Iago is the primary figure of envy, and Othello who is withholding of his "love" is the tragic target of such envy. He examines the underlying oral-destructive nature of Iago's envy and the primitive defense mechanism, projective identification, he employs. Specifically, the projection of bad self aspects into the object, the need to protect against the ensuing persecutory anxiety, and the loss of psychic boundaries are issues of examination. The paper concludes with the argument that primitive envy ensures its own success *and* destruction.

KEY WORDS: Paranoid-schizoid position; Envy; Projective identification; Persecutory anxiety; Shakespeare; *Othello*; and Kleinian theory.

Shakespeare's *Othello* (1963 edition) can be viewed as a tragic example of murderous jealousy. Othello cannot tolerate the belief that his wife, Desdemona, is having an affair with his lieutenant, Cassio, so he kills her in the end. However, he acted out of a related but more primitive attitude than jealousy: namely, *envy*, the intent of which is to destroy the loved object. He would have committed a "crime of jealousy," had he killed Cassio instead. Contrary to what might be a popular belief, then, the play is more aptly a demonstration of the Kleinian concept of envy. Further, the primary envious figure in the play is not Othello, but Iago. Othello is the primary loved object, who withholds his love from Iago, and consequently becomes the target of the latter's destructive envy. Othello's murder of his wife is, as I will argue, simply one manifestation of Iago's envy of him. I differ, in this respect, from Wangh (1970) who proposed that Iago specifically schemed to have Desdemona killed, in order to eliminate her as his rival for Othello's affection (cf. also, Smith, 1970).

In this paper, I take a realist view of Iago, that is, as an individual who might actually exist as a person in our midst (Holland, 1966). I will examine the dynamics of his envy from a Kleinian perspective: (a) the circumstances of his envy, (b) its underlying oral-destructive rage and primitive defense mechanisms, and (c) its manifestations within his object relations. I advance the thesis that Iago functions consistently from a paranoid-schizoid position.

The Dynamics of Iago's Envy

At the very outset of the play, Iago reveals the circumstances of his envy towards Othello. On his behalf, three of his important cohorts made a respectful, personal plea that Othello make him his lieutenant, a position Iago felt he rightfully deserved. However, Othello rejected the plea and proclaimed that he had already chosen Cassio. Iago is enraged.

> But he, as loving his own pride and purposes,
> Evades them with a bombast circumstance,
> Horribly stuffed with epithets of war;
> Nonsuits my mediators. For, "Certes," says he,
> "I have already chose my officer . . . ."
> Why, there's no remedy. 'Tis the curse of service:
> Preferment goes by letter and affection,
> And not by old gradation (I.i., lines 11 ff [f]).

Klein (1975) believed that envy is an experience of rage. It arises out of an awareness that the loved object has the resources to gratify the self, but that the loved object can withhold gratification and keep it to itself. In view of this rejection, Iago experienced Othello as literally full of the desirable titles of war, but also as overly involved with himself and biased in his military appointments. "Bombast circumstance" and "horribly stuffed" suggest that whatever deference Iago had for Othello has now turned to devaluation. Further, the disparaging tone of "epithets of war" suggest that he would just as well spoil the very thing he desires because he cannot get it. This devaluation is a way he defends not only against the frustration in being denied gratification, but also against the injury to his personal worth and military seniority.

Iago soon realizes, however, that simply devaluing Othello is not enough: He privately admits, "I hate the Moor. My cause is [deep-seated]" (I.iii.361). So he stirs up Desdemona's father with a vulgar, inflammatory description of what Othello is doing to his daughter: "An old black ram/ Is tupping your white ewe" (I.i.85f). Othello, for his part, is able to defend himself gracefully in front of her father and the leaders of Venice. In the ensuing movement of the play, Iago resorted to methodic manipulations of his objects in the service of ultimately destroying Othello. I would argue that his primary and most effective defense against a sense of envious rage and injury to his self-esteem is projective identification. It is a testimony to the success of this defense that Iago made virtually no explicit gesture of destruction in the play and that, instead, he was able to make his objects (especially Othello) experience his envy and act upon feelings of rage. (For further discussions of projective identification, see Kernberg [1975]; cf. Tansey and Burke [1989].)

The Kleinian Concept of Envy

Klein (1975) viewed envy as generally bound up with projection. What spoils the loved object, who is withholding and frustrating, is the psychological placement of bad aspects of oneself ("urine and feces") *into* the loved object itself. As a mechanism of envy, projecting with the intent to spoil is clearly what Iago intends to do with Othello when he deliberates, "I'll pour this pestilence in his ear" (II.iii.356). First, the pestilence with which he will spoil the object bears examination. Iago speaks indirectly of his own innate, primitive aggression when he acknowledges the need to "cool our [deep-seated] raging motions, our carnal stings or [uncontrolled] lusts"; otherwise, "the blood and baseness of our natures would conduct us to most prepost' rous conclusions" (I.iii.321 f). The increasingly destructive quality of Iago's hatred of Othello is consistent with what Klein argued, namely, that the deprivation of gratification tends to increase aggression. In essence, this pestilence is the growing, aggressive impulse from within him, clearly a malignant growth which he himself heralds: "Hell and night/ Must bring this monstrous birth to the World's light" (I.iii.395f). These base and "raging motions" are certainly at the root of envy, and have the potential not just to spoil but literally to destroy.

Second, the process of putting these bad self-representations into the good object, as a critical expression of envy, also needs to be examined. Iago's references to *this* pestilence and *this* monstrous birth suggest that he has disowned his aggressive impulse and is psychically ready to project it into Othello. Specifically, Iago schemed to discredit Cassio and make him lose his lieutenantship. He suggested that the best way for Cassio to regain his position was to entreat Desdemona to speak to her husband on his behalf. He then "poured" the belief in Othello "that she repeals [Cassio] for her body's lust" (II.iii.357). When Othello witnesses Cassio furtively leave Desdemona, Iago incisively insinuates that their *tête-à-tête* was adulterous. The success with which Iago lodged his bad self-representations within Othello, thus spoiling him, is evident in a number of instances:

(1) Desdemona's growing impression that "some unhatched practiced.../ Hath [muddied] his clear spirit" (III.iv.141 f);

(2) the remark later in the play that someone "doth abuse [Othello's]

bosom/ If any wretch have put this in your head" (IV.ii.14f), that is, in his believing her to be unfaithful, and;

(3) Iago's own secret disclosure that "the Moor already changes with my poison" (III.iii.322).

Projective Identification as Iago's Primary Defense

The fact that Othello is drastically moved to rageful, destructive envy ("I'll tear her all to pieces!" [III.iii.428]) toward someone as good and innocent as his wife suggests that Iago had not just projected his badness, however, but also identified with that badness via projective identification. Klein believed that in disowning one's aggression and projecting it into the object, the individual risks being persecuted in turn. To manage that sense of anxiety, after his projection, Iago is compelled to *control* Othello in an effort to disempower the latter from destroying *him*, in turn, with the very monstrosity he had projected there. Envy is ultimately experienced as persecutory anxiety, especially for an individual who has never had adequate gratification, and the aggressive spoiling of the once loved object is a defense against this anxiety.

To further examine Iago's projective identification, I cite a pivotal exchange between Iago and Othello, remarks which chart the actual pouring of pestilence. This exchange suggests that this particular defense against envy loosens the boundaries between both of them. Characteristic of the Kleinian paranoid-schizoid object relations, the object is no longer experienced as an object but as the self-representation. Consequently, by psychologically getting into his head Iago is able to anticipate what Othello might be thinking and to discern his very vulnerability:

IAGO	Did Michael Cassio, when you wooed your lady, Know of your love?
OTHELLO	He did, from first to last. Why does thou ask?
IAGO	But for a satification of my thought, No further harm.
OTHELLO	Why of thy thought, Iago?
IAGO	I did not think he had been acquainted with her.
OTHELLO	O, yes, and went between us [i.e., as a messenger] very oft.
IAGO	Indeed?
OTHELLO	Indeed? Ay, indeed! Discern'st thou aught in that? Is he not honest?
IAGO	Honest, my lord?
OTHELLO	Honest? Ay, honest.
IAGO	My lord, for aught I know.

OTHELLO   What dost thou think?
IAGO   Think, my lord?
OTHELLO   Think, my lord?
          By heaven, thou echoest me,
          As if there were *some monster in thy thought*
          Too hideous to be shown (III.iii.94f; emphasis added).

The fact that Iago's echoing here slowly dismantles Othello's faith in his wife is evidence that Iago had effectively entered him and that his own pestilence (envy) had begun to resonate inside Othello, and do its damage. The merging between the two of them is clinched when Othello remarks to Iago, "I am bound to thee forever" (III.iii.213), as though to give explicit proof that he is under the latter's control. Also, Iago later replies, "I am your own forever" (III.iv.476), suggesting that whatever is his own (specifically, his vicious envy) is now Othello's, as well. Furthermore, it is noteworthy to point out that this loosening of boundaries also allows Othello a clear glimpse of the monstrosity within Iago, but, remarkably, he never truly discovers Iago's scheme until the very end. For the bulk of the play, he believes Iago to be his "honest" officer, to whom he is very grateful for uncovering what he has construed as Desdemona's infidelity. In fact, soon after the above exchange, he installs Iago as lieutenant. I argue that Othello's blind trust or myopia is further testimony to the success of Iago's projective identification. At this point, as painful and enraging as the uncovering is, Othello cannot at all consider the possibility that what is truly Iago's envy is something other than his own envy. He is so overcome with envious pain and rage that he becomes disoriented ("falls in a trance"). Projective identification has had a depleting effect on him. His ego resources are so thoroughly diminished that he cannot see through Iago nor act against the monstrosity he glimpsed, let alone manage the rage he feels. The oral-destructive effect of Iago's envy is illuminated in his reflection back to Othello, "I see you are eaten up with passion" (III.iii.368).

The mechanism of envy for Iago seems to make such a defense the only viable one, given that splitting is a defense to which he does not resort. On the surface, the fact that Iago is able to display honesty, loyalty, and love for Othello when they are together suggest that he succeeded in splitting off his bad representations from his good feelings about Othello. However, I would argue that it is, at best, a pseudo-splitting: This display is merely a manipulative guise. His hatred of Othello remains essentially acknowledged and unmitigated throughout the play. In reference to the function of splitting in normal development, Klein (1975) argued that

> since . . . integration is based on a strongly rooted good object that forms the core of the ego, a certain amount of splitting is essential for integra-

tion: for it preserves the good object and later on enables the ego to synthesize the two aspects of it (p. 192).

What I am arguing is, Iago experiences an envy of such destructive magnitude that he cannot at all build up a good object representation of Othello, from which he could then hypothetically split off his monstrosity. The tragedy in the play could be attributed, in one respect, to his failure to split.

Iago's Defense Against Persecutory Anxiety

Othello kills himself in the end, out of a sense of despair at having murdered his wife and at having belatedly discovered Iago's plot. Envy clearly does not have a gratifying end; its ultimate intent is to spoil and destroy the good object. The good object literally can no longer provide any means of gratification, which the individual had enviously sought. Yet, there must be some mechanism that directs this oral-aggressive drive specifically towards the good object. In this regard, Klein (1975) argued, "it is not only food he desires; he also wants to be freed from destructive impulses and persecutory anxiety" (p. 185). Therefore, what is ostensibly gratifying about the envious destruction of the good object is the experience of being freed from this impulse and anxiety. In essence, this object is really no longer good, because it is withholding, selfish, and biased. In other words, because frustration of gratification increased aggression, Iago projected the impulse swiftly into Othello, who drastically became the bad, persecutory object, whom Iago must then destroy to defend himself against the looming threat of annihilation.

In addition, I argue that Othello's inadequate response to Iago's envious machinations ultimately entrapped both of them in an inescapable, destructive web. Given that Othello was devastated so effectively that he was unable to see through the malevolent scheming, he was not able to contain Iago's projected destructive impulse. Consequently, Iago was left unprotected as well as ungratified. Projection in itself could have been a sufficient and non-malevolent defense, were Othello somehow able to protect Iago from feelings of persecution and also to provide him some semblance of gratification. (Had Othello been an analyst, he might have had the wherewithal to do so!) As it were, Iago had to resort to projective identification: The more successful he was in its defensive expression, the more Othello failed to protect and gratify, the more it became necessary for Iago to execute this defense to its fullest. In short, as Klein argued, excessive envy not only destroys the possibility of gratification, but also destroys the self's capacity to be gratified—since enjoyment is founded on the successful establishment of a good object—and thus be alleviated of envy. This self-perpetuating, infectious nature of envy, within which Iago and Othello are caught, is evident in the following remark:

> They are not ever jealous for the cause.
> But jealous for they're jealous. It is a monster
> Begot upon itself, born on itself (III.iv.159f).

Conclusion

There is a good deal of evidence that Iago s excessive envy "indicates that paranoid and schizoid features are abnormally strong" (Klein, 1975, p. 183). The oral quality of his rage, the primitive nature of his defenses, the marked absence of an enduring good object with which to integrate the bad object, his narcissistic object relations (based in projective identification) all suggest that Iago lives wholly within the paranoid-schizoid position. In addition, there is simply no evidence in the play that Iago reached the Kleinian depressive position, if only temporarily: Iago experiences *no* guilt, as would be expected in this position, even in the end when his scheming is uncovered. In rage and despair, Othello observes for Iago. "If that thou be'st a devil, I cannot kill thee" (V.ii.283). He then attempts to stab him to death. Merely wounded, Iago taunts him in turn, "I bleed, sir, but not killed" (V.ii.284) as though to suggest that he *is* the omnipotent devil.

OTHELLO   I do believe it, and I ask your pardon.
               Will you, I pray, demand that demi-devil
               Why he hath thus ensnared my soul and body?
IAGO   Demand me nothing. What you know, you know.
               From this time forth I never will speak word (V.ii.296f).

In conclusion, because Iago fails to split or experience some enduring semblance of a good object, he cannot move up the Kleinian developmental ladder. Depressive integration is not possible. The marked absence of any reparative tendency (motivated out of guilt) in Iago is final testimony to the intensity and destructiveness of his envy and to his developmental arrest within the paranoid-schizoid position.

REFERENCES

Holland, N.N. (1966). *Psychoanalysis and Shakespeare*. NY: McGraw-Hill.
Kernberg, O. (1975). *Borderline Conditions and Pathological Narcissism*. Northvale, NJ: Jason Aronson.
Klein, M. (1975). *Envy and Gratitude and Other Works: 1946-1963*. NY: Dell.
Shakespeare, W. (1963 edition). *The Tragedy of Othello: The Moor of Venice*. NY:

New American Library.

Smith, G.R. (1970). Iago the paranoiac. In M.D. Faber (Ed.), *The Design Within: Psychoanalytic Approaches to Shakespeare*. NY: Science House.

Tansey, M.J. and Burke, W.F. (1989). *Understanding Countertransference: From Projective Identification to Empathy*. Hillsdale, NJ: Analytic Press.

Wangh, M. (1970). *Othello*. The tragedy of Iago. In M.D. Faber (Ed.), *The Design Within: Psychoanalytic Approaches to Shakespeare*. NY: Science House.

ISPP/Chicago Campus
20 South Street
Third Floor
Chicago IL 60603
USA

CALL FOR BOOK AND FILM REVIEWS

The *Journal of Melanie Klein and Object Relations* is accepting book and film reviews, and reviews of several books in the form of essays. Send manuscripts to the Book Review Editor, % jmkor97@aol.com. A list of books scheduled for review is available upon request. All manuscripts should conform to the style of this publication (see "Instructions to Authors" in this issue, pp. 543-544).

BECKETT'S GHOSTS AND FLUXIONS[1]

Jean-Michel Rabaté

Starting from few tantalizing hints alluding to Beckett's brief psychoanalytic treatment with Bion, this paper explores the ways in which Bion's and Beckett's concepts overlap. Bion's notion of "thoughts without a thinker" appears as operative in Beckett's early dialectics of void and emptiness, while Beckett's shadowy and paradoxical narrators seem to surface again in Bion's late novelistic production. This would ideally lead to a detailed investigation of the philosophical underpinnings (passing through Descartes and Schopenhauer) of a "converging vision of spirits" that can only be sketched here. Beyond loss and mourning, the "ghost theme" provides access to a renewed understanding of interpersonal and fictional links.

KEY WORDS: Bion; Beckett; Berkeley; Klein; Kant; Newton; Schopenhauer; Chaos theory; Negativity; Links; Ghosts; Theory of thinking; Hallucinations; Spirits; Divided self; Solipsism; Clairvoyance; and Somnambulism.

Flux and Fluxion: Between Philosophy and Psychoanalysis

In one dense passage of Bion's novel, A *Memoir of the Future* (1991), the narrator, a psychoanalyst of the Kleinian school, struggles with two projections of himself, named Mycroft and Myself, both also engaged in a dialogue with Sherlock Holmes and Watson. Mycroft insists that the author should go back to sleep and let him speak, then starts an impassioned plea for the reality of fictional beings. These he calls "ghosts," noting that the Greeks believed in ghosts, as beings "independent of anatomy yet with a visible counterpart," and "spoke of them frequently and as if they had no shadow" (p. 95). Mycroft's discourse recalls some of Bion's main ideas, especially when he stresses the apparent paradox that we need to build abstract systems that allow us to "learn from experience."

> MYCROFT We can use constructions and verbal transformations of objects derived from what were in origin part of the sensuous domain. For

example, that poor fellow, though he knew better, struggled to transform his religious rubbish into what he called "opticks." Quite erroneous and limited in so far as he was successful. Berkeley had no difficulty; even labouring with the equipment of religious training he could detect the infinitesimal increments and the part they could play in postponing the detection of a fallacy for at least a century (p. 94).

The reference to the "poor fellow" may remain rather cryptic unless we read Bion's *Transformations* (1965), a book that provides a conceptual grid of concepts and systematizes the theses of *Learning from Experience* (1962) and *Elements of Pycho-Analysis* (1963). The "poor fellow" here is Newton, and Bion alludes to the attack of Bishop Berkeley who was trying to prove Newton's *Optics* wrong. Bion quotes from a treatise interestingly entitled *The Analyst* (1734), in which Berkeley attacks Newton's theory of "fluxions" —the term means a derivative of a mathematical function, and was needed by Newton to define differential calculus:

Whatever therefore is got by such exponents and proportions is to be ascribed to fluxions: which must therefore be previously understood. And what are these fluxions? The velocities of evanescent increments. And what are these same evanescent increments? They are neither finite quantities, nor quantities infinitely small, nor yet nothing. May we not call them the ghosts of departed quantities? (Berkley [in Bion, 1965, p. 157]).

Berkeley (1901 edition) acknowledges the truth of Newton's results in so far as differential calculus works, but he questions the method by which he has invented it. Newton's "Method of Fluxions," instead of providing a mathematical key with which he would "unlock the secrets of Geometry and consequently of Nature" (vol. 3, p. 18) multiplies unnecessary fluxions of fluxions of fluxions so that our Imagination is at a loss to conceive them (*ibid*, p. 19). Berkeley firmly replaces these "ghosts" of a vanished matter in their perceptual or phenomenological context, using the difference between qualities and quantities as a conceptual wedge by which he can distinguish between series of perceived impressions in his idealist rewriting of empiricism. This turns Newton's theory into an absurd verbiage:

The incipient celerity of an incipient celerity, the nascent augment of a nascent augment, i.e. of a thing which hath no magnitude—take it in what light you please, the clear conception of it will . . . be found impossible (*ibid*, p. 20).

In another passage from A *Memoir of the Future*, "Myself" returns to the same controversy which seems to have a paradigmatic value:

> You refer to Berkeley's attack in the Analyst on Newton's formulation of the "ghosts" of increments? I have always been impressed by the language in which Berkeley clothed his attack. It is the language Freud might have used to describe a theory of anal eroticism (Bion, 1991, p. 193).

If this explanation remains enigmatic, another reference can bring more light. This time, the speaker is "P.A." (for Psycho-Analyst):

> P.A. Berkeley made fun of these objects whichever way they were growing less or more; even the object that did not exist, the object so small that it was the ghost of a departed increment, or what I describe as the increment of a "ghost" coming into being according to the laws of change whether crescent or decay. All this is easier to formulate if it is talk about the decay or growth of a corporeal object, or a use of the language appropriate to corporeal objects for a purpose for which it was not intended—incorporeal objects, thoughts, minds, personalities. . . . It may be a "nothing" out of which something comes; the increment of a "ghost of a departed increment,"or the disappearing, declining something which is destined to disappear—or both" (*ibid*, p. 315).

It should be necessary to apologize for these lengthy quotations appearing in an essay purportedly about Beckett. By plunging directly into Bion's labyrinthine texts, I wish to imply some connection between Bion, who was Beckett's analyst in the mid-thirties, and the Irish writer (Bair, 1978; Anzieu, 1986, 1992; Rabaté, 1984).[2] My contention is that one can discern a hidden correspondence between the theses of the two writers, especially as they are both concerned with "ghosts," with the issue of an infinitesimal (and ghostly) lessness, and with the question of the positivity of the "void" or "nothing" for the elaboration of a general logic of subjectivity. By a strange coincidence, Bion's novels, written after many difficult and technical studies of psychoanalysis, seem to follow in the steps of the neurotic young Irishman he had sought to cure in London. His trilogy, *The Dream* (1975), *The Past Presented* (1977) and *The Dawn of Oblivion* (1979) can be seen as a third trilogy, following Beckett's two narrative sequences of the fifties and the eighties.

Whenever Beckett evokes his first creative period, he calls up a moment of naive story-telling, indeed evoking a sort of "pre-analytic" time, a moment when it was still possible to believe in traditional fiction. When Moran is told to leave his house and look for Molloy, he muses on the real nature of his previous missions. All those whom Moran has helped or worked for are described tantalizingly as his "patients."

> I lost interest in my patients, once I had finished with them. . . . Oh the

stories I could tell you if it were easy. What a rabble in my head, what a gallery of moribunds. Murphy, Watt, Yerck, Mercier and all the others. ... Stories, stories. I have not been able to tell them. I shall not be able to tell this one (*Molloy*, p. 126).

If Moran embodies the doubting and self-conscious narrator, Murphy is presented as the first "patient" of Beckett's fiction, and he steps forward in a philosophical novel which allegorizes the function of his mind in order to show how the "nothing" can provide a stronger object of desire than the "something." The clearest hint about this novel was provided by Beckett in a letter written in 1967 to Sighle Kennedy to stress the novel's irrationality and negativity. Beckett explains that the real point of departure of any investigation into *Murphy* should be the concept of "nothing," a "nothing" that appears in Democritus' famous "Nothing is more real than nothing," and in Gueulincx' statement, *Ubi nihil vales, nihil velis* ("You will not want anything where you are worth nothing").[3]

However, the discovery of the "nothing" as a fundamental object of unconscious desire was also one of the major discoveries of Bion in the thirties (some time before Lacan—who had always been an admirer of Bion —took it up in his *Seminars* of the 1960s). Bion, who seems at first sight the model for a neo-Hegelian Neary who believes in the centrality of Desire, is in fact, closer to that of the eponymous hero of the novel; for it befalls to Murphy to stress the Nothing as a way of reaching authentic desire. Bion came to London from India where he was born, which may trigger the association of Neary with an Indian sacred river: we learn how his training has been obtained somewhere "north of the Nerbudda" (*Murphy*, p. 6). I have developed elsewhere the hesitation in *Murphy* between the theory of perception that was then developed by the forerunners of Gestaltpsychology and the concept of unconscious desire defined by Kleinian psychoanalysis (Rabaté, 1984). A good summary of this hesitation can be found in the famous scene in which Murphy manages to drink two cups of tea while only paying for one. The scene is described with the precision of a scientific experiment. Murphy has to resist the waitress's seduction and bring the "surgical" quality which Neary and Wylie had already acknowledged in him to bear on her. Having gulped down the first cup, he eructates, complaining that the tea is Indian not Chinese as he had asked. Given a fresh cup, Murphy then asks for a refill and some milk, saying: "I know I am a great nuisance, but they have been too generous with the cowjuice." The text adds:

Generous and cowjuice were the keywords here. No waitress could hold out against their mingled overtones of gratitude and mammary organs (*Murphy*, pp. 50-51).

Murphy deliberately plays on the unconscious register in order to swindle the caterer of a few pennies. His near starvation or unwilling anorexia transforms the psychological experiment into a protracted fight with the very logic of capitalism for Vera is

> a willing bit of sweated labour, incapable of betraying the slogan of her slavers, that since customer or sucker was paying for his gutrot ten times what it cost to produce and five times what it cost to fling in his face, it was only reasonable to defer to his complaints up to but not exceeding fifty per cent of his exploitation (*Murphy*, p. 50),

while staging a confrontation with the maternal principle. This confrontation is oblique, involving as it does an irrational fraction in the final calculus: Murphy has only consumed "1.83 cups approximately" (*ibid*, p. 51). The fact that the waitress is named Vera links her with a "truth" nonetheless humiliated and exploited. The feminine truth her name evokes can be interpreted in Kleinian or Bionian terms as the primitive link established between truth and the "good object" or "good breast."

For Bion, if the relation between the infant and the mother is lacking in truth, the result is a premature weaning or starvation: "This internal object starves its host of all understanding that is made available" (Bion, 1962 [in 1993], p. 115). Bion's fascinating post-Kantian "Theory of thinking" (1962a [in 1993]) opens with an analysis of the dire consequences of a mother's loss of her capacity for reverie and patience which generally creates a perverse couple of mother-infant. The starvation of truth attacks the thinking process which Bion normally explains in terms identical to those describing the digestion of healthy food. For Bion, thinking can only begin if "beta elements"—made up of inchoate impressions, early sense data, raw feelings of loss and anger—are transformed into "alpha elements," which are the conditions for the mental such as it deploys itself in dreaming, memorizing, and thinking *thoughts*. Such a division could evoke the Lockean distinction between primary and secondary qualities, coupled with a variation on Kant's transcendentalism. Bion's theory supposes for instance that most schizophrenic patients lacked "experienced mothers." Their mothers, deprived of any capacity for reverie, could not help the infant transform its inchoate experiences, its early feelings and impressions into real thoughts: they could not work dialectically with negativity.

What remains Bion's distinctive contribution to the Kleinian school, namely a neo-Kantian grid of abstract a priori categories providing the condition for normal and pathological thinking, finally leads to a notion of "thoughts without a thinker." The paper "Attacks on linking" (1959) examines patients who wish to cut all links, in particular the link between themselves and the analyst. They will tend to attack language and thinking to achieve this end. "For a proper understanding of the situation when attacks on linking are being delivered it is useful to postulate thoughts that have no thinker"(Grostein, 1993, p. xi[4]). Bion's argument compares thinking with the concept of infinity: "Thoughts exist without a thinker. The idea of infinitude is prior to any idea of the finite. The finite is 'won from the dark and formless infinite.' Restating this more concretely the human personality is aware of infinity, the 'oceanic feeling.' It becomes aware of limitation, presumably through physical and mental experience of itself and the sense of frustration" (Bion, 1967 [in 1993], p. 165). This also describes Murphy's own plight, when he hesitates between a surrender to the infinite he has discovered in himself, and the acceptance of a sense of limitation, whereas Neary's basic theory aims at unifying Hegelian and Gestaltian features. However, his "sublations" are short-lived and not very satisfactory, precisely because the synthesis he expects has to occur in the field of perception. Neary's drama is the drama of human desire which abolishes its object as soon as it is satisfied. If the object structures the field of perception, is one condemned to the alternative: either keep yearning blindly, in the hope of a redeeming "face," or open one's eyes and discover an abyss of nothingness?

Wylie seems closer to a psychoanalytic truth when he tells Neary that there is no palliation for desire:

> "I greatly fear," said Wylie, "that the syndrome known as life is too diffuse to admit palliation. For every symptom that is eased, another is made worse. The horse leech's daughter is a closed system. Her quantum of wantum cannot vary" (*Murphy*, p. 36).

The biblical reference to Proverbs (30:15) suggests an image of eternal want: want is a quantity which can never change since the world is a "closed system." The second law of thermodynamics introduces entropy, or death by the slow exhaustion of all energy. One might prefer Berkeley's solution of radical idealism, but this is denounced by Neary as a deliberate blindness. Berkeley, called the "young Fellow of Trinity College," has, according to Wylie, found a remedy for another disease than the one he wished to cure ("He thought relief in insulin... and cured himself of diabetes" says Wylie). Neary concurs: "'I don't wonder at Berkeley,' said Neary. 'He had no alternative. A defense mechanism. Immaterialize or bust. The sleep of sheer terror. Compare the oppossum'" (*Murphy*, p. 36). This sketches one of the options for Murphy: to immaterialize and bust, but only after he has undergone an experience of radical destructuration.

The discussion convinces Neary that the possession of his desired object, Miss Counihan, "will create an aching void to the same amount" (*Murphy*, p. 37). Wylie knows that if Miss Counhinan is for the moment Neary's "only symptom," she will soon be replaced by another symptom of the same type.

The only issue then becomes whether it is possible to survive the succession of symptoms, whether one can move smoothly from the field of "faces" and "ground" that perception demands to the unconscious locus of desire postulated by psychoanalysis. Murphy's radical separation, closer to Berkeley's gesture, refuses to unify the field of life, cutting all links between bodies and minds, and prefers the void to the dialectics opposing the "face" to an unorganized chaos. The other option, slightly less suicidal, consists in allowing all the ghosts that are teeming in the unconscious to return as images. This will be, apparently, Beckett's solution after the 1940s, when he reaches beyond Bion and Jung back to the philosophical mediation afforded by Schopenhauer's doctrine of ghosts and spiritseeing. Ghosts will then appear as the nothing that is more real than Nothing, as a resilient "lessness" that manages to survive erasure and oblivion. Ghosts provide the only bridge between the split self and a return of its own affirmation, even if it has to span the void of the abyss.

In *Murphy*, we find a central opposition between Neary who is so afraid of chaos that he is prepared to sacrifice everything to his desiring quest and Murphy, who is originally more ambivalent. He has almost found an imaginary completion, symbolized by his finding a purely mental bliss reached by rocking himself into a sort of trance. After he has met Celia and has had a taste of real love, this cannot suffice. Unhappily, love brings the pressure of real life problems: Celia is a prostitute who refuses to keep selling her body as before, although Murphy, "liberal to a fault," would neither force her nor condemn the practice of prostitution. Celia is a woman in love who expects her companion to work and make a decent living. This sends Murphy into a quest for a job against his will. Now, because this "job" has become the main object of Celia's desire, Wylie's dialectical law applies: as soon as Murphy has found the position that could allow them to live according to her wishes, Celia loses all interest. When Murphy triumphantly tells her that he has at last found *"her* job" (*Murphy*, p. 80) he cannot elicit any response, for Celia is lost in some "impersonal rapture." Symptomatically, she loses interest in the object of her desire by displacing the loss onto another type of mourning: she starts mourning the Old Boy who is nothing to her, but who embodies the principle of an active "Nothing" by having just committed suicide.

Murphy then hits upon the only acceptable compromise to his division: he will live among people who are all locked up within their cells and their selves. He discovers the "small world" of deliberate confinement, and explores it with rapture. The strange happiness discovered by Celia when slipping into the penumbra of rhythmical rocking is now offered to Murphy once more. The Hospital is both a refuge and the end of his exile, above all because the inmates resist the dialectics of desire and possession, and live an autarky that secures total freedom. However, Beckett does not conclude on a happy ending in which Murphy would stay happily as a model-warden among the psychotics. Instead the disquieting encounter with a schizophrenic will lead to his untimely death. Murphy, who knows he could only consummate his "life's strike" by a "slap-up psychosis" (*Murphy*, p. 104) identifies so closely with Endon that he feels a strange homoerotic attraction for him:

> It seemed to Murphy that he was bound to Mr. Endon, not by the tab only, but by a love of the purest kind, exempt from the big world's precocious ejaculations of thought, word and deed (*ibid*, p. 104).

The replacement of Celia with Endon will prove to be Murphy's final undoing. Murphy still labours under the delusion that he has found a "friend" or a reciprocal "partner" in Endon whereas he is just a Pavlovian stimulus—he only evokes the pleasant activity of chess playing. Their last game exemplifies the schizophrenic's lack of human connection with a vengeance: Murphy is ready to sacrifice all his pawns so as to drag him out of his reserve, while Endon moves his in a circular fashion and returns them to their original places. The outcome of the psychotic game is a sort of trance evoked in terms which smack of Gestalt Psychology:

> But little by little his eyes were captured by the brilliant swallow-tail of Mr. Endon's arms and legs, purple, scarlet, black and glitter, till they saw nothing else, and that in a short time only was a vivid blur, Neary's big blooming buzzing confusion or ground, mercifully free of figure. . . . Mr. Endon's finery persisted for a little in an afterimage scarcely inferior to the original. Then this also faded and Murphy began to see nothing, that colourlessness which is such a rare postnatal treat, being the absence (to abuse a nice distinction) not of *percipere* but of *percipi* (*ibid*, p. 138).

The reduction of Endon's body to *a fascinum* inducing a sort of hypnosis is relayed by its being just an "after-image," which also fades and allows an insight into an equivalent of prenatal bliss. Not being perceived by Endon, Murphy discovers in one sensuous ecstasy the pure Nothing that Democritus saw as the keystone of his atomistic philosophy. It seems that Beckett's hero has managed to reach the third zone of his mind, as it is described in chapter six: the third zone is defined as "a flux of forms, a perpetual coming together and falling asunder of forms" (*ibid*, p. 65). The third dark zone connects the mind with a pure irrationality (it is also called "Matrix of surds" [*ibid*, p. 66]), an irrationality which paves the way to freedom, while still being couched in the language of forms. The same expression recurs to depict Murphy's release from "perceivedness" (to use

Beckett's language in *Film*, p. 11) when he slips out of Mr. Endon's consciousness. Having regained consciousness, Murphy puts a catatonic Mr. Endon to bed and stares at his eyes which seem fixed on another Nothing. Murphy sees that he is not seen at all by the psychotic patient. The mental ecstasies Murphy could apparently produce at will when he lived in the third zone of his mind and was a "mote in the dark of absolute freedom" is quite different from this new discovery.

Murphy has reached this radical "immunity" from the pain of being seen, but this creates a feeling of more acute discomfort, for which the term "sorrow" is too weak. The discovery generates a sort of panic which forces Murphy to run away from the scene, strip off his clothes and lie panting on the ground. He then tries to conjure up images, but only produces fragments which call up mutilation and castration:

> He saw the clenched fists and rigid upturned face of the Child in a Giovanni Bellini Circumcision, waiting to feel the knife. He saw eyeballs being scraped, first any eyeballs, then Mr. Endon's (*Murphy*, p. 141).

The imaginary realm reveals here its gaping dehiscence, especially when confronted with the symbolic logic of maternity and paternity. Even the threat of the Father's castration appears unable to restructure this rout of images. All this sounds like a schizophrenic delirium, a moment of crisis which could bring about a positive resolution at the end of a psychoanalytic session or could lead into murder and savage aggression. What remains clear, among so many uncertainties, is that *Murphy*'s plot testifies to a divorce between a philosophical model of the mind as *cogito* and a psychoanalytical topology of the subject that would take the agency of desire into account. Bion's post-Kantian theory of thinking can throw some light on this disjuncture, especially if we read it in the context of Schopenhauer's theory of ghosts.

Haunting for Nothing: The Ghostly Condition of Textuality

Kant had criticized Swedenborg for his "irrational" belief in spirits, when Schopenhauer provided a neo-Kantian rectification of this critique. For Kant, who published His *Dreams of a Seer of Spirits, Explained Through the Dreams of Metaphysics* in 1766, the main illusion to destroy was the Cartesian idea that man consisted of two substances, the body and the soul. Kant's critique refuses to believe that the soul, conceived as an immaterial entity, continues being perceived after death has separated it from the body. For Kant, the soul cannot have the properties of a body: it cannot move in space as a more or less translucent ectoplasm. If he admits that he does not know what the word *"Geist"* means, he accepts that the soul be called *Geist*, only on the condition that it be located in all the parts of the body which it animates. When Kant sums up Swedenborg's philosophy as the "Ecstatic Journey of an Enthusiast into the world of Spirits (or Ghosts),"[5] he points to the difference between a metaphysical dream and his own rigorous investigation of the conditions of possibility of knowledge. However, in his essay on the "vision of spirits," Schopenhauer accepts the premises of Kantian philosophy, but translates the "thing in itself," left by Kant as unknowable and undecidable, into an unconscious Will underlying all aspects of Life. The "Essay on Spirit Seeing and Everything Connected Therewith" develops the main theses of *The World as Will and Representation*. In this essay, Schopenhauer grants some weight to the lore of ghostly apparitions, spectral hallucinations, animal magnetism, and premonitory dream visions which Kant had disqualified.

Always intent upon going beyond the subject of representation to reach the universal Will connected with the body, Schopenhauer examines the physiological evidence provided first by dreams, then by sleepwalking, and concludes that in these two states, the brain is capable of purely internal perceptions: it speaks its own language (Schopenhauer, 1974 edition, p. 237). Schopenhauer uses the English term of "second sight" (a "second faculty of intuitive perception" which does not need the senses) to describe a faculty that covers the whole range of intuitive knowledge. Sleepwalking proves that some perception of reality can be reached without the intervention of actual vision: this "sleep-waking" half-dreams and half-sees the truth of reality in a "True Dreaming."[6] The evidence of clairvoyance is reinforced by the story of a servant who had dreamed beforehand that she would scrub a floor stained by ink (*ibid*, p. 254). Dreams and magnetism show how the body can become totally identical with the Will, for there, the usual categories of time and space do not apply. All the somnambulistic or prophetic soothsayings consist in freeing knowledge from its phenomenological limits. The realm of the "ghosts" refuted by Berkeley is finally given pride of place in a philosophically rigorous system.

However, Schopenhauer grants the "truth" of all these extrasensory phenomena, not their empirical "reality": the ghosts of departed persons are mental images created by the dream-organ, since all the accounts of these visions confirm that they are not bodies or pseudo-bodies, but internal impressions produced by the brain (*ibid*, p. 274). This explains why ghosts and specters are generally seen at night or in darkness: they are like a phosphorescence of the brain whose inner eye sees its proper objects and not external representations. This unconscious activity opens a new realm for investigation, an opening which Freud was to take seriously, resisting only the idea that Will, which defines the link between the thing-in-itself and man's inner being, lies outside the principle of individuation whereby individuals are separated (*ibid*, p. 303). Freud's translation of the Will into Libido or desire reestablishes an uneasy cohabitation of materialism with metapsychological entities such as the Unconscious itself. Schopenhauer's idealist reconciliation of the World and the Unconscious has the merit of philosophical consistency. By squarely admitting as philosophical objects what a purely rationalist mind would term "hallucinations," he bridges the gap between bodily phenomena and a universal Unconscious. My contention is that Beckett could find in Schopenhauer's "spirit-seeing" the hitherto missing link between a theory of the mind (as Murphy's mind) and a theory of desire and of the Unconscious. The conflation between Schopenhauer's philosophy of Desire-as-Will and Bion's theory of Thinking-as-Desire generates the subsequent proliferation of "ghosts" in Beckett's texts.

If Beckett's later works have rightly been called "ghostly,"[7] I would like to suggest that the term spans the entirety of his production from the early Schopenhauerian essay on Proust to the late minimalist prose pieces and poems. Here, ghosts seem to be encrypted words emerging from the deepest layers of the Unconscious, words that limn the dim contours of blurred yet luminous images. Thus the "ghost" has to be described by a voice which reiterates its insistent drone in the "skull," while asserting a difficulty to become visible. An investigation of the parallel and enmeshed "spectrification" of voices and of images can thus take *Texts for Nothing* (Beckett, 1967) as a point of departure. These texts are clearly written in the wake of *The Unnamable*, and keep exploring the famous "impasse" in which Beckett found himself. They are "for nothing" in the sense that they promote the "naught" or void Murphy was still embarrassed with, raising it to the level of a ghostly textuality—a textuality which describes itself in the making through the image of haunting. Like the narrator of *The Unnamable*, the narrator of these texts hears voices or sees images from his past, but continues speaking despite his having reached a point of impossibility:

> Suddenly, no, at last, long last, I couldn't any more, I couldn't go on. Someone said, You can't stay here. I couldn't stay there and I couldn't go on (*Texts for Nothing*, p. 75).

We recognize a familiar predicament, the division of the self into body and soul leaves the "I" dangling in the middle, uncertain of its capacity of synthesis or reunion. However, instead of a reunion, one can observe a pluralization of the narrative agency:

> I should turn away from it all, away from the body, away from the head, let them work it out between them, let them cease, I can't, it's I would have to cease. Ah yes, we seem to be more than one, all deaf, not even, gathered together for life. Another said, or the same, or the first, they all

have the same voice, the same ideas, All you had to do was stay at home (*ibid*, pp. 75-76).

The voices resounding inside the narrator's mind are also described as ghosts or ghouls haunting the enunciating "I." The haunting process prolongs a technique that Joyce would have called "epiphanic" but that is here reduced to "apparitions." Besides, no agency is available to tell whether these apparitions are pure hallucinations or authentic memories. The only sure thing is that they happen, and that between these returns, the speaking voice must find something to chatter about: "How are the intervals filled between these apparitions?" (*ibid*, p. 101). What is left is the necessity to take stock of the traces crowding the space of the skull:

> Ah to know for sure, to know that this thing has no end, this thing, this thing, this farrago of silence and words, of silence that is not silence and barely murmured words. Or to know it's life still, a form of life, ordained to end, as others ended and will end, till life ends, in all its forms. Words, mine was never more than that, than this pell-mell babel of silence and words, my viewless form described as ended, or to come, or still in progress, depending on the words, the moments, long may it last in that singular way. Apparitions, keepers, what childishness, and ghouls, to think I said ghouls, do I as much as I know what they are, of course I don't . . . (*ibid*, p. 104).

What the first Trilogy kept giving names to, in order to provide minimal identities, as when for instance the narrator of *The Unnamable* invents a Mahood, remains "unnamable" here precisely because the speaking subject realizes he or she is constituted by words: ". . . with what words shall I name my unnamable words?" (*ibid*, p. 105). Another passage describes this process in terms of a proliferation of ghosts that appear both as a multiple speaking subject and an absolute exteriority, an outside of consciousness:

> It's a game, it's getting to be a game, I'm going to rise and go, if it's not me it will be someone, a phantom, long live all our phantoms, those of the dead, those of the living and those of those who are not born. I'll follow him, with my sealed eyes, he needs no door, needs no thought, to issue from this imaginary head, mingle with air and earth and dissolve, little by little, in exile. Now I'm haunted, let them go, one by one, let the last desert me and leave me empty, empty and silent (*ibid*, p. 98).

Beckett's virtuosity is nowhere more apparent than in this play with a vortex of whirling positions in a game which never allows any rest to the voice. For, if at times the voice produces the ghosts, at times it is spoken and created ty them. The ghost becomes the symptom of the lack of identity of the self:

> It's they murmur my name, speak to me of me, speak of a me, let them go and speak of it to others, who will not believe them either, or who will believe them too. Theirs all the voices, like a rattling of chains in my head, rattling to me that I have a head. . . . But the phantoms come back, it's in vain they go abroad, mingle with the dying, they come back and slip into the coffin, no bigger than a matchbox, it's they have taught me all I know, about things above, and all I'm said to know about me, they want to create me, they want to make me (*ibid*, pp. 98-99).

However, the haunted self is still presented as writing, even if (s)he (it?) drops the quill at the end of the piece:

> That's where the court [of the phantoms] sits this evening, in the depths of that vaulty night, that's where I am clerk and scribe, not understanding what I hear, not knowing what I write (*ibid*, p. 98).

The ghostly apparatus systematically metaphorizes the act of writing. Another passage of the same "Text for Nothing" confirms this. The narrator is still hoping to become deaf-mute:

> Then what a relief, what a relief to know I'm mute for ever, if only it didn't distress me. And deaf, it seems to me sometimes that deaf I'd be less distressed, at being mute, listen to that, what a relief not to have that on my conscience. Ah yes, I hear I have a kind of conscience, and on top of that a kind of sensibility, I trust the orator is not forgetting anything, and without ceasing to listen or drive the old quill I'm afflicted by them, I heard, it's noted (p. 96).

A trinity of the ear, the eye and the writing hand underpins the strange choreography of ghostly voices or images. The ghosts define a supplement which prevents the "I" from being deaf, blind or even paralysed. The twelfth text describes this curious "trio", thus already pointing toward the later "Ghost Trio":

> . . . and who's this speaking in me, and who's this disowning me, as though I had taken his place, usurped his life, . . . and who is this raving now, pah there are voices everywhere, ears everywhere, one who speaks saying, without ceasing to speak, Who's speaking ?, and one who hears, mute, uncomprehending. . . . And this other now, obviously, what's to be said of this latest other, with his babble of homelessn mes and untenanted trims, this other without umber or person whose abandoned being we haunt, nothing. There's a pretty three in one, and what a one, what a no one (p. 134).

In a very illuminating commentary of Beckett's works, Alain Badiou (1992) takes this stratification of the three selves seriously and distinguishes three levels. There is first the linguistic subject of enunciation:[8] he is the "one who speaks" and who suffers from the terror of solipsism, thus insists upon identifying the voice's origin. There is then the passive subject who hears, the reverse side of the subject of enunciation. The third level is the subject supporting the question of identification, the agency which, through the subject's passivity, insists upon the question of being, and who, for this end, is ready to submit it to an endless torture (p. 340).

Beckett would thus force us to modify our views of a "monologue": a monologue is not just a dialogue with oneself, since it always entails three persons at least. This multiplication derives from theoretical problems bequeathed by the Cartesian *Cogito*. If the evil genie can intervene to dupe me and even inhabit "my" unconscious, the only stable point of identity is not my thought as metaphysical *res cogitans* but my voice, a voice which proves that I am "ego" only as long as I can repeat "ego". Starting from Lacan's reformulation of Descartes's sentence as *Cogito: "ergo* sum" (I think/say: "therefore I am"), Badiou (1992) stresses the links between the ghost and the *Cogito*. The ghostly dialogization of the divided self inverts the postulates of the *Cogito*:

> It is the argument of the *Cogito*, with the ironical nuance that the quest for non-being is substituted to the quest for truth, and that, by an inversion of values, the "inescapability of self-perception" which is for Descartes the first victory leading to certainty, appears here as a failure. The failure of what, to be precise? What fails is the extension to the Whole, which includes the subject, of the general form of being, which is the Void. The *Cogito* stops this extension: there is a someone whose being cannot not exist, and it is the subject of the Cogito (pp. 338-339).

If I am only as long as I say to myself "I think," and this inner soliloquy has to be repeated endlessly, I become the ghost of my speech. My words thus generate images that attempt to cover for this lack in being. This dilemma seems to underwrite the fundamental position of the subject in Beckett's last texts, as we can see in *Ill Seen Ill Said*:

> For the last time at last for to end yet again what the wrong word? Than revoked. No but slowly dispelled a little very little like the last wisps of day when the curtain closes. Of itself by slow millimeters of drawn by a phantom hand. Farewell to farewell. Then in that perfect dark foreknell darling sound pip for end begun. First last moment. Grant only enough remain to devour all. Moment by glutton moment. Sky earth the whole kit and boodle. Not another crumb of carrion left. Lick chops and

baste No. One moment more. One last grace to breathe that void. Know happiness (pp. 96-97).

The "phantom hand" that half betrays itself not only draws attention to the crucial role of a fading "arranger" or conjurer seen slowly drawing the curtain, but also signals a sort of reversal: as voice and eye move towards their fusion and dissolution, they strive not only towards convergence but also try to keep as much of the "final instants" as possible. A paradoxical positivity is granted to life in *extremis*, the happiness of living, of seeing and breathing are asserted precisely at the moment of their fading away.

A similar reversal of the "ghost theme" can be found in the late television pieces. Commenting on the difference between *Eh Joe*, in which the narrator is victimized by the voice of moral conscience which forces him to "Imagine" the ghost of the woman who had committed suicide, and the two television plays produced ten years later by the BBC, *Ghost Trio* and *...but the clouds...*, Katharine Worth (1992) writes:

> . . . the protagonist no longer shrinks from his ghosts but on the contrary seeks them out. These plays focus with the same unremitting intensity which in *Eh Joe* was applied to a state of dread, on the opposite state—of longing for some remembered being to appear. The word "appear" acquires a mystical resonance (p. 66).

Indeed, these companion pieces are similarly haunted by the return of ghosts: in *Ghost Trio*, a male Figure is seen in a room listening to a cassette recorder, while a female voice repeats that he "will think he hears her" (Beckett, 1990, pp. 410-411). The music heard is the Largo of Beethoven's fifth piano Trio, called "The Ghost," it creates the gaps or holes in language, those gaps that language is unable to produce by itself as the German letter of 1937 expresses so forcefully (*Disjecta*, p. 172). At the end of *Ghost Trio*, a young boy dressed in black oilskins glistening with rain appears at the door, shakes his head twice and leaves: is this a sign that the woman will not come, is he a messenger, is he someone who has rung the wrong bell? Is he just suggesting a little more patience? *...but the clouds...* also insists on the positive "apparition," since when the male figure begs for "her" to appear, the female shape really appears, and three times murmurs snatches of verse, the last lines of Yeats's "The Tower" in which the poet seems to be accepting his death as a natural phenomenon.

We realize that these apparitions are thus as much intertextual and literary as visual or auditory hallucinations, they depend on a discourse that rehearses different modalities of apparition, ranging from a glimpse to a lingering vision accompanied with a recitation, including the failure of exhortation. The most common case is the "case nought," when nothing happened:

> ... when I begged in vain, deep down into the dead of the night, until I wearied, and ceased, and busied myself with something else, more... rewarding, such as... such as... cube roots, for example, or with nothing, busied myself with nothing, that MINE, until the time break, with break of day, to issue forth again..." (Beckett, 1992, p. 421).

The apparition introduces a pure supplement, brings a wonderful and unexpected gift to a lonely character who has mastered the various combinations of irrational numbers, or the different uses of the Nothing. From the "mine" of nothingness to the "deepening shades" concluding Yeats's poem and the play, we have gone through the stages of a poetic annulment that hovers ambiguously between the rational and the mystical. This delicate blending of the pastoral and the spectral adequately defines the unique tone of Beckett's last texts and can provide a key to his vision of human thinking and suffering.

NOTES

1. These pages take up material from two chapters of my book *The Ghosts of Modernity*. Gainesville, FL: The University of Florida Press, 1996. I have revised them and condensed the argument, using also some pages from the Preface.
2. The link between Beckett and Bion has been explored by Didier Anzieu (1986), and more recently in his novelistic treatment of Beckett (Anzieu, 1992). For instance on pp. 34-67, Anzieu recreates their parallel diaries and imagines how Beckett and Bion vent their frustrations at each other. Slightly earlier, I had also developed the theoretical implications of the meeting between Beckett and Bion (Rabaté, 1984).
3. David H. Hesla (1971) has brilliantly demonstrated the importance of Gueulincx's occasionalism in Beckett's early works.
4. Grotstein writes: "Bion is often compared with Lacan, not only in terms of the complexity of their contributions, but also in terms of their similar journeys into the origins and nature of *meaning*. They both seem to distrust that truth can emerge from linear prose and therefore appear to induce or radiate meaning by a style that could be called *poetics* [sic])" (p. XI).
5. This is the subtitle of the second half of *Träume eines Geistersehers*, p. 50.
6. Translated as "dreaming of reality" in "Essays on Spirit Seeing...", p. 240, and as "dreaming of what is real on p. 247." See also *Parerga und Paralipomena, vol.* 1 (Zurich: Haffman, 1991) (same pagination as in English).
7. See Worth (1992) and Moorjani (1990). Moorjani links in a very interesting way the paradoxes of the utterance of a "Not-I" with the return of a cryptic

voice of an entombed other, and refers to Abraham and Torok's concept of *cryptonymia*. Katharine Worth's essay describes the last television or theatre plays, from *Eh Joe* to *What Where* (collected in Samuel Beckett, *The Complete Dramatic Works*. London: Faber, 1990, pp. 359-476), as "ghost plays".

8. The term of "enunciation" is used here in the meaning given to it by Emile Benveniste in his *Problems of General Linguistics*. See Moorjani's paper for a useful application of the term. More and more Beckettians feel obliged to use these notions in their approaches; see above all the excellent unpublished thesis of Daniel Katz (1993).

REFERENCES

Anzieu, D. (1986). Beckett et Bion. *Revue de psychotherapie*, 5-6: 21-30.
—— (1992). *Beckett et le psychanalyste*. Paris: Éditions Mentha.
Badiou, A. (1992). L'ecriture du generique: Samuel Beckett. In *Conditions*. Paris, pp. 329-366.
Bair, D. (1978). *Samuel Beckett*. New York: Harcourth Brace Jovanovich.
Beckett, S. (1967). *Stories and Texts for Nothing*. New York: Grove.
—— (1969). *Film*. New York: Grove.
—— (1990). *The Complete Dramatic Works*. London: Faber.
Benveniste, E. (1966). *Problèmes de linguistique générale*. Paris: Gallimard.
Berkeley, G. (1734). The Analyst. In *The Works of George Berkeley, vol. 3*. Oxford: Clarendon Press, 1901.
Bion, W.R. (1962a). A theory of thinking. In *Second Thoughts* [1993 edition].
—— (1962). *Learning from Experience*. London: Heinemann.
—— (1963). *Elements of Psycho-Analysis*. London: Heinemann.
—— (1965). *Transformations. Change from Learning to Growth*. New York: Basic Books.
—— (1967). *Second Thoughts*. London: Heinemann. (Reprinted by Jason Aronson, Northvale, NJ, in 1993.)
—— (1975). *A Memoir of the Future*. Book 1: *The Dream*. Rio de Janeiro: Imago Editora. (Reprinted by Karnac Books, London, 1991.)
—— (1977). *A Memoir of the Future*. Book 2: *The Past Presented*. Rio de Janeiro: Imago Editora. (Reprinted by Karnac Books, London, 1991.)
—— (1979). *A Memoir of the Future*. Book 3: *The Dawn of Oblivion*. Rio de Janeiro: Imago Editora. (Reprinted by Karnac Books, London, 1991.)
Grotstein, J.M. (1993). Preface to *Second Thoughts* by W. R. Bion. Northvale, NJ: Aronson.
Hesla, D.H. (1971). *The Shape of Chaos*. Minneapolis, MN: University of Minnesota Press.
Kant, I. (1975 edition). *Träume eines Geistersehers*. Hamburg: Felix Meiner Verlag.
Katz, D. (1993). *Summing Up: Subiectivity and Consciousness in the Prose of Samuel*

Beckett. Unpub. doctoral diss.

Moorjani, A. (1990). Beckett's devious deictics. In *Rethinking Beckett*. London: Macmillan, pp. 20-30.

Rabaté, J.M. (1984). Beckett et le deuil de la forme. In *Beckett avant Beckett*. Paris: Presses de l'Ecole Normale Superieure, pp. 135-151.

Schopenhauer, A. (1974 edition). Essay on Spirit Seeing and everything connected therewith. In *Parerga and Paralipomena: Short Philosophical Essays*. Translated by E.F.J. Payne. Oxford: Clarendon Press.

Worth, K. (1992). Beckett's ghosts. In Wilmer, S.E. (Ed.), *Beckett in Dublin*. Dublin: The Lilliput Press, pp. 62-74.

University of Pennsylvania
School of Arts and Sciences
Department of English
Philadelphia PA 19104
USA

Need to get in touch with us?
E-mail us at: jmkor97@aol.com.
It's fast and convenient....

BECKETT'S *THAT TIME*:
EXILE AND "THAT DOUBLE-HEADED MONSTER... TIME"

Bettina L. Knapp

In Samuel Beckett's *That Time* (1976), the "double-headed monster of damnation and salvation–Time" (p. 1) is the antagonist. The mutant and miscreant Time is the enemy that forces the protagonist's exile from life and his slow deterioration. Time, unceasingly and eternally, eats voraciously into every second, hour, day, year, decade, century. Past, present, and future in *That Time*, like three black holes in the heavens, expand when called upon to articulate thoughts and feelings, only to contract seconds later, in what becomes a final gravitational collapse at the play's conclusion (Capra, 1975). Because of Time, life is viewed by the protagonist as a loss and an insult: a dominating, enslaving, imprisoning, and torturing indignity. Worst of all, it feeds illusions; it breeds the fossilization of ideologies, dogmas, and behavioral patterns, forever luring and alluring mortal minds to grasp at deceits in their attempt to arrest the nonapprehensible.

Because the story in *That Time* begins at the end, audiences are not imprisoned in linear time as in traditional drama, waiting and wading through an accumulation of sequences, observing the inexorable march of decrepitude in an increasingly helpless and hopeless protagonist. As humanity's foe, Time has already eliminated, pulverized, reduced Beckett's protagonist, the Listener, to virtual nothingness. Born into Time, a product of the finite universe, he has failed, as does everyone and everything else in the manifest world. Yet his mind, like that of other mortals, also attempts to fit events and ideas into a series of partitions, concepts, illusions, deceptions, catching him up in what the Hindus call *maya's web*.

Although memory gives structure to *That Time*, it does not give it meaning. Associations and suggestions pull the Listener (and reader) into the story (Asmus, 1986, p. 349). Because, for Beckett, the artistic process proceeds via contraction, intuition, and perception, and not via intellectual or rational concepts, no grand construct—as in the dogmas of organized religions, or of political, social, or artistic institutions—is acceptable. On the contrary, these palliatives are viewed as blinders, illusions, traps. Only doubt is real. Thus the artist, at best, is only a translator of, or Listener to, inner murmurings. He is not a creator.

That Time. Curtain. The stage is dark. A light shines on the Listener's haloshaped white hair. Only the head is visible: "about ten feet above stage level midstage off centre." Silent and nameless, the archetypal Listener listens to the three disembodied voices (A, B, C) emanating from loudspeakers placed to the left, to the right, and above the stage space. Identityless, he exists only in terms of the succession of voices echoing from his past. Neither affirming nor rejecting a point of view or a way of life, the Listener submits to existence: fate, death. Yet every now and then, reactions are indicated though always with reserve: by the audibility or inaudibility of his rhythmical breathing and the opening and closing of his eyes. Both are barometers able to measure the impact the voices make on his invisible interior clime. His *being there* is sufficient to point up the anguish and feeling needed to create drama.

Although there are three voices, they are one. Each, representing a period in the Listener's life, is isolated from the others, imprisoned in its own dimension, limitations, time-frames, levels of understanding. As such, each is exiled in its own world: A, the middle-aged man; B, the youth; C, the old man. The trinity's speeches are sounded four times, in a different order each time, during each of the three cycles.

While listening to three segments emerging from his past, the Listener, like an eavesdropper, absorbs the fragmented unfoldings as if from a transpersonal sphere. A supreme consciousness, he hears the words, tones, and diapasons that help him redefine his existence: viewed as a slow divestiture of free will, an expiation for the original sin that was his birth into the world of consciousness. Objective, neither rebelling against Time nor siding with it, like Job he experiences his reality, his slow decomposition, as a fact of life: "Thought he slay me, yet will I trust in him: but I will maintain my own ways before him" (Job, 13:15).

There are times, nevertheless, when pain becomes acute. It is then that the Listener takes comfort in precedents: musing, say, about the child that he once was or about his trip back to his hometown in his middle age. Although aware that any attempt to escape the "cancer-Time" is to no avail, the Listener's voices, nevertheless lapse momentarily into dreams, loves, and ideations. "They modulate back and forth without any break in gene ral flow except where silence is indicated." As each voice introduces its own score, instrument, rhythm, and shading, it recollects instances from the unending memory bank that is the psyche. These retreats are only momentary in the Listener's harrowing descent/exile from the human sphere.

Despite the fragments of past happenings given in *That Time*, the play deals in universals. The city to which the voices return in their foray into the past is Dun Laogaire, south of Dublin on the coast, but it could be any city. The stories flow into a present, they encapsulate a panoply of moods and feelings, ranging from distress to elation. When, for example, the Listener reflects on the child that he was, the flashback seems comforting at first, like a habit. In *time*, it takes on harrowing dimensions: a period that once was and is no more is viewed as a painful deception, a "great deadener," a constant reminder that life consists of perpetual deaths, each moment driving one closer to the finale.

That Time 1

The play begins. Darkness is transformed into Light fading up to the Listener's face. From death to birth: from the Void (that is, the formless, the unarticulated, the potential embedded in the collective unconscious) to the created, the differentiated articulations of the ego (the center of consciousness). From no word to the word. The miracle of transformation is perhaps best conveyed by two Hebrew words: *ain* (nothing) and *ani* (I, or something). Merely changing the position of one letter, one breaches the gap between the uncreated and the created (Scholem, 1961, p. 218).

The voice of "A," the middle-aged man, speaks: "that time you went back that last time to look was the ruin still there where you hid as a child when was that." That the Listener's eyes close during A's meditation suggests a descent into an archaic past, an exploration into absence, a slow absorption into earlier comforting, feeling tones. He has recourse, momentarily, to illusion-filled mental constructs existing in a time-riddled world. By situating or making concrete a period that had been, with such statements as "that time'n aback," or "that last time," A endeavors to fill the limitless emptiness of his present, the aloneness of the Listener's old age, the meaninglessness of his individual existence in an impersonal universe. Allusions to penultimate and ultimate time-frames, although seeming to give structure to abstractions, instead further emphasize universal flux. Passing moments are incarnated into present modes with such words as "ruin," which may be interpreted symbolically, as something that has fallen, crashed, been damaged, or collapsed from age; it represents the end of an era, culture, or life.

From the very outset, the "child," running through (what had perhaps once been a Druidic temple or sacred grove of stones), puts into juxtaposition the archetypal images of young and old. Within the Child exists the Old Man; within the Old Man exists the Child. That Beckett focuses on the archetypal child in *That Time* and in so many of his other works intimates a need to emphasize fluidity, rather than rigidity, of attitudes. The child to which A alludes is special in that he is what the Listener once was. Imagination roams supreme in this child: as if inhabiting fairy tales. Everything for him, be it a stone, a picture, the sky, the sun, water, has the power to alter in form and substance. Dreams, excitement, and the impossible exist in this child's actuality. Undifferentiated, unlimited, and unimprisoned unconsciousness overflows into consciousness and vice versa, inviting unimpeded communion.

Because the child throughout history has been viewed as the hope of the future, a common and universal concept is that of the divine child (Moses, Buddha, Christ) and the child-hero (David, Roland, Siegfried). As a primordial figure, *filius ante patrem*, the child represents unity and plurality; as a messiah, the beginning and the end, *renatus in novam infantiam*. Psychologically, children represent pre- and postconsciousness (Jung and Kerenyi, 1969, p. 27). Vested with infinite power, these saviors of the world are capable of establishing continuity and eternality in families. The child in *That Time*, however, is identified in psychological terms with the ego; it has never been born. It has lived its specterlike existence in an unmanifested psychic state.

That the Listener closes his eyes, descending more deeply into his meditation, allows him better to absorb the welcome intrusion of past moments—those of the child in particular—into a present reality. Although he cannot situate the precise time when he stepped into the tram on the "grey day took the eleven to the end of the line and on from there no trams then all gone long ago that time," he reacts affectively upon learning that since that time the trams have turned into ruins. The only proof of their existence is in the "old rails."

Grey, like ash or embers, suggests residue; for the alchemist, the quintessence that remains after all excess has been burned off: the death of the flesh and the retention of the skeleton, the end of linear time and the even flow of cyclical or eternal time.

Through the image of the tram, a machine adhering to a time schedule as well as to a mapped-out trajectory through space, A experiences past and present as two distinct psychological and cultural phases. While permitting communication on a collective level, the tram also imposes its impersonal laws and rhythms on the individual. What remains of a once functioning tram are its "old tracks," its skeleton (or organizational system and methodology), divested of its livingness. Tracks, coordinators of segments of a once-viable network, may also be interpreted as visible replicas of a once-productive inner psychic organizational pattern, operating according to its own mysterious and inexorable plans. A observes these unworkable, unusable tracks as so many rusted and useless carcasses, as a metaphor for old age.

The voice of C recounts another legend: "when you went in out of the rain always winter then always raining that time in the Portrait Gallery in off the street out of the cold." In the world of analogies, the winter season represents the cold, barren, stark period when nature withdraws into the earth, seeking nurturing and warmth. So, too, does the Listener dig within for comfort against the congealing rigors. Fluidity, in the form of rain, also enters C's reminiscences. For alchemists, water solves the unsolvable by dissolving it. When a stumbling block in life is broken down through liquification (as when sugar or salt is placed in a bowl of water), a smoother, more objective, and more comprehensive attitude is created. Thus, an individual and his or her problems, when blended into the whole, may be viewed from a distance, with fewer details but with greater perspective.

That C went into the Portrait Gallery for shelter from the cold and rain indicates further interiorization, hence, distancing from an inclement outside world: "in off the street out of the cold and rain slipped in when no one was looking and through the rooms shivering and dripping till you found a seat marble slab." C yearns for protection against a stormy, grim, unpitying exterior world relentlessly dominated by Time. Designed to exhibit replicas of God's creations, the Portrait Gallery, like any museum, exists in order to arrest Time, in this case, by the re-creation of the human form realistically, imitatively, or diagrammatically. Is C oblivious to such deceptions and snares? C, like the egoless child he once was, takes the same route: penetrates the inner rooms of the Portrait Gallery, surreptitiously, unseen. Shivering and wet, he wanders through the rooms until he finds "a seat marble slab," sits down, and dries off.

Is the "marble slab" referred to by C a tombstone? a dolmen? a prehistoric monument dating from patriarchal Druidic times? Is he referring to his own past? The Irish countryside is peppered with stones that symbolize continuity, cohesion, hardness, unity, and strength, as opposed to the fragmentary, fleeting formlessness of sand. Unlike the human body, the "marble slab" is not subject to rapid change. Let us also note that the juxtaposition of stone and water ("rain") brings to mind a psychological condition. When identified with Noah and the turbulent winds and waters of the Flood, the inner oceans of the collective unconscious come to mind. During moments of chaos, when "suffering" overpowers consciousness, opacity prevails; after the waters subside and calm sets in, the treasures of the deep may be glimpsed and the light of consciousness clarified. Thus is the invisible transformed into the visible, the unheard into the heard, and unconscious into conscious contents.

Affectivity (turbulent waters) is the primal mover needed to stir the inert matter, the treasures, of the deep. But cerebralness must not be overwhelmed if consciousness is to be expanded. The inert matter of the depths, recognized as treasure as it enters consciousness, may be symbolized by the marble slab—possibly Irish Connemara stone—upon which C sat. Marble is heavy and hard to move, but may also be very valuable. Highly polished thoughts, with their veins of feeling, are as beautiful as marble.

The stone may even be sacred to C, as is the case of other legendary stones: the Kaa'bah, the Emerald Table, the Omphalos, the pillar of God's house (Genesis, 28:22), the cornerstone (Acts, 4:11), dolmens, and so on. Within these seemingly hard and unfeeling relics of ancient times, there lives a sacred power. Did not Orpheus's sweet tones move stones? Did not stones, equated with bones in the Deucalion myth, become a source of life? Does not the Zohar tell us about Adam's descendants who recorded in hieroglyphics astronomical data on two stone tablets, one of which Noah found at the foot of Mt. Ararat? (Eliade, 1960, p. 169). Nor should the stone tablets upon which the Ten Commandments were written be omitted from the list of hierophanies. Understandably, C takes momentary comfort in these universal and timeless traditions.

The third voice that the Listener hears is that of B, the young man, who lives in a dreamland: his future (Asmus, 1986, p. 346). It is no longer winter: "on the stone together in the sun on the stone at the edge of the little wood and as far as eye could see the wheat turning yellow vowing every now and then you loved each other." Another trap. Two polarities come into being: the stone is warmed by the sun, but also shaded by the little wood where Mother Nature burgeons without design as *massa confusa*. Yellowing wheat, symbolizing birth and death, as did the previous archetypal images of the child and the old man, suggests the beginning of the end of life. Once something enters the world of Time (manifestation), it takes on mortality. The ripened wheat, ready to be picked and transformed into food, reflects the apostle John's optimistic view of eternal rebirth: "Except a corn of wheat fall into the ground and die, it abideth alone: but if it die, it bringeth forth much fruit" (12:24). Within this same image exists its contrary, the agony experienced by Jeremiah: "They have sown wheat, but shall reap thorns: they have put themselves to pain, but shall not profit" (12:13).

Rebirth is just another lure, as are the love vows to which B refers. Taken when a youth, "you loved each other just a murmur not touching or anything of that nature you one end of the stone she the other long low stone like millstone." All was purity in those days and there was faith in the future, in the legends and tales where goodness and happiness prevail. In *time*, the joy of romance turned into a "millstone," a grinding experience, a heavy burden. Love, like yellowed wheat, became jaded, dated, outmoded, a tiresome habit. And all the yesterdays are the same: clusters of unendingly ripening fantasies about love concluding as pulverized fictions and fabulous fables. With "eyes closed all still no sign of life not a soul abroad no sound," the fictions of youth slowly erode. Life, sound, and sight have atomized, sunk into the unincarnated timeless, spaceless collective unconscious: the Void, that inner cemetery, that "charnelhouse" of being.

The round of disembodied voices speaking to the Listener begins anew, with the voice of A recounting another legend: of taking his "nightbag" on the ferry and walking onto "the high street neither right nor left not a curse for the old scenes the old names" onto the wharf, where the previously mentioned old rails exist in their now-rusted condition, "when was that was your mother ah for God's sake all gone long ago." This second incursion into a past marks an even greater demolition of illusions, a more cutting mockery of religious ideations. Mother and God figures, once indispensable, are now experienced dispassionately. Assessing their damage on his spirit and psyche, the speaker regards their deceit with contempt. He now experiences the "old scenes the old names" like so many overhanging rusted and unusable tram wires. Rust. Corrosion: "last time you went back that last time to look was the ruin still there where you hid as a child someone's folly." Only in the preconscious, egoless world of the child, where connections with timelessness and spacelessness take root, can "folly" exist. Does this unevolved period in a child's life spell madness? Or, like the clowns of old, are children the only ones to speak the truth?

C again looks at his past, and life in general, but in a harsher light: "for God's sake all gone long ago all dust the lot you the last huddled up on the slab... in the old green greatcoat." Here, too, images deceive: the beautifying green grasses of Ireland cover ruts and gulleys, dangerous stumbling blocks. Love arouses passion, but also conceals a future of routine and boredom. C walks on; "not a living soul in the place only yourself and the odd attendant drowsing around in his felt shufflers not a sound." The impact of death, decay, isolation, and alienation takes on actuality, emphasizing a soul in exile. All returns to dust, particles of a past, diffused experiences, disparate and powdery residues of earthly life, relics and products of disintegration. As Beckett (1931/1957) wrote: "We are alone. We cannot know and we cannot be known" (p. 49).

B still believes in a future of burgeoning leaves, sheaves of wheat, and love retaining the glow of its vows. Thoughts of sadness do not yet intrude, though love will dry, falter, and fall. Feelings of warmth and well-being tinge his outlook, as he rekindles the memory of the time he and his sweetheart took their vows to love each other always.

A muses on Foley's Folly, "a bit of a tower still standing all the rest rubble and nettles." Towers, constructed in the Middle Ages as lookouts for observing enemies, were protective constructs, but also took on ascensional symbolism: the tower places humans far above the madding crowds, feeding them inflated ideas. It also cuts them off from the mainstream, isolates and alienates them from society. Built in the form of a tower was the alchemist's *athanor:* the stove in which the various operations leading to transmutation of metals took place. Designed to elevate base metal (lead) to its purest form (gold), the tower may also be said to unvitiate the vitiated. That A remembers the tower, though all else has turned into "rubble and nettles," suggests the sameness of mankind's yearnings: a search for final answers, the finite's need to understand the infinite.

Linear, or historical, time associated with such constructs as towers, trams, and walls, or humanized, as in family enclaves, fragments what was once unified and connected. Stone becomes rubble, bricks tumble and crack, and mortals vanish, as the whole mass of worthless and decayed detritus piles up. The fables of faith taught to the young slowly turn to dust; pain, in the form of piercing "nettles," stings and abrades tender and vulnerable flesh. Bitterness burgeons with each succeeding laceration by those coarse herbs flourishing throughout the countryside, hidden beneath a beautiful coat of green grasses.

A can't remember where he slept: "where did you sleep no friend all the homes gone was it that kip on the front where you no she was with you then still with you then." Was it with her or not? Did it really matter, as it was for only one night and the ferry would be back in the morning? The ruin where he had hidden as a child is again mentioned, as is the stone, perhaps wistfully this time. Each is a sacred affective presence, memento mori.

C recalls peering out onto "a vast oil black with age and dirt someone famous in his time some famous man or woman or even child." The soot of an industrial life that has taken over is juxtaposed with the luster of a famous person who lived in these same environs. In the Portrait Gallery, behind the glass, pictures of "famous man or woman or even child such as a young prince or princess" peer at him, only to swivel, turn, and vanish. Did they ever exist? Or were they *eidola:* fragments, glimpses, like so many scintillae, of continuously mobile atoms?

B voices anew what he had seen, said, and felt: sun, wheat, sky, vows, love. What is love? Then archetypal figures are constellated and conflated syncretistically: Lao-tzu. Chuang-tzu, and Confucius, with the Western Christ: "suddenly there in whatever thoughts you might be having whatever scenes perhaps way back in childhood or the womb worst of all or that old Chinaman long before Christ born with long white hair."

C continues to interweave Heraclitean formulas into speech patterns: "never the same after that never quite the same but that was nothing new." The eternalness of the unknown, its sameness, and its motility in the universal flow, although nonapprehensible, is forever resurrected by memory.

Similarly with words: although they sound alike, A intimates, each takes on different meaning, depending upon text and context, mood and atmosphere, the tonality and tempo of the individual voicing them. Some are spoken with more *feeling* than others.

B, near the window, "in the dark harking to the owl not a thought in your head till hard to believe harder and harder to believe you ever told anyone you loved them." He must have been blind when incarnating his feelings in words of love at that *time*. Just as the owl is identified with sadness and melancholia, so B's thoughts are painful. Even worse, the owl, according to the ancient Greeks, carried out the dictates of Atropos, cutting the string of life, and hence was identified with death. Another question arises. Was B referring to the pain caused by love for reasons of adultery? For the Welsh, Blodeuwedd, the unfaithful wife of Llew, was transformed into an owl as a punishment for her adultery and for having betrayed the secret of her husband's vulnerability. Are not these tales, segments from a collective past, also examples of a personal agony? Or are they "just another of those old tales to keep the void from pouring in on top of you the shroud"? Were they once, but no longer, true? "The aspirations of yesterday were valid for yesterday's ego, not for today's" (Beckett, 1931/1957, p. 42).

That Time 2

After ten seconds of silence the Listener's breath becomes audible. His eyes open. He is ready to undertake the "ex-foliation" of his being. Elements of his inner world become more palpable as sound waves infiltrate the stage space. Like those mysterious *eidola*, vision upon vision constellates before the Listener's mind, not in accordance with Cartesian or Newtonian rational and logical processes, but following the Listener's inner network of acausal pulsations emanating from his unfathomable and suprapersonal depths.

The Listener has no illusions about the meaningfulness of the triadic dialogue, which is really a monologue, nor is he deceived into thinking that it will stem the course of his progressive decline. He knows that whatever he is, thinks, and feels is contingent upon his past, which he is absorbing and reabsorbing through the voices of a world that was. As elliptical and repetitious incantations pass into the empty caverns of the Listener's decrepit old brain, their impact on his subliminal world is evident. He closes his eyes once again, enabling his reverie to proceed. As his verbal patternings fill the moment, the paradoxical degradation endured by a virtually nonexistent ego becomes increasingly heavier to bear. He understands now that life is emptiness, and to prolong it is, as Beckett's protagonist maintained in *All That Fall* (1957), to see oneself slowly burn out under the heat of an ever-smaller fiame.

Twice C refers to a "turning-point" in life, once in the singular and once in the plural ("always having turning-points"), implying mankind's obsessive need to structure and give mathematical logic to the world in a frantic attempt to grasp its meaning. There is no understanding, however, of the unfathomable. Democritus suggested: "We know nothing in reality; for truth lies in an abyss" (in Hesla, 1971, p. 9). Are C's references to turning-points to be understood as realities in eschatological time-frames? Is he adding further to his ironies in the phrase "the one the first and last that time"? Is the unstable oceanic journey that is life also a construct of the mind, like Descartes' triangle? Are both to be understood as concrete? In his seminal letter to Sighle Kennedy, Beckett wrote: "If I were in the unenviable position of having to study my work my points of departure would be the 'Naught is more real . . .' end the'Ubi nihil vales'" (Beckett quotes Arnold Geulincx: 'Ubi nihil vales, ibi nihil velis' [where you are "worth nothing," you "want nothing"]) (Kennedy, 1971, p. 304; originally published in *transition*, March 1932, pp. 148-149).

C's "point" (or "points"), although determined in space and time, are dimensionless and directionless. Yet, he wants. Theologians, such as Clement of Alexandria, considered the positionless point as indicating primordial unity; for Angelus Silesius, the point contains the circle; Kabbalists view it as the space from which the hidden manifests itself; the Hindu sees the point (*bindu*) as the germ or drop from which incarnation takes root.

Because everything emanates from and returns into a subjectless "turning-point" (or "points"), C's metaphor, "that time curled up worm in slime when they lugged you out and wiped you off"—may refer to the inception, that is, the birth and death process in an endless round. Didn't Beckett write in "Dante . . . Bruno. Vico . . . Joyce" that "transmutations are circular"? Programmed existence, or the alpha and the omega, operates prior to the point's emergence, as is implied in the image of the worm curled up in the fetal position in slime. Such viscous deposits, when associated with primordial matter and the circularity of the earth's configurations, take on womblike form; and the worm takes on the form of a phallus. Although C "never looked back" then, he does now, to that birth-day in time or in "another time."

B, once radiant in his naiveté, again refers to stone, sun, towpath, sand. All are subject to change during the course of the dramatic unfolding: "facing downstream into the sun sinking and the bits of flotsam coming from behind." No longer outspoken nor quite so sure of himself as he once was, he recalls a past that resonates and reverberates through the Listener's cavernous brain. B has begun to experience time as a "sinking downstream," leading to confusion and absurdity, as when making something out of nothing through projection, or when stamping one's days with meaning in a meaningless universe.

What remains of all the dreams? B speaks of "flotsam coming from behind and drifting on or caught in the reeds the dead rat." Plans, ideas, works, events, are like so much floating detritus: wreckage of ships, miscellaneous materials lumped together carried along by the shifting tide and the rhythms of the waters. Everything drifts, forced here and there by the currents, or caught, ironically, by thin, swaying, fragile reeds. The "dead rat" not only conjures up images of humanity's ultimate end, but of the sameness of its aggressive and destructive habits. Like mankind, this fearsome, nocturnal, forever famished rodent eats its way into anything and everything, killing not out of hunger alone, as do other animals, but like human beings, for blood. This chthonian creature, nevertheless, suggests duality: in the *Illiad*, Apollo's other name, Sminthee, signifying "rat," suggests both a God of vengeance (as sender of the plague) and a healer of disease. So, too, in the Orient, is the rat viewed positively and negatively: although vicious, its presence in agrarian societies is considered to be a good omen of a plentiful harvest. Thus is the initial Naught followed always by the Aught.

Like a leitmotif, the images of the ruin insinuate themselves into C's monologue with growing poignancy; C, "waiting with the nightbag till the truth began to dawn," yearns for answers. But there is no truth any more than there is a final word: just continuous comings and goings of sunrises and eventides, beginnings and endings, expectations and disappointments, "coincidences of contraries" (Beckett, 1929/1972, p. 6). In the world of contingencies, affirmation is inseparable from negation, position from opposition, the visible from the invisible, the audible from the silent: all constructs of the mind. Without one there is no others. Without life there is no death.

C regresses: "not knowing who you were from Adam." Who is he? Whence came he? and when? From the flotsam of eternal duration prior to the formation of ego-consciousness, prior to awareness, to the world of contradictions, antagonisms, and oppositions. The fact of "not knowing" invites him to sink back to prototypal man, the *anthropos*: Adam (*adamah* in Hebrew) was fashioned from earth/dust (Genesis, 2:7). So the artist, replicating the Creation, brings forth his own work from his flesh and blood, amalgamating linear and nonlinear, spatial and nonspatial frames into the incarnated mixture and animating matter.

Since C mentions Adam twice, he may be referring to the two Adams: the second Adam, although referred to as the first in the Bible, and the Kabbalist's Adam Kadman, who was really the first and the purest symbol of God in human form. Because the "fullness" of the Divine Light flowing through Adam Kadman was too great, it shattered that which contained him. Thus did the first cosmological drama, alluded to as "The Breaking of the Vessels," come to pass.

When C mentions the "skull you were clapped up in whose moan had you the way you were was that time," he may be referring to the pain following the Breaking of the Vessels. When the protective coverings of dogma and systems are shattered, and thoughts and feelings wander alone in pleromatic spheres, they are vulnerable to attack by contents in both conscious and subliminal spheres.

Alone in the Portrait Gallery again, C observes the images of those who have died, like so many black spots imprinted on sheets of paper, like so many pages in a child's picture book, or signs and codes in ancient collections of magic spells. The dirt, dust, or earth of Creation, like today's DNA, serves to link the contemporary with the ancient, thus becoming another of mankind's methods of structuring and ordering what is in the last analysis outside of its dominion. To crave order, dates, and facts upon which to base each "point of departure," is for nought as much as it is for aught. Yet, from one century to another, from one pouring rain to the next, theories evolve and dissolve, dredging up the flotsam until "closing-time," when disintegration causes everything to flow back into primordial earth—*adamah*—the first again becoming the last.

For B, there is "no sight of face or any other part." Did the invisible face ever exist? Isn't each being a product of another's projection and thus without identity? Graven images must not be made, nor must a name be allotted to that which is unnamable. Letters only—YHWH—for the name of God are acceptable, as signs of that which is infinite.

B affirms that he "never turned to her nor she to you always parallel like on an axle-tree never turned to each other just blurs. . . ." The axle refers to both the world of contingencies (trams, carts) and the cosmic spheres (Tree of Knowledge, Tree of Life). The image of the axle bar (phallus) and wheels (earth, womb) conflates sexual polarities with mystical ones (and is perhaps an allusion to Ezekiel's vision of the Divine Chariot, which allowed him to glimpse God's appearance on the throne) (Scholem, 1961, pp. 265-266). Once again, such images, though they structure and comfort, allow "space between." The unfathomable and unnamable will always be out of reach of the finite mind, and the inch separating the former from the latter will never be obliterated, no matter how concerted the "pawing." Memories of a dead past and the once-tender vows taken are "no better than shades no worse" and cannot obliterate the gaping Void.

"Bowed half double," A experiences life as the Stations of the Cross, as a perpetual and mounting agony. After years of prayer, hoping in vain to regain that lost paradise, A faces only the "Doric Terminus of the Great Southern and Eastern all closed down and the colonnade crumbling away so what next." Cultures have come and gone: among them the Dorian invaders of Greece (twelfth century B.C.E.), colonizers of Asia Minor, organizers of Sparta, creators of the stark columns of ancient temples. Meaningful and meaningless. The austere and striking Doric colonnade adorning the train station, a paradigm for a network of confluences, may represent evolution, but for A it spells desuetude, collapsing points of departure and returning crumblings and vanishings in the flotsam and jetsam of existence.

C recalls "the rain and the old rounds," the whirls of water moving downstream, the circular dances and songs, referring perhaps to ancient Druidic stone burial monuments in the round. Roundness may be associated with the head, and by extension with the inner circuits of the mind. Linear time-frames are hurdled as C spans, syncretistically, centuries, cultures, and religions. No longer new and dynamic, no longer creative and innovative, they have left behind stones and other residues of sacred relics, now useless old forms, like the "tottering and muttering" C. Entropy has set in.

B now stands "stock still" as he looks back again at "that time on the stone" or at "that time" in the sand and sun, observing the "blue or closed blue dark blue dark stock," still dreaming, believing in the scene of love floating up into consciousness. To be "stock still," ideationally or otherwise, is to encourage stasis with its stock mental contents, its stock phrases, its stilled cerebral constructs that in time become facile mental coordinates. Or does the "stock still" refer to the arrested notion of primordial mankind from which all others descended? As A takes stock of himself, he begins to understand that his stock, once hardy and creative, is no longer so. Development has been arrested. But for him who is so young the end is not yet in sight: "still side by side scene float up and there you were."

The voice of A remembers that he "gave up and sat down on the steps in the pale morning sun," his eyes following the trajectory of the circular fireball through the heavens. Now A is pale, seated as he is in the shade, or midway through life, no longer bathed in the glow of the sun's infinite luminosities. But in the past, he recalls, he "gave up and off somewhere else," always elsewhere, perhaps on a "doorstep" entering into another sphere of being, another time-level, another spatial dimension, forever wandering through the initiatory phases of the life/death experience. Soon, A will take the "night ferry," leaving that childhood world of hide-and-go-seek, with pain but also with anger; the past, although dead, still has the power to move him effectively. The passionate cry of "to hell out of there" allows him to abreact to the "old scenes the old names," the "passers pausing to gape": is he not, like them, just such a passerby, gaping, observing, looking in from the outside, transient but not transcending? Gaping, open-mouthed, staring fixedly, gazing stupidly: all suggest new, multiple openings of chasms, abysses, yawning maws, *vaginae dentatae*. Does A refer to the boatsman Charon, who transported the dead over the Styx, in his utterance "pass pass on pass by on the other side"?

B, still "stock still," in the sun or outside of its radiant glory, observes it sinking out of his line of vision. His thoughts are also descending, as are his feelings, which until now have rarely stirred out of the categorical confines of habit and imperatives, caught up in the blissful safety of doctrines. Somewhat between "the two knobs on a dumbbell," B seeks balance rather than intellectual exercise; such exercise displaces, brings vertigo and the terror of disorientation. Stasis is simpler; unthinkingness more comfortable; numbness more protective.

C utters his soliloquy, "always winter then always raining always slipping"—as he totters along, looking here and there, seeking to remove himself from the cold, the rain, and the solitude. His "green holeproof coat" inherited from his father, not only keeps him warm and dry, but this same cloak (*brat*) is a royal attribute, in Celtic tradition, part of a person's patrimony, handed down from one patriarchal generation to the other. Both protective and isolating, this special holeproof coat permits the wearer, like the god Lugh, to remain invisible. By donning the holeproof coat, one accepts, outwardly, the will and consciousness of the collective. Only when the seemingly solid coat is cast aside and its worn threads are examined can systems and doctrines reveal their imperfections.

Wearing the holeproofcoat, C, like a shadow, passes through all the old places, such as the Public Library and the Post Office, freely, unquestioned by anyone. Yet the Public Library is the very place that breeds opposition, that arouses contention, that reveals apertures in the finest of protective garments and the most veiled of arguments. The Post Office, like the railroad terminus, is the focus of infinite networks of outgoing and incoming dialogue and activity.

A, "huddled on the doorstep in the old green greatcoat in the pale sun" on his knees, perhaps praying, yearns for direction. Increasingly depersonalized and displaced, with a slowly disappearing memory, he has forgotten the details of his beloved's meanderings, and his own. He is virtually divested of ego. The "green greatcoat" of his fathers has smothered and stifled whatever burgeoned within, crushing his very being as he passes into the nothingness of death.

Life, for the Listener, a series of "points of departure" from present to past through the mediation of voices resounding in the inner corridors of his own emptiness, has taken him through two of the three zones of life: the Light of youth and the semilight of middle age. The darkness leading into the terminus remains to be lived out.

That Time 3

Ten seconds elapse. Three more seconds, and the Listener's eyes open on to another verbal foray into an increasingly contracting anterior world. As various archetypal patterns emerge and collide in Beckett's trialogue, the ego's attempts to burgeon, to find a direction, to establish its points of departure, seem to falter. Words, such as *stone, wheat, blue, towpath, rat, floating, sunset,* although used in the first two parts of the play, take on additional affectivity at this juncture. Their varied placements in the clauses lend greater ambiguity to the Listener's plight, thus increasing the terror of a world constructed on continuously shifting quicksands.

Words, such as *ghosts* and *mules,* introduced by B for the first time in part 3, add to Beckett's thematics of time. When B states "or alone on the towpath with the ghosts of the mules the drowned rat or bird or whatever was floating off into the sunset," he is recasting the already well-worn notion of death, posited in such images as drowned, floating, etc. The French word for ghost, *revenant,* means the soul returning or coming back from the dead. Like contents sunk beneath the waters of the collective unconscious, certain words and images now return to consciousness, peopling the Listener's world with the shades of those fallen into oblivion. The Listener sees silhouettes of memorabilia floating in his mind's eye. Visions of bygone eras, they are a whole population of ghosts embedded in an inner landscape. These invisible atomizations, materializations of sound and light waves, provoke associations and recollections, perceptions so powerful that they can redirect libido (psychic energy).

The Listener's eyes close again in an attempt to block out, as if once and for all, the whole conscious/rational world. That B refers to "the ghosts of the mules the drowned rat or bird" reinstates nonhuman patterns of behavior. The mule, a hybrid animal, implies sterility, as well as stubbornness; the bird, the tapping of spiritual, aerated, and nonearthly levels; the death-dealing, fertile rat connotes dangerous polarities. That mule, bird, and rat are dead may represent a premonitory image of mental barrenness, aridity, impassibility, and the final detachment from it all.

A continues: "none ever came but the child on the stone among the giant nettles." Although the child-image once implied youth, zest, and a world of infinite possibilities, no such meanings now prevail; staid and stunted voices have taken over. The child, as ego, has aborted. The giant nettles, like the crown of thorns, have pierced A's flesh and psyche, cutting away, slowly and incisively, the once-fixed protective walls surrounding him. Now he is withdrawn into the library, where pale, shadowy, and diffused "moonlight" penetrates onto his book, "breaking up two or more talking," thus fragmenting what once appeared to be unified and impervious. Divisiveness, fostered by the brilliant and blinding rays of patriarchal consciousness *(logos)*, has not insinuated itself into the book; instead, dimmer, more subdued luminosities, echoing from subliminal spheres, have shone the light of their lunar matriarchal powers *(eros)* upon him. Such feeling forces, "moods," are allowed to flow forth with increasing abandon.

But, as C notes, the mood of openness does not last. Instead, "always winter endless year after year." Coldness. Congealing. Nature goes underground again, in search of interior warmth, while bequeathing barrenness to the outside world. Opposition, however, implicit in the world of contingencies, brings "bustle," despite the rigidity and fixity of the ghostly winter. Images of the Post Office and Christmas activate the staid atmosphere: perpetual movement (of the mail) in and out of town merges with feelings of yearly renewal and expectation of the rebirth of the archetypal divine child.

B looks back again, imagining himself alone, lying on his back on the sand, prior to or after having taken his empty vows of love. Sand, when associated with time, as in Zeno's paradox of the heap of millet, or as in Beckett's *Happy Days* (the play in which sand progressively fills the stage with every passing minute, burying the protagonist up to her neck), cannibalizes life. The cycle begins anew: as linear time gives way to preconscious levels, an "old scene" comes into view, along with time-embossed symbols of the rat feasting on the ripened wheat, or the bird gliding over the sands casting its ominous shadow over events in and out of time. Repetition and habit, like a spreading cancer, leave the once-zestful B hybrid and sterile.

A increasingly seeks to anchor time in linearity: "eleven or twelve in the ruin on the flat stone." Cause and effect are steadying powers, as are all barriers erected to stave off the floodwaters of the unknown. In a lastditch attempt, A seeks further to clarify, increasingly to differentiate ideations within the world of the intellect in order to stay on top of things. In so doing, he lapses back into petrified schemes and formalized units of time. Yet, here, too, energy patterns remain. Eleven, the penultimate, before twelve, the number of completion; as well as the conjunction of 5 and 6, the microcosm and the macrocosm, still reveals struggle and action. So does 12: although it represents the end of the yearly cycle of months, en route back to the beginning, the number's digits taken singly indicate dynamism: 1 (unity) and 2 (duality, differentiation, in the unending birth/decay syndrome).

As childhood, youth, middle age, and old age move on simultaneously with the dimming sun, A pursues his "moonlight muttering," paralleling the continuous march of a degenerating mind and body. And "clutching the nightbag and drooling away out loud eyes closed and the white hair pouring out down from under the hat," on he walks. His imaginings feature him still wearing his hat, perhaps like the archetypal wise old man. An object used frequently by Beckett, the hat, identified with the intellect, as was the crown in ancient days, is now seen as covering for a forgetful and failing mind.

The decrepit form enclosing the faltering mind, seen by "passers pausing to gape at the scandal there" continues on. (The word "gape," indicating a wide-open mouth, like that of Kronos/Saturn when devouring his children, is also reminiscent of the medieval replicas of the Inferno, its voracious jaws open wide, waiting for the bodies of the sinful.)

Fearing "ejection having clearly no warrant in the place," C understands that he no longer belongs to this town or any other: there are no ties, no bonds, no links—but also no chains. Any relationships that he might have had, like "thin air," are no longer.

A, still walking, "making it up on the door step... again for the millionth time" recapitulates, reassesses, reviews, rethinks. The "doorstep," threshold of the inner world, leads from one time zone to the next from the known to the unknown. It must be passed if he is to pursue his initiation and step from life to death, thus confronting the two-faced Janus, the Roman God who looks east toward the rising sun and westward to its setting. Determining beginnings and endings, Janus stands guard at doorways and gates, opening and closing them *once* during the year.

C refers again to the Library, to the dust, "the big round table with the bevy of old ones poring on the page and not a sound," while B recalls the time he gazed out of the window into the dark and saw "the owl flow to hoot at someone else or back with a shrew to its hollow tree." The hollow tree, emptied of its life force, serves as the owl's protection. And "not another sound hour after hour not a sound when you tried and couldn't any more no words left." Aridity, sterility, nothing but an outer core remains.

A is anxious to leave, "not a curse for the old scenes the old names not a thought in your head only get back on board and away to hell out of it and never come back." C's last words confess to endless emptiness: "not a sound only the old breath and the leaves turning and then suddenly the dust... only dust... and not a sound only what was it said come and gone." Infinite deaths and rebirths. As Beckett noted, "In the one movement is unidirectional, and a step forward represents a net advance: in the other movement is nondirectional—or multi-directional, and a step forward is, by definition, a step back."

The Listener's eyes open. He smiles, "toothless for preference." Is he smiling at himself? at the thought that he has taken himself too seriously? Does his grin spell triumph, for having finally accepted himself and his life such as they are? Or is the rictus a sign of pain? Did not Beckett (1958) himself define the essence of his art when he wrote, "Nothing is funnier than unhappiness" (p. 18).

Enigma faces the Beckettian explorer, confirming Roger Thin's statement: "Beckett's theater's very ambiguity makes for its richness" (Beckett, 1953/1986, p. 35). To attempt to explain and define *That Time* or any other Beckettian work is to try to clarify mystery. At best, one can offer only a personal reading for one's own edification.

Beckett's sense of exile in *That Time*, his feelings of aloneness and lack of identity, of irremediable hopelessness as life pursues its continuously coruscating and abrasive struggle against the supreme antagonist time, is perhaps best conveyed by the dramatist himself. At the conclusion of a lecture by Jung that Beckett attended, he wrote:

> He [Jung] spoke about one of his patients, a very young girl. . . . At the end, as the people were leaving, Jung remained silent. And, as if speaking to himself, astonished by a discovery he was in the process of making, he added:—Actually, she was never born. . . . I had always had the feeling that I, too, had never been born (Juliet, 1986, p. 31).

REFERENCES

Asmus, W.D. (1986). Rehearsal notes for the German premiere of Beckett's *That Time* and *Footfalls*. In Gontarski, S.E. (Ed.). *On Beckett: Essays and Criticism*. New York: Grove Press.

Beckett, S. (1929). Dante. . . Bruno. Vico. . . Joyce. *transition*, June 1929. Reprinted in *James Joyce/Finnegans Wake: A Symposium*. New York: New Directions, 1972.

—— (1931). *Proust*. London: Chatto and Windus. [Reprinted by Grove Press, New York, 1957.]

—— (1953). "Le froc d'Estragon." Letter from Samuel Beckett to Roger Blin, 9 January, 1953. [Printed in *Magazine Littéraire*, June 1986, p. 35]

—— (1958). *Endgame*. New York: Grove Press.

—— (1976). *That Time*. London: Faber and Faber.

Capra, F. (1975). *The Tao of Physics*. Berkeley: Shambhala.

Eliade, M. (1960). *Myths, Dreams, and Mysteries*. New York: Harper Torchbooks.

Hesla, D.H. (1971). *An Interpretation of the Art of Samuel Beckett*. Minneapolis, MN: University of Minnesota Press.

Juliet, C. (1986). *Rencontre avec Samuel Beckett*. Montpellier: Editions Fata Morgana.

Jung, C.G. and Kerenyi, C. (1969). *Essays on the Science of Mythology*. Princeton: Princeton University Press.

Kennedy, S. (1971). *Murphy's Bed*. Lewisburg, PA: Bucknell University Press.

Scholem, G. (1961). *Major Trends in Jewish Mysticism*. New York: Schoken Books.
The Zohar (1933 edition). Translated by Harry Sperling and Maurice Simon. London: Soncino Press, vol. 2.

Hunter College
Romance Languages Dept.
695 Park Avenue
New York NY 10021
USA

JOURNAL OF MELANIE KLEIN AND OBJECT RELATIONS
Volume 15, Number 3, September 1997

Missing Back Issues?

Complete your collection of the *Journal of Melanie Klein and Object Relations*

Order now while they last!

Esf Publishers—JMKOR
1 Marine Midland Plaza
East Tower – Fourth Floor
Binghamton, New York 13901-3216, USA

| *Tel.*: (607) 772-6116 | *E-mail*: jmkor97@aol.com | *Fax*: (607) 723-1401 |

BECKETT & LA PSYCHANALYSE & PSYCHOANALYSIS

Ed. by Sjef Houppermans

Amsterdam/Atlanta, GA 1996. VII,174 pp.
(Samuel Beckett Today/Aujourd'hui 5)
ISBN: 90-420-0066-X   Hfl. 55,-/US-$ 34.-

Table des Matières/Table of Contents: Sjef HOUPPERMANS: Introduction. 1. Ciaran ROSS: La "Pensee de la Mère": Fonction et structure d'un fantasme. 2. Jean-Michel RABATÉ: Beckett's Ghosts and Fluxions. 3. Sjef HOUPPERMANS: À cheval. Daniel KATZ: "Alone in the Accusative": Beckett's Narcissistic Echoes. 5. Tom COUSINEAU: The Lost Father in Beckett's Novels. 6. Mary BRYDEN: The Schizoid Space: Beckett, Deleuze, and *L'épuisé*. Kate Martin GRAY: Beckettian Interiority. 8. André FURLANI: Samuel Beckett's *Molloy:* Spartan Maieutics. 9. Ralph BISSCHOPS: Entropie et *Elan Vital* chez Beckett. 10. Jeanette den TOONDER: *Compagnie:* Chimère autobiographique et métatexte. 11. Julian GARFORTH: A Trilingual *Godot*.

USA/Canada: Editions Rodopi B.V., 2015 South Park Place, Atlanta, GA 30339, Tel. (770) 933-0027, *Call toll-free* (U.S. only) 1-800-225- 3998, Fax (770) 933-9644, *E-mail*: F.van.der.Zee@rodopi.nl

All Other Countries: Editions Rodopi B.V., Keizersgracht 302-304, 1016 EX Amsterdam, The Netherlands. Tel. + + 31 (0)20-622-75-07, Fax + + 31 (0)20-638-09-48, *E-mail*: F.van.der.Zee@rodopi.nl

OTHERWISE THAN LANGUAGE

Gerald L. Bruns

> For the god Orpheus, who lives in-finitely in the Open, song is an easy matter, but not for man (Heidegger, "What Are Poets For?")

> Do we intend with this reference to shake the foundations of all philology and philosophy of language, and to expose them as a sham? Indeed we do (Heidegger, *What is Called Thinking?*)

Lingering

What goes on in the writings of the later Heidegger cannot truthfully be called a reasoning of any sort. From the standpoint of progressive, systematic, calculative thinking, it is certain to appear repetitious, opaque, pointless or unproductive. It is not (like this paper) an attempt to get straight about anything. It may not even be the sort of thinking that Heidegger talks about in *What is Called Thinking?* And no one who had ever given a thought to poetry would call it poetry. One could call it, loosely, reflection, but Heidegger would probably say that it doesn't need to be called anything at all. His motto is, "leave everything open."

His writings on language and poetry do not represent the unfolding of a theory. They are rather a lingering with a subject matter, where lingering means holding back, not seeking advancement or mastery, refusing to determine the subject conceptually, acknowledging Plato's judgment "that everything that lies before us is ambiguous" (WD, 123/201[1]). Which means that it is not just Heidegger who holds back; it is his subject, which refuses to be put into words. At the beginning of "The Way to Language" (1959), Heidegger's final lecture on language, and my present text for study, Heidegger introduces the following formula *(Wegformel,* he calls it): *"Die Sprache als die Sprache zur Sprache bringen"* (US, 242/112). What would it be to bring language as language to language? What would it mean, if not a final effort to get language into words?

At the obvious risk of repetition, let me begin by going back (and forth) over where we have been, or where we are, which is what Heidegger would call lingering in the neighborhood. We know, for a start, that for Heidegger truth is not a matter of statements and concepts; it is an event. The German word for event is *Ereignis,* which becomes a crucial (possibly uninterpretable) word in "The Way to Language," where it is translated, for reasons not really clear, as "appropriation." In "The Origin of the Work of Art," Heidegger speaks of the self-divided nature of truth as, on the one hand, *alētheia* or disclosure, and, on the other, as "constant concealment in the double form of refusal and dissembling" (Hw, 43/54). *Alētheia* is not unconcealment pure and simple. The word itself is a pun that inscribes a darkness that is "older than truth" (SD, 78/71): *a-lētheia.* Truth occurs in the work of art in this self-divided way epitomized as the rift of earth and world. Thus Heidegger says that the *work* of the work of art, what happens with it, is unconcealment, the opening up of a world, but this is not an opening that occurs in front of us, before our eyes, the way a prospect opens up before the gaze of sightseers; better to say that it is a momentary clearing in the woods, and there we are. The Open cannot be conceptually determined; it is not anything objective that can be represented by (or to) consciousness. It is not a Kantian world. On the contrary, as Heidegger says in the essay, "What Are Poets For?" [*Wozu Dichter?*—Whereto Poets?] (1946), by putting himself *before* the world, man is excluded from it (Hw, 262/107). Our relation to the Open, or for that matter to the work of art, is not one of knowing; it is not just seeing it there in front of us where we can analyze it. And of course this leaves us not knowing where we are, especially if we know no other mode than analysis.

As for the work of art, Heidegger speaks of it as "self-standing," that is, as something reserved unto itself, something that has "cut all ties to human beings" (Hw, 54/66). The work of the work is disclosure, but strangely so: call it disclosure as estrangement. This estrangement is not something that occurs in addition to opening or unconcealment; the work does not work dialectically. We must shake the idea that *alētheia* means revelation. Rather, Heidegger says, "the stronger and the more solitary the work becomes . . ., the more simply does it transport us into the open and thus at the same time transport us out of the realm of the ordinary [*Gewöhnlichen*]. To submit to this displacement means: to transform our accustomed ties to world and to earth and henceforth to restrain all usual doing and prizing, knowing and looking, in order to stay within the truth that is happening in the work" (Hw, 54/66). The work, the world, breaks free; we must learn to let go, to step back and linger awhile. Or, in other words, we have to become more like the god, or poet, Orpheus.

In its self-standing, solitary, nonhuman character, the work of art is very like the thing. The thing, as Heidegger speaks of it, is not an object of representation; it is simply that which, against all reason or rules of grammar, *things: Das Ding dingt.* Now it happens that the work *works* just as the thing *things.* The work is not an object of art, not an aesthetic object made up of formal properties, but something whose "createdness" reserves the work to itself. The work is earthly as well as worldly, *phūsis* as well as *logos,* darkening as well as lightening, and in this wise it withholds itself, closes itself up, withdraws into its materials (the poem hiding itself in its words). Of course, in its everyday, familiar, objective character, art is the property of collectors, curators, connoisseurs, critics. For none of these, however, does it make sense to speak of the *truth* (that is, the *work)* of the work of art, just as normal philosophers—empiricists, Kantians, Husserlian phenomenologists, analytic philosophers of language, nonreaders of Heidegger, for short—cannot in any sensible or philosophically serious way speak of the truth (the *thinging*) of things. Philosophically, all of this (all of the later Heidegger) is just sillytalk. Nevertheless, for Heidegger, the work works, the thing things, and in this same event, called *Ereignis,* the world worlds.

Now this event, the worlding of the world, is the event of language. Heidegger calls it the speaking of language. *Die Sprache spricht is* a sentence to be taken in the same spirit (it belongs to the same funny line of locutions) as *Das Ding dingt* and *Die Welt weltet.* Heidegger is relentless in insisting that the speaking of language is not our speech, at least not what we think of as speaking: singing, if we could say what *that* is, might be something else. Language is reserved, withholds itself, solitary and strange, no less than work or thing. It is *not for us,* even though in its everydayness we take it as ready-to-hand and always at our disposal, and we study it, objectify it, take it apart, gerrymander it, reconstruct it according to its logical forms, there is no end to what we can do. Heidegger wants us to understand, however, that language, in the midst of its everydayness, is not familiar and ordinary but *überwältigung und unheimlich,* overwhelming and uncanny. As indeed we know very well in those moments when we try to speak and words fail or run away with us.

Part of this uncanniness is that language, as it speaks, has nothing to say, nothing to express, nothing to do with meaning. Rather, Heidegger says, "*Language speaks as the peal of stillness*" (US, 30/207). Moreover, he says, "The peal of stillness is not anything human [*nicht Menschliches*]" (US, 30/207). Here uncanniness turns sinister. The phrase, "not anything human," makes Heidegger sound ugly. It is hard not to recoil from the dehumanization of anything, much less of language. Somehow, as the philosophers say, Heidegger is not one of us.

It is certainly true that Heidegger ranges very far from the program of romantic or aesthetic humanism that begins by conceptualizing man as a consciousness on the way to becoming fully itself, fully self-possessed and in command of its processes and productions, its knowledge and its art: consciousness free from falseness or forgetfulness (*lēthē*). The whole emancipatory project of the Enlightenment is designed to get man out from under the forces that seek to repress him and estrange him from himself: call these forces the Unconscious, or the Other, or (on a certain view of language) language, whose grammar is not just syntax and semantics but also culture and ideology. Anyhow there is no mistaking Heidegger as a figure of the counter-Enlightenment, a man of darkness, as when he says: "it is not we who play with words, but the nature of language [*Wesen der Sprache*] plays with us" (WD, 83/118). And of poetry and thinking, two undeniably human activities, he has nothing progressive to say. On the contrary, poetry and thinking are remystified in his hands; he shrouds them in darkness, turns them over to enigma and ambiguity. They are no longer operations of the spirit but rather participants, whatever that means, in the event, *Ereignis*, of language. We enter into poetry and thinking, not by acts of the mind, but by relinquishing the will-to-power, that is, the will to speak and to explain. The key word with respect to poetry and thinking is "renunciation" (*Verzichten*), where *Verzichten* is a sort of Saying called *Sichversagen* or self-refusal (US, 228/247), which defines the poet's relation to language. *Verzichten* belongs to the same neighborhood as *Gelassenheit*, letting-go, "openness to the mystery" (G, 24/55), and it shows itself in listening and in *not* asking questions (in the sense of probing), that is, in thinking. It means keeping still, as if entering into "the peal of stillness." It means stepping-back from the manipulative mode of representational-calculative thinking, the mode of rationality of the *Ge-Stell* or En-framing of technology. It means the end of philosophy, insofar as philosophy since Descartes knows no other mode.

Aesthetic humanism is in many respects the subject of Heidegger's essay on Rilke, "*Wozu Dichter?*"—"What Are Poets For?," although it is not clear how *wozu* is to be translated. For Heidegger, Rilke's poetry shows the dominance of subjectivity that alienates us from the world, excludes us from what is near by enframing us in a state of affairs in which everything—the world, the Open—has been "raised to consciousness." "The higher the consciousness," Heidegger says, "the more the conscious being is excluded from the world" (Hw, 264/108). This sounds like Owen Barfield or romantic primitivism, and on a certain view it is, as in the following, with its powerful wordplay on Heidegger's keyword for the modern age, *Ge-Stell*:

> Man places [*stellt*] before himself the world as the whole of everything objective, and he places himself before the world. Man sets up [*stellt*] the

world toward himself, and delivers nature over to himself. We must think of this placing here, this producing [*Herstellen*], in its broad and multifarious nature [*Wesen*]. Where Nature [*Natur*] is not satisfactory to man's representation [*Vorstellen*], he reframes or redisposes [*bestellt*] it. Man produces [*stellt*] new things where they are lacking to him. Man transposes things [*stellt die Dinge um*] where they are in his way. Man interposes [*verstellt*] something between himself and things that distract him from his purpose. Man exposes things [*stellt die Dinge aus*] when he boosts them for sale and use. Man exposes [*stellt aus*] when he sets forth [*herausstellt*] his own achievement and plays up his own profession. By multifarious producing [*vielfaltigen Herstellen*], the world is brought to stand and in position [*Stand*]. The Open becomes an object [*Gegenstand*], and is thus twisted around toward the human being. Over and against the world as object, man stations himself [*stellt sich*] and sets himself up as the one who deliberately pushes through all this producing [*Herstellen*] [Hw, 265-266/ 220].

Here is man in his assertive mode, or mode of logic. Logic, let us say, is an affair of places (*Stellen*). It is made of posits, positions, propositions, oppositions, suppositions, expositions, impositions, transpositions, and the desire for repose (called certainty); it is a matter of putting questions and settling them; of locating things in their proper categories and knowing their standing relative to the scheme of things (knowing their names); of systems and rules; of grounds and reasons (knowing, for example, what poets are for); it knows only relations, representations, and frames of reference.

What is logic for? Its business appears to be to construct a safe place for (or from) objects of consciousness, or what man knows (what doesn't get away from him). Maybe a good name for such a place is "metaphysics," the place of places, where everything has a foundation and nothing flies in your face—a vast place of noncontradiction and freedom from ambiguity (mere wandering with no place in mind). The famous line in "What Are Poets For?" is: "Only within metaphysics is there logic [*Nur innerhalb der Metaphysik gibt es die Logik*]" (Hw, 287/133). Only within metaphysics is everything under control; everything is in order, even language. Logic keeps language from happening on its own, makes it safe to use, puts it into man's hands for safekeeping "as a handle for his representations [*als Handhabe seine Vorstellens*]" (Hw, 287/133). Language is for grasping things. This is language as *logos*, which puts everything out in front of us at arm's length where we can keep an eye on it. Language as logos is for making propositions, putting things where they belong and where we won't need to look twice for them; where they won't get away from us, slipping away into ambiguity. Language as logos is an affair of foreseeable, and resolvable, predicaments. Even metaphors belong to language as logos; they are part of the rationality of propositions, a way of bringing ambiguity under control. Metaphor allows us to say, of what is not, that it is, without getting confused as to what is and what is not the case. Only, as Heidegger says in the *Introduction to Metaphysics,* "All by itself the logos does not make language" (EM, 132/145).

When in "What Are Poets For?" Heidegger speaks of "the conversion of consciousness" [*die Umkehrung des Bewnssteins:* the turning-round of consciousness] (Hw, 284/129), it sounds like he is counseling the abandonment of logic, and it is true that the theoretical structure of this essay is built upon a traditional opposition between the logical proposition and song, where the one is assertive and productive, whereas the other is, of course, nothing of the sort. The poet nothing affirmeth. Two lines from Rilke's *Sonette an Orpheus* summarize for Heidegger the whole point about song:

In Wahrheit singen ist ein anderer Hauch.
Ein Hauch um nichts. Ein Wehn im Gott. Ein Wind.

To sing in truth is another breath.
A breath for nothing. An afflatus in the god. A wind [Hw, 292/139].

"A breath for nothing": the poet is the one who gives himself up to language, throws in with it, doesn't try to bring it under control but lets it go, lets it sound itself through him, and so lets himself be drawn into it as into an event or game in which he is the one who is played: drawn, in other words, into the Open, where the open shows itself as something different from logical space or the places of consciousness—different, say, from the Kantian world where everything answers to our concepts. Here the poet is the answerable one: think of him or her in the traditional character as responsive to what is unseen and unheard, who is not under his or her own power but is carried away, frequently bereft of reason (blind, say, or outright mad), the song singing itself through the sounds the poet's voice makes without knowing how or why. Song is not so much the abandonment of logic as the limit of it; it shows us where the limit is, where philosophy is. And at the limit of logic there is, Heidegger says, *risk*. Hence his name for the poets: "the venturesome ones [*die Wagenderen*]," he calls them: they dare, he says, "the venture with language" (Hw, 287/133). They play its gambling game.

"The more venturesome ones," Heidegger says, "dare the Saying [*Die Wagenderen wagen das Sagen*]" (Hw, 287/133). But what sort of risk is this, exactly? Possibly it is just the usual risk of nonsense, silliness, or madtalk—or just what poetry always sounds like to philosophy, namely something naive and trivial. The poet is a light and winged thing, says Plato, stupid, cheerful, never in touch with reality (*Ion*, 534b-c). So what's the risk?

Heidegger's answer to this question is by way of death. Death is of all things human just that which cannot be objectified and brought under control, that which is strangest of all, that which is just where logic, and therefore human knowledge, or say philosophy, ends. At the limits of logic man encounters his own mortality (call this his otherness, or that which is uncontainable in any theory or explanation)—but this is only to say that here man enters into his own, finds himself, or finds where he has always been, where his own place or *ethos* is, his own proper nature *(phūsis)*. Mortality is our experience *with* ourselves as that which gets away from us. For the point is that death is always *near*; we are always mortals, dwelling with it, even though in good logic and for serious practical purposes we picture ourselves differently and labor to exempt ourselves, putting mortality at a distance.

Putting mortality at a distance is the whole end of medical technology, which takes us to that limit where it is no longer possible to determine objectively the point at which death occurs. At the limit of technology (at the very frame or border of the *Ge-Stell*), death withdraws itself, withholds itself, so that now we can no longer say, with the sort of certainty philosophy calls for, *now* it has happened ("Ah, the distinguished thing!"). What is it *not* to be able to say this? How came we to this pass? But Heidegger would say that mortality, like stillness, is always sounding, even though we cannot hear it or even cease to listen for it. Somehow we don't acknowledge our mortality quite the way the Greeks did when without blinking, seeing they were not gods, they came right out and called themselves mortals. The word belongs to an archaic or forgotten way of speaking; it's no longer in our vocabulary, no longer part of our self-understanding. Call it a word whose meaning we no longer know, define it as we will. But of course no one is under the illusion that the Greeks got it wrong: "mortal" is our proper name. There is a sense in which it is the *only* thing we know. Death is the limit of skepticism.

Heidegger's effort is to emancipate language from our theories of it, where our theories always picture language as constituting the logical possibility of our discourse. And of course language does avail itself to us in this fashion. We do speak, after all, and we do make sense to one another. Heidegger has never repudiated his earlier idea that we are constituted historically as a conversation *(Gespräch)*.[2] But now he wants us to understand language as, nevertheless, *not human*—not in the way speech or conversation is. Language, like death, is the limit of the human. Heidegger wants to disconnect man and language in order to reconnect them in the archaic way in which he reconnects us to our mortality. Thus he asks us to think of language in the same breath as death ("A breath for nothing"), that is, he wants us to think of it as belonging to the same region or neighborhood as death: think of our mortality as the way we connect up with language and, therefore, with the world.

This is how Heidegger ends his third lecture on "The Nature of Language": "The essential relation between death and language flashes up before us, but remains still unthought" (US, 21 5/107). Think of language as belonging to the same neighborhood as our mortality. This is what Heidegger's strange talk about the fourfold (*Geviert*) comes to. Language as Saying is the event (*Ereignis*) in which world and thing are called into the Open. This thinging and worlding of thing and world is the event of the fourfold, the dwelling together, round dance, and ringing of earth and sky, gods and mortals. The fourfold is not some imaginary realm. It is *our* world, and we are nowhere but in it. We are the mortals Heidegger is talking about, dwelling together with earth, sky, and divinities, strange as it is to say so. Entering into this realm means exposing ourselves to our own darkness, which is to say the truth (the dark truth or *a-lētheia*) of our mortality, our being mortal, or that which we cannot bear to think.[3] Or say that we enter this realm when we *are* exposed to the darkness, that is, to the otherness of earth and sky, mortality and divinity. The strangeness of the fourfold, its otherness, its dif-ference from the familiar and the reliable, its singularity, is just that it is irreducible to explanation, ungraspable, outside the laws of intelligibility. "Gods" and "mortals," "earth" and "sky" belong to a forgotten lexicon, say the savage mind from which Plato emancipated us. So we are ashamed to talk of such things. We assign such talk nowadays to poetry, madness, or myth—whatever is on the nether side of logic. It is no longer serious to wonder about gods. The gods withhold themselves from the discourse of modernity, that is, from language as objectifying and analytical logos, the *parole* of the *Ge-Stell*. There are no such beings as gods, just as there are no such beings as words. We can only represent gods as figures of imagination, Hölderlin's mythology. Perhaps they resound in Nietzsche's word, "God is dead." But what sort of talk is Nietzsche's word? Is he speaking literally or metaphorically? For Heidegger, Nietzsche's word has the character of uncanny discourse; it is the cry, or call, of the madman, but the ear of thinking, so under the control of the eye, cannot hear it. "It will refuse to hear it so long as it does not begin to think. Thinking begins only when we have come to know that reason, glorified for centuries, is the most stiffnecked adversary of thought" (Hw, 247/112). Nor is the task of thinking to seek the overthrow of reason; it is perhaps no more than it has always been, namely to seek the limits of reason. But for Heidegger this means that thinking must enter into its own darkness and perhaps lose itself in its wandering, as if overtaken by madness; that is, it must expose itself to its other. This means that it must acknowledge the rift that binds it to poetry; that is, it must acknowledge its belongingness to this other— something philosophy could never bring itself to do.

Signs

Heidegger's final text on language, "The Way to Language," was originally a lecture given in 1959 as part of a series of lectures on language by various scholars from different disciplines. Heidegger was preceded, for example, by C. F. Weizsacker, who spoke on information theory. "The Way to Language" has a familiar Heideggerian look: it does not represent an advance or conceal a change in Heidegger's thought but is once more a going back and forth along the same path. It begins with the customary "break" with tradition, where tradition (here figured in the name of Wilhelm von Humboldt) means the Kantian tradition that wants to know how meaning is possible. In this tradition, language is the formative, structuring, systematically signifying activity of the spirit. It is that which holds totalities together, makes totality possible. According to the famous distinction, language is not a work (*ergon*), that is, not a product of consciousness, but the activity (*energeia*) of the subject as such. In this tradition, meaning is form (whatever has form, that is, possesses formal fitness, makes sense), and consciousness is formative. Meaning is not correspondence to an object but the way objects hang together in a total composition (*Gestell*). Nothing is ever of any significance (has any reality) all by itself; rather, things are for us only insofar as they belong to an ensemble of relations. The ensemble has been figured in a variety of structuralisms: (1) epistemologically as a system of symbolic forms (Cassirer); (2) linguistically or semiotically as a diacritical system of differences (Lévi-Strauss); (3) socially or, say, grammatically as a network of intersecting language-games (Wittgenstein); (4) logically as a holistic framework of interlocking true sentences, or conceptual schemes (Quine); (5) politically as an ideological system or as the cultural constitution of the subject (Althusser, Lacan); (6) hermeneutically as a temporal horizon of presuppositions or world held in common (Heidegger, *Being and Time*, section 32).

In "The Way to Language" Heidegger parodies this structuralist tradition by speaking of the "web of relations" (*ein Geflecht von Beziehungen*) in which we find ourselves whenever we try to think about language or speak about it as such (US, 242/112-113). Language *is* the ensemble in which everything hangs together, only of course we are not outside the web but are enmeshed in it as part of everything else, woven into the weaving of it, entangled and certainly bewildered as we listen to so many efforts to unweave the web. The task of thinking, however, is not to solve the problem of language; it is not to unweave the intricate latticework or hopeless tangle but just to separate the threads a little, loosen them here and there to create an opening. "Perhaps," Heidegger says, "there is a bond running through the web which, in a way that remains strange, unbinds and delivers language into its own [*in ihr Eigentümliches entbindet*]. The point is to experience the unbinding bond within the web of language [*Es gilt, im Geflecht der Sprache in ihr das entbindende Band zu erfahren*]" (US, 243/113). So we are not to think of language as our prison house; emancipation is not our theme. The web is rather something we should enter into, perhaps to wander through, listening as we go (it being too dark to see) for what Heidegger calls "a soundless echo which lets us hear something of the proper character of language [*ein lautloser Anklang, der uns ein Geringes vom Eigentümlichen der Sprache hören lässt*]" (US, 243/113).

In the Kantian tradition the concept of concepts is that of the sign or its equivalents (the significant form, the logical term, the element as nexus, gap, place, or difference in the chain, fence, frame, system, or totality of signifiers, signifieds, or conceptual determinations). But instead of speaking of the sign (*Zeichen*), Heidegger, wholly into the spirit of parody, recurs to his mysterious word, *Riss*, that is, the sign as rift, which here takes the form of *Aufriss* or (in its rifted or disseminated version) *Auf-Riss*, the design or de-sign which structures what Heidegger calls the *Sprachwesen*, which is something like a word for the essence or nature of language. "Most of us," he says,

> know the word "sign" ["*Riss*"] only in its debased meaning—lines on a surface [*Riss in der Wand*]. But we make a design also when we cut a furrow into the soil to open it to seed and growth. The de-sign is the whole of the traits of that drawing which structures and prevails throughout the open, unlocked freedom of language [*Der Auf-Riss ist das Ganze der Züge derjenigen Zeichnung, die das Aufgeschlossene, Freie der Sprache durchfügt*]. The design is the drawing of the being of language, the structure of a show in which are joined the speakers and their speaking: what is spoken and what of it is unspoken in all that is given in speaking [*Der Auf-Riss ist die Zeichnung des Sprachwesens, das Gefüge eines Zeigens, darein die Sprechenden und ihr Sprechen, das Gesprochene und sein Ungesprochenes aus dem Zugesprochenen verfugt sind*] (US, 252/121).

Riss: there is probably no coming to terms with this word. First (remember) there was the antagonistic and even violent rift of earth and world ("The Origin of the Work of Art"); then there was the gentler but still painful rift of world and thing ("Language"); and then the still more "delicate and luminous" rift of poetry and thinking ("The Nature of Language"). Now we have the rift *in* language itself—or, more accurately, in the *Sprachwesen*, call it the "being" of language, although now it is otherwise than being, that is, no longer *das Wesen der Sprache* but something else, something more *phūsis* than *logos*, namely the *rift:* say the rift between the spoken and the unspoken, or between language as speaking (saying something, putting something into words) and language as Saying (*Sage*), where, in something less than a manner of speaking, nothing gets said, language withdraws itself, although something happens. In whatever context, the task, or event, of the rift has been roughly to hold things apart, to create a "between" between things without determining the difference between them, as between the literal and the metaphorical. Call rift, therefore, (loosely) a figure of indeterminacy in deference to all those cases in which things don't (or can't) quite get put into words, that is, cases where, for whatever reason, you stop or come up short of conceptualizing things, or saying (exactly) what something means—cases, or say failings or failings in which the darkness of Saying appropriates our discourse and puts itself, if that is the right way of putting it, into our words. Call this appropriation, or this event, *Dichten.*

In *Being and Time* (section 34), Heidegger speaks of the task of "liberating grammar from logic" (SZ, 1651-66/209).[4] Parody is the mode of liberation in "The Way of Language," in which we get something like a Heideggerian "grammar," that is, an account (of sorts) of what language is made of, how it is put together, how it works, what its "deep structure" is. *Der Auf-Riss des Sprachwesens* means, roughly, how language, on its own, is, that is, how it is with it, or say how it speaks, even though there's no determining the logic of it. Thus Heidegger the paragrammarian draws or sketches the *Auf-Riss* of language for us in the form of a pun, a little piece of indeterminacy— namely *Zeichen-Zeigen* (sign-show). The rift in language, taken on its own (*Sprachwesen*), can be traced in the difference or dif-ference that this pun inscribes. It is perhaps something like the dif-ference, impossible quite to determine, between word and term that Heidegger talks about in *What is Called Thinking?* (WD, 89/130). Or, again, the dif-ference can be traced in a line of puns that the word "sign" sets in motion: *Zeichen–Zeigen–Eigen–Eignen–Ereignis*. In ways that we may never quite grasp, this line of puns shows the way to language.

For now, however, let us trace this line as follows: We speak, let us say, by means of the manipulation of signs, that is, in terms of language, and according to its systematic operations, but what gets said cannot be accounted for simply by a doctrine of signification, since it is always the case that what we say gets away from us and more gets said, something other gets said, than is simply spoken (not to say stated). "The Way to Language" picks this up by stressing what Heidegger calls the "manysidedness" of what is spoken: *Das Gesprochenes bleibt indes vielfältig* (US, 251/120). It is this manysidedness that logic is meant to bring under control. This was the whole point about constructing artificial languages obedient to reason—calculi in which the deep structure of language can finally be laid bare. Grasp this structure and you are in command of the secret workings of language, that is, you have the makings of an ideal or logically perfect language, a language of pure syntax and transparent terms. Natural languages, for their part, refuse to do what they are told. They remain opaque, dense (*dicht*), closed to view: it is impossible to give a coherent description of natural language, in which our expressions are always excessive with respect to meaning. Their words resist our efforts to make them transparent. This is the upshot of Heidegger's distinction between words and terms (*Worte* v. *Wörter*): the term means one thing and not another, but not the word, which resonates so as to sound not like one word but many. Words are more like puns than terms. As Gadamer says, besides the Platonic dialectic of the One and the Many that makes possible the fragile unity of predication, "there is another dialectic of the word, which assigns to every word an inner dimension of multiplication [*Vervielfachung*]: every word breaks forth as if from a center and is related to a whole, through which it alone is a word. Every word causes the whole of the language to which it belongs to resonate and the whole view of the world that lies behind it to appear. Thus every word, in its momentariness, carries with it the unsaid, to which it is related by responding and hinting [*winkend*]" (TM, 415-416).

Here is structuralism with a difference. For what is it for a word to have "an inner dimension of multiplication"? It is not just that words are polysemantic and capable of being used in radically different contexts; it is that it is hard to tell where one word leaves off and another begins. This is so especially when we take words as sounds rather than by sight. As Heidegger says, "It is just as much a property of language to sound and ring and vibrate, to hover and to tremble, as it is for what is spoken to carry a meaning" (US, 205/98). Heidegger asks us to imagine a language whose each word internalizes, not so much its own meaning, its own structural difference from other words in the system, as the sounds of all the other words in the language (perhaps, *Wake-like*, in every language). Sound a word and others answer, as in the pun. Hence the uncanniness of ordinary language where no word is just itself but is always threatening to turn into another, or always carries others clinging to it wherever it goes. In this event it is not enough to characterize words as elements in a signifying system. Language is not a network of implications that differential analysis could explicate. Words are not discrete particles or made of such things but, like puns, they are multiple and dialogical, hetero- rather than polysemous. Imagine language as an infinite conversation in which words talk endlessly back and forth, picking up hints from one another, playing to one another and on one another, internalizing one another, parodying one another, sounding and resounding, echoing and reechoing so that nothing can ever be said purely and simply but is always in excess of itself, spilling over and spreading in every direction. One could not write a grammar for such a language; that is, one could not say in what the logic of such a language could consist. One would have to say that "in the Nichtian glossary which purveys aprioric roots for aposteriorious tongues this is nat language at any sinse of the world" *(Finnegans Wake,* 183). It is otherwise than language.

Heidegger turns back deliberately from linguistics and philosophy of language toward an antique way of taking language, say before there was a word for language—namely the way of mystery rather than system. "Everything spoken," Heidegger says, "stems in a variety of ways from what is unspoken" (US, 251/120). Or, again,

> What is unspoken is not merely something that lacks voice, it is what remains unsaid, what is not yet shown, what has not yet reached appearance. That which must remain wholly unspoken is held back in the unsaid, abides in concealment as unshowable, as mystery. That which is spoken to us speaks as saying in the sense of something imparted, something whose speaking does not even require to be sounded [*Das Zugesprochene spricht als Spruch im Sinne des Zugewiesenen, dessen Sprechen nicht einmal des Verlautens bedarf*]" (US, 253/122).

This is very strange, this talk, but to situate it one could say that before Aristotle, with his *Organon* (that is, before the invention of a logical grammar), there was Heraclitus, whose words we can sound but no longer understand, and whose theory of the sign is like nothing we know because it has nothing to do with meaning, or what we think of as meaning, that is, signifying, determining something as this or that. "The Oracle at Delphi does not speak, it gives a sign [*semainei*]" (Fr. 93). Only this is not the sign of anything, it is nothing logical, nothing semiotic, nothing that can be determined or put into a statement (made to function semantically). The Heraclitean sign is dark, more word than term; it is, as Heidegger emphasizes every time he takes up Heraclitus, something like a hint *(Wink).* What is a *Wink?*

What it is, is close to what "The Way to Language" is about. *"The essential being of language,"* Heidegger says, *"is Saying as Showing [Das Wesende der Sprache ist die Sage als die Zeige]"* (US, 254/123). He then adds: "Its showing character [*deren Zeigen*] is not based on signs of any kind" (US, 254/123). Signs belong to human speaking, that is, to the making of statements (or of metaphors); they belong to the logos, but not to language. And so it hurts the mind when we try to imagine what it would be like to speak such a language. But speaking, Heidegger says, is finally *not* making statements (or metaphors) or anything at all—not the use of signs. Oh, it is *that* in some sense, anyhow there's no other way (in theory), to figure it.

But speaking is at the same time also listening [*zagleich Hören*]. It is the custom to put speaking and listening in opposition; one speaks, the other listens. But listening accompanies and surrounds not only speaking such as takes place in conversation. The simultaneousness of speaking and listening has a larger meaning. Speaking is itself a listening. Speaking is listening to the language which we speak. Thus, it is a listening not *while* but *before* we are speaking. This listening to language also comes before all other kinds of listening that we know, in a most inconspicuous manner. We do not merely speak *the* language—we speak *by way of it* [*wir sprechen aus ihr*]. We can do so because we always have already listened to the language. What do we hear there? We hear language speaking [*das Sprechen der Sprache*] [US, 254/123-124].

Die Sprache spricht: language speaks, but nothing gets said, that is, nothing gets signified; rather, in the peal of the stillness of nothing spoken, things make their appearance in the sense of coming into their own (as against coming into view), that is, they *thing* in the manner of self-disclosure or self-showing (*Sichzeigen = Das Ding dings*). The thinging of things is not a revelation; it is the worlding of the world, the ringing of the fourfold, the round dance of earth and sky, gods and mortals—and *there* we are: that's us moving among them, mortal as we are.

Only here we are getting away from "The Way to Language," which (strangely) doesn't say a word about these things, I mean doesn't so much as hint at earth and world, the near and the remote, thinging things and worlding world, the simple onefold of the fourfold: not a word of it. What is striking about this text is that the idiom of the later Heidegger, put into play as long ago as "The Origin of the Work of Art," and carefully elaborated in the early lectures on language and in the collateral texts on "Building Dwelling Thinking" and "The Thing"—the whole lingo is dropped. Or rather not quite the whole. All that remains is *der Riss,* echoing in the quasi- or paragrammatical notion of *der Auf-Riss des Sprachwesens,* the rift of sign and showing, the spoken and the unspoken, speaking and saying, sounding and stillness. What remains strange, or anyhow unphilosophical, is the priority of listening, and even this Heidegger makes an effort to turn to philosophical account: "Language," he says, "speaks by saying, that is, by showing [*Die Sprache spricht, indem sie sags, d. h. zeigt*]. . . . We, accordingly, listen to language in this way, that we let it say its Saying to us. No matter in what way we may listen besides, whenever we are listening to something *we are letting something be said to us* [*Sichsagenlassen:* letting Saying happen to us], and all perception and conception are already contained in that act. In our speaking, as a listening to language, we say again the Saying we have

heard. We let its soundless voice come to us, and then demand, reach out, and call for the sound that is already kept in store for us [*Wir lassen ihre lautlose Stimme kommen, wobei wir den uns schon auibehaltenen Laut verlangen, zu ihn hinreichend ihn rufen*]" (US, 254-255/124).
What is this *Sichsagenlassen*?

Er-eignis

In the essay, "Logos (Herclitus, Fragment 50)," Heidegger picks up on the pun in *gehören*: "We have *heard* [*gehört*] when we *belong to* [*gehören*] the matter addressed [*Zugesprochenen*] (VS, 207/66). In "The Way to Language" he picks up on this again: "We hear Saying," he says, "only because we belong within it [*Wir hören sie nur, well in sie gehören*]" (US, 255/124). And "all perception and conception," he says, "are contained in that act."

Say that our relationship to the world is not first that of seeing but of listening. Not that we don't (can't) see and conceive how things are, but because of how we are situated (in the mode of hearing) we may not be in a position to get a good look at things; we may not be able to produce the picture we want (for example, an exact likeness). Seeing and conceiving are already contained in listening, not so much in the sense of implied as in the (darker) sense of being situated in an alien mode. For listening is not the spectator's mode. Listening means involvement and entanglement (as in the web of language). It means participation or belonging (*gehören*) for short. The ear's mode is always that of conspiracy, that is, of getting caught up in something (a tangled plot), being overtaken or taken over and put to use. The ear is exposed and vulnerable, at risk, whereas the eye tries to keep itself at a distance and frequently from view (the private eye). The eye is the agent of surveillance. It appropriates what it sees, but the ear is always expropriated, always being taken over by another ("lend me your ears"). The ear gives the other access to us, allows the stranger to enter us, occupy and obsess us, putting us under a claim, driving us mad or something like it, as when we let (cannot do otherwise than let) "a soundless voice come to us, and then demand, reach out and call for the sound that is already kept in store for us." Imagine hearing such a thing! Seeing is objectifying and possessive; hearing means the loss of subjectivity and self-possession, belonging to what we hear, owned by it. Think of the call. The ear puts us in the mode of being summoned (*belangen*), of being answerable and having to appear. It situates us. It brings us into the open, puts us, like the poet, at risk, whereas the eye allows us to stand off and away, not on the way but out of it—seeing but unseen, eminently philosophical.

What is it to be taken over (call it appropriated) in this way? It is usual to think of appropriation (*Aneignung*) as an act of possessive individualism, as one subject appropriating another: I make my own what belongs to someone else, that is, I take ownership of another's property, even take another as property. For Heidegger, however, appropriation is *Ereignis* rather than *Aneignung*. It is the word for event and also a complex pun, as we know from "The Thing": *Das Spiegel-Spiel von Welt ist der Reigen des Ereignens* (VA, 173/180), where the round dance is a "figure" of belongingness. Think of *Ereignis* not as a subjective act of appropriation but as an event in which we are caught up—appropriated, if you like, or say expropriated: no longer self-determining but taken out of ourselves and put into play.

Play is a good analogy. As Gadamer has shown, play is like (but not quite the same as) the event of appropriation. Play, he says, "is not to be understood as a kind of activity. . . . The actual subject of play is obviously not the subjectivity of the individual who among other activities also plays, but [is] instead play itself" (TM, 99/93). He says, "all playing is a being played. The attraction of the game, the fascination that it exerts, consists precisely in the fact that the game tends to master the players. . . . The game is what holds the player in its spell, draws him into play, and keeps him there" (TM, 101-102/95-96). One could explicate listening as a kind of play, as against the seriousness of seeing, which hasn't time for play except as a spectator sport.

Think, however, of the difference between hermeneutical and empirical or psychological experience (*Erfahrung* v. *Empfindung* and *Erlebnis*). This is the distinction Heidegger has in mind when he speaks about "undergoing an experience with language."

> To undergo an experience with something . . . means that this something befalls us, strikes us, comes over us, overwhelms and transforms us. When we talk of 'undergoing' an experience, we mean specifically that the experience is not of our own making; to undergo here means that we endure it, suffer it, receive it as it strikes us and submit to it. It is this something itself that comes about, comes to pass, happens" (US, 159/57).

And naturally one thinks here of "the gambling game of language, where our nature is at stake" (WD, 87/128). Hermeneutical experience is not a cognitive event. It does not add to the subject by enlarging its store of knowledge. On the contrary, it is more likely that the subject is bereft of its store, is divested of all that belongs to it, including itself, and left exposed to what happens.[5]

However, this loss of subjectivity does not mean self-annihilation. On the contrary, Gadamer speaks of the buoyancy, the sense of abandonment and freedom from constraint, that is possible when one enters fully into the spirit of the game. Gadamer wants to say: the essence of play is freedom.

The game does not so much annihilate the subject as let it go; the game takes us out of ourselves and, putting us into play, brings us out into the open, not in the sense that we are therefore objectified—playing is not self-expression or making inwardness visible. Rather, play puts us at risk. But it is also true that in playing what is in reserve is called upon and brought out. As in the fulfillment of a task or in responding to a challenge, we come into our own (*eigen*).

The loss of subjectivity means self-annihilation only if we hold to the Cartesian outlook of the pure subject—pure in the sense of disembodied and free of all environment and contingency. Descartes's motto, "I think, therefore I am," carries with it the angelic corollary that thinking, and therefore being, can do without the body, has no need for it, cannot, in any case, picture itself that way as having or being in a body; has no language of embodiment in which to sort out the tangle of whether one is "in" or whether one "has" a body—does it belong to us or we to it?—which is just the age-old question of ownership or mastery. How we connect up with the body is just as mysterious as how we connect up with language. The body on the modernist or Neoplatonist view is (like language) a negative entity; it is just that which gets in the way of knowledge—and of being, since the body always lets us down when we want to live, as when it grows old and weak and dies. But of course there is no limit to the ways in which the body can get away from us. The body is a satire upon rationality. The body means historicality and finitude. It means belonging to horizons. One cannot say either that one has or is in a body, as if the body were something objective, an entity apart, a form of containment or prison house. It is true perhaps that in virtue of our bodies we are brought up against otherness, our own temporality, where we are always turning into someone else. But this just means that the body does not seal us off from whatever is other; rather, it is just our mode of being temporal, which is to say mortal. It is in virtue of our bodies that we come into our own, that is, appear as we are—situated, historical, contingent, mortal. The body (the outward and visible sign, not of the soul, but of mortality) catches us up, absorbs us, incarnates us and carries us along, not, however, as its burden or passenger but as its dancer. Think of the dance as a carrying-away, bodily, as by the sheer exuberance and overflowing of embodiment. Dance is the excess of the body. It is no accident that Heidegger figures the belonging-together of earth and sky, gods and mortals (that is, the world) as a dance.[6] The body is our mode of dancing, that is, our mode of belonging to the round dance of the fourfold; it is our mode of belonging to the world, being with it, being appropriate to it, owning up to it, acknowledging it. One could say: the body is our mode of belonging to Saying, whose "soundless voice" calls upon us to speak aloud or sing, as with the body.

This suggests that we should think of the body not Platonically as imprisonment but hermeneutically as releasement in Heidegger's sense of *Gelassenheit* or the letting-go of beings. Heidegger says:

> Saying [*Sage*] sets all present beings *free* into their given presence, and brings what is absent into their absence. Saying pervades and structures the openness of the clearing [*das Freie der Lichtung*] which every appearance must seek out and every disappearance leave behind, and in which every present or absent being must show, say, announce itself [*sich hereinzeignen, sich einsagen muss*]" (US, 257/126).

One should say: the truth of Saying is the event (*Ereignis*) in which everything comes into its own, even that which withdraws itself or conceals itself—*phūsis*, for example, or whatever loves to hide: and there is nothing that does not love to do so. Which means that there is nothing that does not belong to Saying, whose essence is withdrawal: Saying, which will not, Heidegger says, "let itself be captured in any statement" (US, 161/59). As if Saying were freedom.

Even Being itself is caught up in this play, this song and dance of Saying. This was Heidegger's point in *Identity and Difference* where *Ereignis* is the event in which "Man and Being are appropriated to one another [*Mensch und Sein sind einander ubereignet*]" (ID, 19/31). The relationship of Man and Being is not to be thought of as a formal connection or a grounding in some primal unity; rather, it is a *"belonging-together* [Zusammen-*gehören*]" in which the notion of ground gives way to the notion of mutual participation in which Being makes a claim upon Man and itself "arrives" only insofar as Man "listens to" the claim, answers to it, belongs to it, as if Man and Being were partners in a dialogue and were nothing apart from it: either in play or nothing. We can, Heidegger says, enter into this mutual appropriation, that is, experience it, but what is required from us is something like the letting-go of the dance—a

> spring away from the ground and into the abyss, where the abyss, however, is no longer a metaphysical void but is now the realm or open place between Man and Being, the region of their mutual belonging [*Der Sprung ist die jähe Einfahrt in den Bereich, aus dem der Mensch und Sein einander je schon in ihrem Wesen erreicht haben, weil beide aus einer Zureichung einander übereignet sind*]" (ID, 20-21/33).

This region cannot be conceived topologically; it is an event rather than a ground: *Ereignis*. Man and Being are not beings but occurrences in the event of appropriation—but now even *Ereignis* is no longer simply what it names, that is, it is no longer to be taken simply as "event" in the usual sense; rather, the word "is now to be used as a *singulare tantum*" (ID, 25/36): the word is no longer a term in a lexicon (*Ereignis*) but is now rifted or different, namely *Er-eignis*, a singular, dark, or untranslatable word like the *Tao* of Lao-tzu or the *logos* of Heraclitus (where *logos* and *phūsis*, like Man and Being, belong together as in a dance instead of in a relationship of domination and subjection). *Ereignis* as *Er-eignis*, Heidegger says, "is that realm, vibrating within itself [*in sich schwingende Bereich*], through which Man and Being reach each other in their nature, achieve their nature by losing those qualities [say subjectivity and objectivity, or master and slave] with which metaphysics has endowed them" (ID, 26/37). The English translation of *Ereignis* as "event of appropriation" is thus, not wrong, perhaps, but neither is it quite saying what *Er-eignis* is, since that word no longer "means" event or appropriation or anything that can be put into words. Like Saying, *Ereignis* cannot be captured in a term or statement, that is, there is no other way of putting it. It has the unspeakability, the uncontainability, of the pun.[7]

Basic to *Er-eignis* as pun is *Eignen*, owning, in which, of course, *Zeichen* and *Zeigen* also resound. Heidegger says, "The moving force in Showing of Saying is Owning [*Das Regende im Zeigen der Sage ist das Eignen*]" (US, 258/127). It is as if it were the *eigen* in *Zeigen* that gives *Zeigen* its force; or perhaps not "as if," but just so: *Das Eigen*, Heidegger says, "is what brings all present and absent beings each into their own [*in sein jeweilig Eigenes*], from where they show themselves in what they are, and where they abide according to their kind. This owning which brings them there, and which moves Saying as showing in its showing, we call Appropriation [*heisse das Ereignen*]" (US, 258/127). And again, echoing *Identity and Difference:* "The appropriating event is not the outcome [*Ergebnis*] (result) of something else, but the giving yield [*Er-gebnis*] whose giving reach alone is what gives us such things as a 'there is' ["*Es gibt*"], a 'there is' of which even Being itself stands in need to come into its own as presence" (US, 258/157). Like *Er-eignis*, *Er-gebnis* has been removed, in the Heideggerian manner, from "usual and customary usage." It is as if the meaning of the word were inscribed by the hyphen, the rift of the dif-ference or *mark of the pun* that turns *Ergebnis* into a word *(Er-gebnis)* for the dissemination (*Es gibt*) "of which even Being itself stands in need to come into its own as presence."

And not Being only, but also language: *Die Sprache als die Sprache zur Sprache bringen* (US, 242/112). Recall the figure of the web at the outset of "The Way to Language": "Perhaps," Heidegger had said, "there is a bond running through the web which, in a way that remains strange, unbinds and delivers language into its own. The point," he added, "is to experience the unbinding bond within the web of language" (US, 243/112). This "unbinding bond" is the rift within the solitary nature of language (*der Auf-Riss des Sprachwesens*) that both divides and joins, brings together and sets free each into its own, Saying and speaking, the unspoken and the spoken, showing and signification, earth and world, world and thing, poetry and thinking. Put it as follows: for us to come into our own means to enter into a dialogue, not with Being, but with Saying. In Saying, nothing gets said, but this does not mean that Saying remains out of hearing. Saying appropriates us in the sense that we now enter into the event of Saying and give voice to it. Saying claims us for its own, and we respond—answer with what is *our* own, namely, as Heidegger says,

> the sounding of the word. The encountering saying of mortals is answering. Every word spoken is already an answer: counter-saying, coming to the encounter, listening Saying [*Gegensage, entgegenkommendes, hörendes Sagen*]. When mortals are made appropriate for Saying, human nature is released into that needfulness out of which man is used for bringing soundless Saying to the sound of language [*Die Vereignung der Sterblichen in die Sage enlässt das Menschenwesen in den Brauch, aus dem der Mensch gebraucht ist, die lautlose Sage in das Verlauten der Sprache zu bringen*]" (US, 260/129).

Here, however, is the surprise: What Heidegger calls "the way to language" turns out to be, not *our* way, that is, not a way of getting at language, getting the right idea about it or the hang of it—not the "right approach" that might serve us as an alternative to linguistics or philosophy of language. The "way to language" is not anything for us to hold to or follow. The way to language, Heidegger says, "belongs to Saying," not to us. So "way" is not method or theory. Heidegger uses the word idiomatically rather than philosophically. "Way" is the *wëgen* of the Alemmanic-Swabian dialect where it means "way-making [*Be-wëgung*]" (US, 261/129-130), which is to say not just moving along a path, making one's way, but breaking open, setting-free, wandering off the straight and narrow.

For Heidegger, *Ereignis* (taken singularly as *Er-eignis*) is to be understood as *Be-wëgung*. It is the "way-making" event that "lets . . . Saying reach speech": "*Das Ereignis lässt in der brauchenden Vereignung die Sage zum Sprechen gelangen. Der Weg zur Sprache gehört zu der aus dem Ereignis bestimmten Sage*" (US, 260/129). Letting Saying go this way, letting it reach speech, is the meaning of the formula that Heidegger introduced at the outset of his lecture: *Die Sprache als die Sprache zur Sprache bringen*. Er-eignis is the way-making (call it the punning) in which language as language is brought to language. This event has nothing to do with the process of objectifying language, giving a picture of it, framing a theory of it, raising it to consciousness. Language is untheorizable. Indeed, perhaps philosophy of language shows as much in spite of itself with its distinction between natural and formalized or gerrymandered languages: it throws the one away because it is only possible to frame a coherent theory for the other, that is, to produce theories of meaning and truth that will explain how language can be said to hook onto reality. But Heidegger is not to be thought of as intervening in philosophy of language with a counter-theory. On the contrary, in the way-making or punning that brings language as language to language, the being or nature or reality of language, or whatever *Sprachwesen* means—what belongs to language essentially— *conceals itself*: "*In diesem Weg, der zum Sprachwesen gehört, verbirgt sich das Eigentümliche der Sprache*" (US, 260-262/129). As if the philosophical term *Wesen* had now been reenchanted or remystified, returned to its Heraclitean sense of *phūsis*, or that which loves to hide.

So the way to language belongs to Saying. *Er-eignis is* the event in which Saying reaches speech. This setting-free of Saying—this letting go or releasement—is what bringing language as language (*Sage*) to language (*Sprache*) amounts to. "What looks like a confused tangle," Heidegger says, "becomes untangled when we see it in the light of the way-making movement [*Bewëgung*], and resolves into the release [*Befreiende*] brought about by the way-making movement disclosed in Saying. That movement delivers Saying to speech. Saying keeps the way open along which speaking, as listening, catches from Saying what is to be said, and raises what it has thus caught into the sounding word" (US, 263/131). And that word is the lowly pun, the other of the noble concept, the letting-go of language as against the fixing of its sense that bends it to assertiveness.

It is worth emphasizing (once more) that we don't produce puns; they catch us up in an uncanny hermeneutics: we hear them, let them happen to us (*Sichsagenlassen*), pick up on them and sound them out *(er-läutern*—where *erläutern* no longer has to do with explanation). The event, as it catches us up in it, is hermeneutical rather than poetic in the sense of *poiēsis*, and it is bound to bother us that we can't see it this way, can't see ourselves clearly in this event—can't pick ourselves out, identify ourselves at work. Indeed, what is frustrating about Heidegger's thinking is that he doesn't hold up the mirror we're accustomed to, doesn't hold up any mirror, either to language or to ourselves as expressive agents, masters of *poiēsis*, discursive egos, conscious or unconscious subjects in a linguistic process. The "way-making movement ... delivers Saying to speech": we don't do it. The way-making movement is not a performative activity; it is an event in which we are caught up, to which we belong—in which, let us say, we disappear. We can't picture ourselves in what Heidegger has to say with respect to language, can't recognize ourselves, because that is what it means to belong to language. What belongs to language *essentially conceals itself*, and so it is with us:

> In order to be who we are, we human beings remain committed to and within the being of language [*in das Sprachwesen eingelassen bleiben*], and can never step out of it and look at it from some where else. Thus we always see the nature of language [*Sprachwesen*] only to the extent to which language itself has us in view, has appropriated us to itself. That we cannot know the nature of language [*Sprachwesen*]—know it according to the traditional concept of knowledge defined in terms of cognition as representation—is not a defect, however, but rather an advantage by which we are favored with a special realm, that realm where we, who are needed and used to speak language, dwell as *mortals* [US, 266/134].

To belong to language means that we disappear into the event of way-making as consciousness disappears into play, as spectatorship is dissolved by participation, as speaking turns into listening, or as the dancer is carried away by, disappears into, the dance. Or as Orpheus is carried away or appropriated by his song. Or as the thinker disappears into the darkness when consecutive progress gives way to wandering or way-making without why. But of course philosophy was invented to keep this from happening.[8]

Indeed, belonging to language in the way Heidegger speaks of it, with his emphasis on darkness—on withdrawal, on refusal or dissembling, on the disappearance of the subject as a cognitive and vociferous consciousness—is what philosophy has always recognized as the condition of skepticism, or rather the condition that the skeptic always bends our minds to: what Stanley Cavell, distinguishing the skeptic from the nihilist, calls "the truth of skepticism," which is that our belongingness to the other calls upon us to forgo or "disown knowledge."[9] Of course, we do not know the consequences of such disownment, unless perhaps it is the *Eignen*, or perhaps *Ereignis*, of which Heidegger (darkly) speaks. Anyhow, as Cavell reminds us, tragedy is knowing (too late) the consequences, or limits, of knowing. Comedy is not knowing; comedy is risking it—risking the consequences of exposure to the dark. What remains to be understood— perhaps this is the lesson that remains to be drawn from the later Heidegger —is that skepticism, although far from cheerful, edifying, or even practical —is comic rather than nihilistic, as if the finitude or failure of *theōria* were the releasement of *phronēsis*, or *Gelassenheit*: the letting-go of the ground, the risk of wandering, the uncertainty of listening, the gambling game of language, the venturing of Dichten.

Notes

1. References to Heidegger's works are cited in the text, where the first number in parentheses refers to the German text, the second to the English transla-

tion.
AD *Aus der Erfahrung des Denkens, 1910-1976. Gesamtausgabe*, vol. 13). Frankfurt: Klostermann, 1983. The title section, "Aus der Erfahrung des Denkens" (1947), has been translated as "The Thinker as Poet" by Albert Hofstadter, *Poetry, Language, Thought.* New York: Harper & Row, 1971, pp. 1-14.
ED *Erlauterungen zu Hölderlins Dichtung.* Frankfurt: Klostermann, 1951. (3d ed., 1963.) Contains:
"Hölderlin und das Wesen der Dichtung," pp. 31-46, and "Heimkunft/An die Verwandten," pp. 9-30. "Hölderlin and the Essence of Poetry" and "Remembrance of the Poet." Translated by Douglas Scott, *Existence and Being.* Chicago: Henry Regnery, 1949, pp. 233-291.
EM *Einfahrung in die Metaphysik.* Tubingen: Max Niemeyer, 1953. (3d ed., 1966.) *Introduction to Metaphysics.* Translated by Ralph Manheim,Garden City, N.Y.: Doubleday, 1961.
G   *Gelassenheit.* Pfullingen: Günther Neske, 1959. (8th ed., 1985). *Discourse on Thinking.* Translated by John M. Anderson and E. Hans Freund. New York: Harper & Row, 1966.
ID *Identität und Differenz.* Pfullingen: Günther Neske, 1957. (7th ed., 1982.) *Identity and Difference.* Translated by Joan Stambaugh. New York: Harper & Row, 1969.
Hw *Holzwege.* Frankfurt: Klostermann, 1950. *(Gesamtausgabe,* vol. 1.) Contains the following:
"Der Ursprung des Kunstwerkes," pp. 7-68. "The Origin of the Work of Art," *Poetry, Language, Thought,* pp. 15-87.
"Nietzsches Wort, 'Gott ist tot,'" pp. 193-247. "The Word of Nietzsche: 'God is Dead.'" Translated by William Lovitt. *The Question Concerning Technology and Other Essays.* New York: Harper & Row, 1977, pp. 53-112.
"Wozu Dichter?," pp. 248-295. "What Are Poets For?" *Poetry, Language, Thought,* pp. 91-142.
"Der Spruch des Anaximander," pp. 296-343. "The Anaximander Fragment," translated by David Farrell Krell and Frank A. Capuzzi. *Early Greek Thinking.* New York: Harper & Row, 1975, pp. 13-58.
NI *Nietzsche I.* Pfullingen: Günther Neske, 1961. *Nietzsche.* Translated by David Farrell Krell. New York: Harper & Row, 1979. Vol. 1: *The Will to Power as Art.*
SD *Zur Sache des Denkens.* Tübingen: Max Niemeyer, 1969. Contains "Des Ende der Philosophie und die Aufgabe des Denkens," pp. 61-80. "The End of Philosophy and the Task of Thinking," translated by Joan Stambaugh, *On Time and Being.* New York: Harper & Row, 1969, pp. 55-73.
SZ *Sein und Zeit.* Tübingen: Max Niemeyer, 1984, 15th ed. *Being and Time,* translated by John Macquarrie and Edward Robinson. New York: Harper

& Row, 1962.
TK *Die Technik und die Kehre*. Pfullingen: Günther Neske, 1962. "The Turning," *The Question Concerning Technology*, pp. 36-49.
US *Unterwegs zur Sprache*. Pfullingen: Günther Neske, 1959. (7th ed., 1982.) Contains the following:
"Die Sprache," 11-33. "Language," *Poetry, Language, Thought*, pp. 189-210.
"Die Sprache im Gedicht," pp. 37-82. "Language in the Poem: A Discussion on Georg Trakl's Poetic Work," translated by Peter D. Hertz, *On the Way to Language*. New York: Harper & Row, 1971, pp. 159-198
"Aus Einem Gespräch von der Sprache," pp. 85-155. "A Dialogue on Language," *On the Way to Language*, pp. 1-54.
"Des Wesen der Sprache," pp. 159-216. "The Nature of Language," *On the Way to Language*, pp. 57-108.
"Des Wort," pp. 219-238. "Words," *On the Way to Language*, pp. 139-156.
"Der Weg zur Sprache," pp. 241-268. "The Way to Language," *On the Way to Language*, pp. 111-136.
VA *Vortrage und Aufsätze*. Pfullingen: Günther Neske, 1954. (4th ed., 1978.) Contains the following:
"'... dichterisch wohnet der Mensch ...,'" pp. 181-98. "'... Poetically Man Dwells,'" *Poetry, Language, Thought*, pp. 213 - 229.
"Die Frage nach der Technik," pp. 9-40. "The Question Concerning Technology," in *The Question Concerning Technology and Other Essays*, pp. 3-35.
"Bauen Wohnen Denken," pp. 139-156. "Building Dwelling Thinking," *Poetry, Language, Thought*, pp. 145-161.
"Des Ding," pp. 157-180. "The Thing," *Poetry, Language, Thought*, pp. 165-186.
"Logos (Heraklit, Fragment 50)," pp. 199-221. "Logos (Heraclitus, Fragment 50)," *Early Greek Thinking*, pp. 59-78.
"Aletheia (Heraklit, Fragment 16)," pp. 249-274. "Aletheia (Heraclitus, Fragment 16), *Early Greek Thinking*, pp. 102-124.
WD *Was heisst Denken?* Tübingen: Max Niemeyer, 1961. (4th ed., 1984.) *What is Called Thinking?* Translated by J. Glenn Gray. New York: Harper & Row, 1968.
Wm *Wegmarken*. Frankfurt: Klostermann, 1967 *(Gesamtausgabe*, vol. 9). Contains the following:
"Was ist Metaphysik?" pp. 1-20. "What is Metaphysics?" translated by David Farrell Krell, *Martin Heidegger: Basic Writings*, ed. David Farrell Krell. New York: Harper & Row, 1977), pp. 95-112.
"Vom Wesen der Wahrheit," pp. 73-98. "The Essence of Truth,"

translated by John Sallis, *Basic Writings*, pp. 117-141. "Brief über den 'Humanismus,'" pp. 145-194. "Letter on Humanism." Translated by Frank Capuzzi and J. Glenn Gray, *Basic Writings*, pp. 189 - 242.

2. This is a main theme of "Hölderlin and the Essence of Poetry," which tries to elucidate this fragment:

Viel erfahren hat der Mensch.
Der Himmlischen viele genannt,
Seit ein Gesprach wir sind
Und hören konnen voneinander.

Much has man learnt.
Many of the heavenly ones has he named,
Since we have been a conversation
And have been able to hear from one another [ED, 36/277].

Conversation is what draws us into the orphic event and maintains us there. Heidegger writes: "Since we have been a conversation—man has learnt much and named many of the heavenly ones. Since language really became actual as conversation, the gods have acquired names and a world has appeared. But again it should be noticed: the presence of the gods and the appearance of the world are not merely a consequence of the actualisation of language, they are contemporaneous with it. And this to the extent that it is precisely in the naming of the gods, and in the transmutation of the world into word, that the real conversation, which we ourselves are, consists" (ED, 37/279). However, *Gespräch* in this social and historical sense seems to drop out of the later Heidegger's thinking. It appears that for the later Heidegger the crucial conversation is between poetry and thinking, where conversation is not a mutual exchange but a mode of belonging to Saying. At all events the relation of poetry and thinking is not social.

3. See Joseph P. Fell, "Heidegger's Gods and Mortals," in *Research in Phenomenology*, 1985, 15: 31: "For one who has walked Heidegger's path from his early thinking forward, the term 'mortals' is richly evocative. It calls up my death, an unsurpassable boundary which throws me right back to my other boundary, my own beginning. Encountering darkness—nothing—as both my 'whence' and my 'whither.' I am thrown right into my own time as my true place and the place of the only truth I can possibly experience. It is in this time alone, then, that I can ask about the gods. Might, therefore, a necessary step in the question of the role of the gods for Heidegger consist in meditating on death, and so on nothing?"

4. See Michael Murray's discussion of this liberation in *Modern Critical Theory: An Introduction*, pp. 143-202.

5. See Gerald L. Bruns, "On The Tragedy of Hermeneutical Experience," in *Research in Phenomenology*, 18 (November 1988).
6. See David Michael Levin on the dance in Heidegger, in *The Body's Recollection of Being: Phenomenological Psychology and the Deconstruction of Nihilism*. London: Routledge & Kegan Paul, 1985, pp. 317-349.
7. Professional Heideggerians are apt to find my account of *Er-eignis* a bit bizarre. Even Jacques Derrida, when he heard me present an earlier version of this paper at a conference in Jerusalem, questioned my insistence on listening for the pun in Heidegger's words. My impression is that Derrida would prefer to think of Heidegger as being soberly unaware of his puns, which is highly implausible but consistent with the way Derrida once read Heidegger, namely as reinscribing in his metaphors the metaphysics he wants to destroy. As I indicate elsewhere in this book, I see, or hear, Heidegger as being closer to Derrida, or vice versa, than Derrida perhaps does, because I hear more (or something other) than metaphysics in Heidegger's puns. For a proper view of *Ereignis*, see Otto Poggeler, "Being as Appropriation" (1959), trans. Rudiger H. Grimm, *Philosophy Today*, Summer 1975: 152-178; reprinted in *Heidegger and Modern Philosophy*, pp. 85-115, and esp. pp. 101-102. "Being as the event of appropriation [*Ereignis*]: with this definition Heidegger's thinking has arrived at its goal." For a more disseminated view, see John Caputo, *Radical Hermeneutics*, pp. 200-201, although even for Caputo *Ereignis is* more term than word. With all respect to the philosophers, I take *Ereignis* as a pun (*Er-eignis*) rather than as a concept, definition, or name (in the sense of designation)—and so, I think, does Heidegger. See, for example, "The Turning" (1950), where, in addition to the puns I've picked up on, Heidegger adds another: *Eräugnis* (TK, 44/45). I confess, however, that Heidegger is more philosophically sober on this subject in "Time and Being" (1962; SD, 20-25/19-24), but even here he makes it clear that in the phrase "Being as *Ereignis*" the "as" is a term of dissemination like the "hermeneutical 'as'" discussed in section 32 of *Being and Time*. The "as" (like the pun) cannot be contained within propositional discourse. I discuss this "as" in "The Weakness of Language in the Human Sciences," in *The Rhetoric of Inquiry: Language and Argument in Scholarship and Public Affairs*, ed. Allan Megill, Donald McCloskey, and John Nelson (Madison: Univ. of Wisconsin Press, 1988), pp. 239-262. I think that Francis Ambrosio's essay, "Dawn and Dusk: Gadamer and Heidegger on Truth," is very valuable for its discussion of *Ereignis*. See *Man and World*, 1986, 19: 21-53.

And even when in Heidegger it appears that "Being *is* Ereignis" after all, it is plain that we are still slip-sliding on drifting or moving ground, as in Heidegger's poem, "Gefahrten," with its parodistic archaisms and self-circling, self-canceling "propositions":

Einstige kommen
vom Seyn übernommen

Sie wagen
Das Sagen
der Wahrheit des Seyns:

Seyn ist Ereignis
Ereignis ist Anfang
Anfang ist Austrag
Austrag ist Abschied Abschied ist Seyn (AD, 31).

Here the word for Being is no longer (or is in excess of) the word for Being. See the conclusion on the parodistic relation of the archaic to the customary.

8. At the end of "The Way to Language" Heidegger says, in a line that is easy to misinterpret, that "All reflective thinking is poetic, and all poetry in turn is a kind of thinking [*Alles sinnende Denken ist ein Dichten, alle Dichtung aber ein Denken:* not a *kind* of thinking, but a thinking on its own, a singular thinking rather than a particular sort]" (US, 267/136). This is not a remark about style or form, or about the resemblance of poetry and thinking. I take it as a statement about letting-go with respect to language, where letting-go means departing, entering into one's apartness or singularity, getting free. I think it would be a mistake to map this line back onto Heidegger's prose in order to figure Heidegger's writing as an exhibition of thinking that has turned to poetry. But his writing does reflect an openness to the pun, a listening, that also belongs to poetry. The question is, Where does this listening take us? The answer is: Elsewhere, where to be always elsewhere is what being on the way comes round to. The vagueness and pointlessness of this answer is repugnant to philosophy. In an essay on "Heidegger and Metaphor", Gerald Casenave says that "To the end, [Heidegger's] thought remains tentative; he is always on the way and never arriving." Casenave speaks for philosophy when he rejects this state of affairs. "Can fundamental thinking be brought to completion and remain fundamental thinking?" he asks. The answer, he thinks, is yes. "It may be the case that thought can become fully explicit only by becoming representational. That is to say, thinking moves through the break out of metaphor to a more fundamental level of thought, experience, and language, but then it returns to stability with the achievement of a new order of things. A new break-through to fundamental thought ends with the elaboration and definition of a new realm of discourse." And so a new "break-through" is required in turn, to be followed by a new elaboration and establishment of a discursive realm; and so on without end. See *Philosophy Today*, 1982, 16: 147. I think Heidegger would reject this picture of the history of thinking as being nothing more

than a picture of the history of philosophy, with its endless construction and deconstruction of systems. For Heidegger, thinking, once on its way, never "returns to stability with the achievement of a new order of things." Casenave (speaking, as I say, for philosophy) cannot picture thinking except in terms of searching, whereas I think Heidegger figures the thinker as a wanderer who can never settle anywhere, whose being-on-the-way (to use that expression) cannot be contained within the romantic concept of the quest, but is Cain-like in its resemblance to pure exile. There is no place where the thinker is not a stranger.

9. See Cavell, "Thinking of Emerson," in *The Senses of Walden*, expanded edition (San Francisco: North Point Press, 1981), pp. 133-134; and *Disowning Knowledge in Six Plays of Shakespeare* (Cambridge: Cambridge Univ. Press, 1987), pp. 3-5, and esp. pp. 92-97.

University of Notre Dame
Department of English
356 O'Shaughnessy Hall
Notre Dame IN 46556
USA

Change of Address?

If you are anticipating a change of address, please notify us as soon as possible to ensure uninterrupted delivery of your issues.

Send change of address to:
JMKOR, 1 Marine Midland Plaza
East Tower – Fourth Floor
Binghamton, New York 13901-3216 USA

Notes on Contributors

RICHARD P. ALEXANDER, M.D. is Training and Supervising Analyst at the Psychoanalytic Center of California. He is the author of several psychoanalytic papers and book chapters, and is in private practice of psychoanalysis in Beverly Hills, CA.

JOSEPH H. BERKE, M. D., F.A.B. Med. Psych. is the Co-Founder and Director of the Arbours Association and Arbours Crisis Centre, London, and is a psychoanalytic psychotherapist in private practice in London. He is the author of many articles and books including *The Tyranny of Malice*, and *Sanctuary. The Arbours Experience of Alternative Community Care* (co-editor). His forthcoming book, *Even Paranoids Have Enemies* (co-editor) will be published by Routledge in 1998.

HAROLD N. BORIS (1932-1996) was a nationally recognized and respected teacher, a member of the Psychology Faculty in the Department of Psychiatry of the Harvard Medical School, Cambridge Hospital. His research has been supported by NIMH, the Ford and the Field Foundations. He has published many articles, and several books: *Passions of the Mind: Unheard Melodies, A Third Principle of Mental Functioning*; *Envy*; and *Sleights of Mind: One and Multiples of One*. He was in the private practice of psychoanalysis with adults and children in Lexington and Boston, MA.

GERALD L. BRUNS, Ph.D., the William and Hazel White Professor of English at Notre Dame University, is concerned with the philosophy of interpretation. In addition to articles and book chapters on subjects ranging from legal theory to the literary cannon, he is the author of several books: *Modern Poetry and the Idea of Language*; *Inventions: Writing, Textuality, and Understanding in Literary History*; *Heidegger's Estrangements*; *Hermeneutics Ancient and Modern*; and *Maurice Blanchot: The Refusal of Philosophy*. He has won several NEH and Guggenheim fellowships.

MICHAEL EIGEN, PhD is the author of *Psychic Deadness*, *The Psychotic Core*, *The Electrified Tightrope*, *Coming Through the Whirlwind*, *Reshaping the Self*, and of many published articles and reviews. He teaches and supervises at the National Psychological Association for Psychoanalysis and the New York University Postdoctoral Program in Psychoanalysis. He is in private practice in New York City.

EDWARD EMERY, Ph.D. is a psychoanalyst in private practice in Northampton, MA. He is the author of several papers and book chapters, and is presently working on a series of papers on the problematics of mourning.

BETTINA L. KNAPP, Ph.D. is Professor of French and Comparative Literature at Hunter College and the CUNY Graduate Center, New York City. She is the author of numerous articles and book chapters, while her most recent books include, *Machine, Metaphor, and the Writer; Music, Archetype, and the Writer; Women in Twentieth-Century Literature,* and *Exile and the Writer.*

JEAN-MICHEL RABATÉ, Ph.D. is the Marjorie Ernest Professor of English at the University of Pennsylvania, Philadelphia. He is the author of numerous articles and book chapters, and books. His most recent volumes include *James Joyce Authorized Reader, Ethik der Gabe Denken nach Jacques Derrida, Ghosts of Modernity,* and *Writing the Image after Roland Barthes.*

RICHARD E. VILLEJO, Ph.D. is Professor of Psychology at the Illinois School of Professional Psychology, Chicago Campus. He is the author of several articles and book chapters.

Would You like to Help Your Colleagues
Get Acquainted with the Journal?
Send Us Their Addresses
and We Will Send Them Information about the Journal.
They Will Appreciate it and So Will We.

INSTRUCTIONS TO AUTHORS

MANUSCRIPTS should be sent to: Prof. O. Weininger, PhD, Editor, Department of Applied Psychology, The Ontario Institute for Studies in Education, 252 Bloor Street West, Toronto, Ontario M5S 1V6, Canada. E-mail file attachment(s) to: jmkor97@aol.com. Authors residing in South America, send manuscripts to: Paulo C. Sandler, MD, Associate Editor for South America, rua do Livramento 274, 04 008 São Paulo SP, Brazil. E-mail file attachment to: sandler@uol.com.br. Please specify in the text of your e-mail the file format used for text and graphics (if any).

MANUSCRIPTS should be typewritten (preferably laser quality), double-spaced, including quotations and references, with one-inch margins on all sides. Send a clearly marked, PC or Macintosh (*high density*) diskette of the manuscript accompanied by two print-outs on white paper. Provide on a separate page a SUMMARY of a maximum of 250 words, a list of maximum of 30 KEY WORDS, and a brief BIOGRAPHICAL NOTE with the author(s) degree, title, affiliation, publications and mailing address.

THE EDITORIAL COMMITTEE welcomes manuscripts which contribute to our understanding of object relations. The length of the paper is usually determined by the content. This may include, for example, critical analyses of concepts, literature reviews leading to creative proposals, empirical research, and historical analyses. The manuscripts may be either theoretical or practical and applied. Notes about cases and treatment procedures, ideas concerning theory, and book and film reviews are invited as well. The highest ethical and professional standards must be observed in protecting the confidentiality of patients, families, and groups. Special attention should be given to the *clarity and pertinence of the language* used in the paper.

TEXT DOCUMENTATION: Titles of books should be in *italics*, while titles of articles and book chapters in double quotation marks: "...". All notes should be endnotes only with clear and consecutive superscript numbering in the text of the paper. Notes and references should conform to the style in this issue of the publication. References in the text should provide the author's name, and in parentheses, the year of the publication of the paper or book. *Example*: Klein (1945) wrote.... If the author's name is not included in the sentence of the text, place in parentheses the author's name, followed by a comma, and the year of the publication. *Example*: The focus of my contribution is on ... the emotional mathematician (Bion, 1965). For two or more publications, use semicolons to separate the names of authors. *Example*: I have later discovered that the term has been used by others (Kant, 1789; Heidegger, 1931; Wittgenstein, 1933-1935). Whenever material is quoted in the text, cite a page reference, in parentheses, at the end of the quotation. *Example*: If it went . . . could not endure it and must perish (p. 586).

REFERENCES should be arranged alphabetically by author. References from the same author should be listed in chronological order, beginning with the earliest source. If there are several papers by the same author, type after the first reference a double em line——. Names of journals should be in *italics* and abbreviated as in the *Index Medicus*, or in this issue of the publication. Names of books should be in *italics*. For Sigmund Freud's works, indicate the volume number and the pages of the paper from the *Standard Edition*. *Example*: Freud, S. (1915). Observations on transference love. *SE*, 12: 157-172. However, the first reference to a paper or book by Sigmund Freud from the *Standard Edition* should indicate the editor's name and the complete title of the edition. *Example*: Freud, S. (1915). On beginning the treatment. *SE*, 12:123-144. In: J. Strachey (Ed.), *Standard Edition of the Complete Psychological Works of Sigmund Freud*, 24 volumes. London: Hogarth Press and The Institute of Psycho-Analysis, 1953-1974. Authors using a different edition or their own translations, should indicate so.

ILLUSTRATIONS AND COPYRIGHTS: All illustrations should be sent in black and white, camera-ready format only. If the illustration is not in camera-ready format, the authors will be billed for the costs incurred by the publisher. The authors of papers published in this journal agree to indemnify this journal and its publisher against any expenses, damages, or losses resulting from the use by the author of any unauthorized photographs, words, names, illustrations, sketches (but not limited to) protected by copyright or trademark. Authors are solely responsible for the opinions and views expressed in their papers and do not necessarily reflect the viewpoints of the editor, associate editors, book review editor, editorial committee, or the publisher.

A COMPLIMENTARY COPY of the issue in which the paper appears and a REPRINT ORDER FORM will be sent to the author(s).

Visit our WEB site at: **http://tier.net/esfpub/**